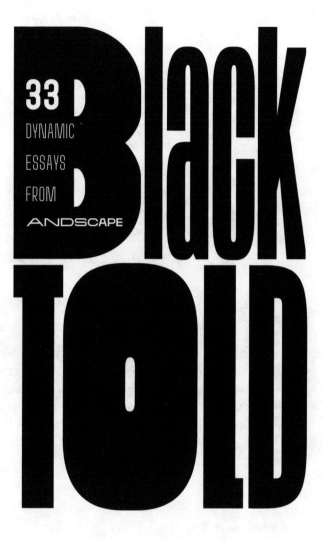

Black Told

33 DYNAMIC ESSAYS FROM ANDSCAPE

STEVE REISS, *EDITOR*

FOREWORD BY **RAINA KELLEY**

ANDSCAPE

LOS ANGELES   NEW YORK

First Edition, October 2022
10 9 8 7 6 5 4 3 2 1
FAC-004510-22231
Printed in the United States of America

This book is set in Acta, TT Hoves, and Tp Andscape
Book design by Amy C. King
Cover and part opener designs by Gail Anderson

Library of Congress Control Number: 2022936735
ISBN 978-1-368-07663-0
Reinforced binding

Visit www.AndscapeBooks.com

CONTENTS

FOREWORD BY **RAINA KELLEY** *ix*

BLACK LIVES MATTER

George Floyd's mother was not there, but he used her as a sacred invocation
LONNAE O'NEAL
1

I look at Breonna Taylor and see myself
JENISHA WATTS
5

For corporations, is Juneteenth about profits or progress?
WILLIAM C. RHODEN
10

America is facing a reckoning over race, but we've seen this before
MICHAEL A. FLETCHER
15

Victim No. 79: America's homicide crisis claimed my childhood friend
DWAYNE BRAY
26

The "comma effect" on bias and Black lives
DOUG GLANVILLE
53

AMERICAN HISTORY

The Waco horror
JESSE WASHINGTON
65

Ali–Frazier was more than a fight, it was part of my awakening as a Black man
WILLIAM C. RHODEN
85

A blessing and a curse: The rich history behind "Black Twitter"
DAVID DENNIS JR.
90

The gut-wrenching history of black babies and alligators
DOMONIQUE FOXWORTH
114

MLB elevating the status of Negro Leagues is the problem, not the solution
CLINTON YATES
119

A national lyching memorial recognizes the domestic terrorism that killed my great-great-grandfather
KARIN D. BERRY
124

If you truly knew what the N-word meant to our ancestors, you'd NEVER use it
BRANDO SIMEO STARKEY
137

ARTS & CULTURE

The low-key cool of "Jake, from State Farm"
LONNAE O'NEAL   145

For Shock G, the man who made room for everyone on the dance floor
MINDA HONEY   151

Can a black heroine fix the racist stereotypes infecting *King Kong*?
SORAYA NADIA MCDONALD   157

"Game, Blouses"
JERRY BEMBRY   167

Wake up! In this #BlackLivesMatter era, Spike Lee's *School Daze* is still relevant
KELLEY L. CARTER   172

Diddy's White Party kicked in the door, announcing "we up in here"
ROGER REEVES   176

Toni Morrison made me stop wanting to be white
RAINA KELLEY   182

Whitley's world: a brief history of bad and boujee Black girl style
DANIELLE CADET   185

An ode to *Jet* magazine's "Beauty of the Week"
MARTENZIE JOHNSON   196

Uncle Phil from *The Fresh Prince of Bel-Air* may be the best TV dad in history
JUSTIN TINSLEY   202

What Michael K. Williams taught me about being a man
DAVID DENNIS JR.   211

The unbearable whiteness of *Oklahoma!*
SORAYA NADIA MCDONALD   216

SPORTS

Under the coronavirus lockdown, a father and son rediscover their love for baseball
DWAYNE BRAY   *227*

A PGA veteran's callous joke about blackface and Tiger Woods turned into a lesson on empathy
MICHAEL WILLIAMS   *234*

The Thanksgiving an imprisoned Jack Johnson fought two men at Leavenworth
ROBERTO JOSÉ ANDRADE FRANCO   *249*

Kaepernick and the debate over "authentic" Blackness
MICHAEL A. FLETCHER   *256*

The moral argument for keeping Barry Bonds out of Cooperstown doesn't hold up
JUSTIN TINSLEY   *263*

What reporters can learn from Kyrie Irving calling them "pawns"
MARTENZIE JOHNSON   *271*

How Black Utah Jazz players embraced Salt Lake City
MARC J. SPEARS   *275*

Black men do cry—in the NCAA tournament
JESSE WASHINGTON   *289*

AFTERWORD 293

CONTRIBUTORS TO **BLACKTOLD** 295

FOREWORD

Let me just put this right out there. I am using this foreword to make a point–or rather to put forward a different point than one normally makes in a foreword. I'm just saying that I need to put the *reason* for this collection of essays front and center over the collection itself. And I'm not just pulling a bit of rhetorical sleight of hand to get you to buy a book that you could get for free with a laborious lean on Google. I'm also doing it to make sure that its raison d'être is neither misunderstood nor taken for granted–two of the twenty-first century's greatest metaphysical nightmares and hence to be avoided at all costs. So, I write this foreword to tell you that this book is the harbinger of and a balm for a world transformed.

It is not, in ways small, large, fundamental, and irrevocable, the same world it was when *Andscape* (then known as *The Undefeated*) came into existence. That was on May 17, 2016. The President was biracial. Pandemics were overblown plot points in blockbusters and there was no TikTok. This was *several* racial reckonings ago. Black was lowercase, and the ability to live on a spectrum instead of at the sharp end of a dichotomy was considered exceptional. These essays stand together as a portrait of what was *Before* and how we got to *Now*.

Not that I'm minimizing the importance of the actual essays themselves. I most certainly am not. These are your maps to navigating this strange new world. How strange? (Is that an undercurrent of boredom I detect? With a top note of cynicism?) We now live in a world where "real" is considered a point of view. Where truth can be stood in but no longer sworn upon. There is no certainty in a place where talk of *all of this is a computer simulation* is now a matter for the experts. This place we find ourselves where the five pillars of storytelling–ironic, funny, tragic, soul-killing, and senseless–have crumbled and rebuilt themselves anew using different mirrors. See "America is facing a reckoning over race, but we've seen this before" by Michael A. Fletcher:

> Reconstruction tried and failed to get the nation to recognize the humanity of African Americans. Following World War I, African Americans who had proven their valor in the trenches of Europe were returning home and hundreds of thousands of others were moving north to flee racial terrorism and abject poverty in the South. They found opportunity, but also murderous white hostility.
>
> After World War II, as civil rights lawyers found once-unthinkable success chipping away at state-sanctioned segregation, the old order was maintained by redlining, massive resistance and white flight. Even as the Black middle class grew, educational levels increased and Black officials filled thousands of political offices, culminating in the election of Barack Obama as the nation's first Black president.... That structure is now being challenged in unprecedented ways. But what will become of this moment?

It seems both unseemly and pointless to wave you down only to tell you that we were here first and please use us for safe passage on the journey. Because this is real. We saw this. Why do you think we changed our name? Because the way we see ourselves now is so different as to demand a new, more flexible vessel to pour ourselves into. Here I quote myself from "Toni Morrison made me stop wanting to be white" in this collection:

> Slavery took our bodies. Cultural hegemony tries to take our minds–and destroy our hair. [Toni] Morrison gave it all back to us–if we have the strength to take it. What did she say in *Beloved*? They do not love your body. So you have to love it and love it hard.
>
> This is not about being *seen*–a watered-down approximation of affirmation if ever there was one. We are seen every day and seen wanting, thanks to the economic demands of a scientifically ignorant people who built a sweet land of "liberty" on the backs of other, darker humans. It's not right to own people. But it seems almost worse to convince yourself and those you enslaved and their descendants that it has something to do with their own inferiority. That's twisted.

So please use us for safe passage on your journey. We are here to ensure the path stays lit and to reassure you that you are correct. The path *is in* your hands. You need these essays, and you need them in this handy dandy *curated* collection to guide you–lest you become misunderstood or taken for granted.

I am certainly not saying that this is going to be easy, or that you will never be angry again, though I do wish that for you. But I am telling you to be optimistic. And I offer these essays, once again, as an aid. They are a reminder that though the other thing is true too, Black means more than resistance. It also means every single other thing that you bring to it. We do not live as a cautionary counterpoint to White. We are simply living. And then we put a little hip-hop on it, because not just surviving but thriving under such circumstances is what one would call flexing. Or, as Soraya Nadia McDonald writes in "Can a black heroine fix the racist stereotypes infecting *King Kong*?"

> Pitts's Ann is adventurous, independent and determined. But she's also a Black woman who, like Kong, is ensconced in a production that doesn't seem to have taken full account of what that means beyond a mealymouthed, post-racial conclusion that anyone can play anything! And it's totally fine! Progressive, even! Perhaps, more than anything else, that's what ties Kong and his Black Darrow together on Broadway, even more so than their victimization at the hands of the arrogant Denham. Both remain suspended in a parable that, however well-intentioned, remains grafted onto a fundamentally racist foundation.

You are not suspended or rather you are no longer suspended in another's parable that, however well-intentioned, remains grafted onto a fundamentally racist foundation. You and all your Ands (pardon the branding) create the Scape we have created in this collection of essays. (See what I did there? Explaining again what Andscape means and what it matters. But we are sowing hearts and minds, not just reaping rewards.) And to paraphrase the great James Baldwin, please also use this collection as proof that you have earned this Scape of your own. This Scape. Your Ands have been bought and paid for by those of us who came Before but are not here Now.

We are the ballast. The anchors. A way for those who are close to the edge to find their way back, or their way home. This is true for Black mothers, who are especially tested and learned in all the dread fates of Black bodies. We are the hedge against the people who don't see us. We are an assertion of Black life.

For Black people who feel they are about to be taken from themselves, we are the assurance of memory, of justice, of ten-hour waits to cast our ballots at polling places. We will not be moved.

That's how Lonnae O'Neal puts it in "George Floyd's mother was not there, but he used her as a sacred invocation." But she is right for all of us, not simply our mothers. We will not be moved.

Life is infinitely stranger than anything that the human mind could invent. Our ancestors could not even begin, would not even dare, to conceive the things that are really the mere comings and goings of existence. If we could fly and somehow hover over this wild world and peep in at the goings-on, the strange coincidences, the planning, the cross-purposes, the wonderful chains of events, working through generations and leading to the most outré results, it would make all fiction with its conventionalities and foreseen conclusions most stale and unprofitable. This essay collection seeks not to remind you that truth is stranger than fiction but to remind you to care. And that your life *really, truly* does depend on that.

–*Raina Kelley*
April 14, 2022

GEORGE FLOYD'S MOTHER WAS NOT THERE, BUT HE USED HER AS A SACRED INVOCATION

With his dying breaths, Floyd called for her as an assurance of memory.

BY LONNAE O'NEAL

THE VIDEO frame of George Floyd on Facebook, handcuffed, on his stomach as a Minneapolis police officer presses his knee into Floyd's neck, feels narrowed.

Floyd lies immobilized, groaning, on the pavement as cars rush by, police radios beep, and bystanders gather, yelling that Floyd's nose is bleeding, that he is subdued, cursing and entreating the officers. "Let him breathe, man!" one bystander yells.

"Please, man!" Floyd begs as he is ground into the pavement and his pleas mix with the ambient noises around him. They are the disjointed sounds that result from the clash of belief systems and competing visions of sovereignty, of ownership, of authority over Black bodies compressed into the narrow frame of Floyd's last moments.

"Momma! Momma!" Floyd, forty-six, calls out. "My knee. My neck. I'm through," the dying man says, and I recognize his words. A call to your mother is a prayer to be seen. Floyd's mother died two years ago, but he used her as a sacred invocation.

"He is a human being!" comes an anguished plea from someone in a desperate attempt to engage the officers' reason or compassion or oaths of office. But in that moment, those officers are beyond the reach of humanity. Not Floyd's, but their own.

I didn't want to click on the video. I didn't want to see another police snuff film. I didn't want to watch whatever it is that compels someone to put his knee into a man's neck until he can no longer draw breath. But I heard this Black man call out to his momma as he lay dying, and I too am a Black mother. One of the ones who since time immemorial have had to answer the sacred call. Who have to answer the call for the divine sisterhood of Black mothers. Even when they are not our own, we are asked to bear witness.

I was in the delivery room with my son, in pain, with no medication, save the one that magnified my contractions. As my vision narrowed, I focused on a point above me and I heard the nurses talking about me as if I wasn't there. I stared at the ceiling and over and over I called out for my mother. There are moments when it feels like life hangs in the balance, and in those moments, we want to go back to the beginning, when we were known.

Dying soldiers called out for their mothers, according to Civil War battlefield reports. A recent article from the *Atlantic* cited a hospice nurse. "Almost everyone is calling for Mommy or Mama with the last breath."

We are the ballast. The anchors. A way for those who are close to the edge to find their way back, or their way home. This is true for Black mothers, who are especially tested and learned in all the dread fates of Black bodies. We are the hedge against the people who don't see us. We are an assertion of Black life.

For Black people who feel they are about to be taken from themselves, we are the assurance of memory, of justice, of ten-hour waits to cast our ballots at polling places. We will not be moved.

I have often imagined fourteen-year-old Emmett Till calling for his momma, Mamie Till-Mobley, as he was kidnapped, tortured, and killed as a result of the false witness of Carolyn Bryant Donham, whom America had imbued with the savage idea of white womanhood. The Black mother's answer was to throw open her son's casket and change the nation.

It is the duty of Black mothers made sacred by all the ugly Karens (Beckys, Katies, et al.) who threaten to call the police on Black people because they understand the country we live in. It has been made sacred by all the admonitions and prayers–all the side deals we try to cut with our God when Black boys cross streets, or play in parks, or get into cars, or grow into men who do anything at all while being Black.

It is made sacred by our need to protect against all the people who think they hold dominion over Black lives. Who overpolice or underfund or overreport or wag their fingers in our faces. The vacant-looking father and son with rifles in Georgia, the masked female portfolio manager waving her cellphone in New York, the reptilian officer who has learned how to "kneel" a man to death in Minnesota, may not see themselves. But we, the Black mothers, see you.

As bystanders scream at Minneapolis officers, "He's dying. You're f–ing killing him," Floyd is no longer moving. He is perhaps already dead. In the ways Black people have trained themselves to look at these things, in his final breaths, he has already won.

To call out to his mother is to be known to his maker. The one who gave him to her. I watched the Floyd video, for us, the living. It's my sacred charge. I am a Black mother.

Originally published May 28, 2020

I LOOK AT **BREONNA TAYLOR** AND SEE MYSELF

Every day that Louisville fails to arrest those officers, they devalue my life and others like me.

BY JENISHA WATTS

I CAN'T stop thinking about Breonna Taylor. Like her, I love well-coordinated outfits, saucy red lipstick, and big hoop earrings. Her round, brown-sugar face with her strong eyes dressed in lashes sticks in my mind, even as I try to tuck her image away, as if to close a jewelry box.

She had big dreams, her mama, Tamika Palmer, said. "Breonna had her head on straight." Palmer used the common language of proud Black Southern mamas and aunties. That's what my mama and aunties said about me too.

Taylor, an emergency medical technician, was shot to death in her apartment by Louisville, Kentucky, police who were executing a no-knock warrant as part of a drug investigation that allowed them to enter without warning or identifying themselves. Taylor and her boyfriend, Kenneth Walker, were awakened by a loud banging, and Walker, a licensed gun owner, fired as the men forced their way inside. The cops responded with ten shots, eight of which hit Taylor. No drugs were found.

Taylor lived an hour away from my hometown of Lexington, Kentucky, and as I look through her timeline, I think her tweets could've been mine. She was "Staying Afloat!" according to her Twitter bio. In my twenties, as a first-generation college graduate, I too was just trying to stay afloat. Like Taylor, I was a Black girl trying to "stay true to herself regardless." Black women in the South are taught to be modest. But Taylor, who called herself "PrettyN_Paidd" on Twitter, was having a tug-of-war with modesty, wanting to "brag so bad just one time but my humbleness won't allow me . . . just ain't me."

And Taylor was trying to be cautious when it came to how she let men treat her or who she dealt with, which is important when you got "lil sisters and cousins looking up to ya."

I'm the oldest of five children and I know my sisters and cousins look up to me. My youngest sister, Ebony, was born a year before Taylor. As I scanned the photos taken in Taylor's apartment, two things in her bedroom reminded me of my other sister, Shay. The first was Taylor's hot-pink-and-black iron, because my sister loves a hard crease in her clothes. Second were the aphorisms glittering in black-and-metallic-gold letters on Taylor's wall telling her to "pray more." My sister has posted quotes throughout her house asking God to bless her home.

I've tried to set a good example for my sisters, but I wasn't always cautious when it came to men, a necessary wisdom Taylor emphasized herself on Twitter. After college, I left Kentucky to move to New York City, and my first few years were tough. I was a freelancer in my mid-twenties, making ten dollars an hour and struggling to get by. A friend from college would send me money when I was short.

"You helped me when I was down," he would say over the phone, after confirming he had sent me money through Western Union.

But I felt terrible, because I was accepting drug money. He sold crack, the same drug my mama has been addicted to on and off since I was in elementary school. A drug so powerful it robbed me and my siblings of a childhood with her leading the family. One day when I was back visiting family in Kentucky, my friend picked me up and we drove to his apartment. As we reminisced about college, I opened his glove compartment and a gun stared back at me. We never talked about it. But I knew why he had it.

Unlike me, Taylor was clear earlier in life about dodging men with questionable backgrounds. And even though she was intentional in her choice to date "a law-abiding citizen," this desire didn't save her. Unnecessary deaths creep in our shadows, even when we walk a straight path. The cops still kick in our doors looking for drugs and kill us.

At twenty-six, Taylor was coming to understand her worth and how radical it is to love your Black female self. "I ain't better than nobody, but I am too good for certain s–– period!" As I take in Taylor's words, I think about some of my own sloppy life decisions and how it is true I'm not better than anyone else. But like Taylor, I still don't deserve to die.

I'm one of a cohort of Black women trying to find their way in the world.

There are a lot of us who, in the words of poet Nikky Finney, "never had it made, but made it." There's the lawyer who was raised by her grandmother and now lives in Atlanta. The University of Kentucky economics graduate who decided to teach underprivileged children in New Orleans. The writer with a master's degree in social work who planted her life in Kentucky. The only daughter who left Shelbyville to work for our first Black president.

We aren't all the same, but we carry similar scars. Some of our mamas work as cashiers at Walmart, a newly defined essential job during COVID-19. One of our sisters collects food stamps, and that's okay because she's trying to make sure her kids have healthy meals, perfect spelling tests, and clean sheets every night. These Black women from Kentucky learned to thrive in a racist world. And all of them, in Taylor's words, are "a f–ing vibe."

On Twitter, she emphasizes changing area codes from Michigan to Kentucky. I remember feeling a similar shift when I packed three suitcases, hopped on a Greyhound bus, and headed to the Big Apple. I felt hopeful and strong, even though my grandmother tried to talk me out of it. "New York is too big for you," she said in her last attempt to get me to stay in Kentucky.

I wonder, like Taylor did in a tweet on February 19, what her life would've been like if she had never moved. "Where would I work? Would I have kids?"

I have that same thought. What would I be doing right now in some sister-life where I had stayed home? I know I would have joined my grandmother and mother, who decided to march, even during a pandemic, on Taylor's birthday, so "that they could get something done about those officers that killed her," as my grandmother told me.

The ghosts of white supremacy haunt me as the months go by since the police killed Taylor and blew out her Black girl sparkle.

Every day that Louisville fails to arrest those officers, they devalue my life and others like me.

She's my sister, my niece, and all the other Black girls who love their community and family. Breonna is me and I am her.

Originally published June 26, 2020

FOR CORPORATIONS, IS **JUNETEENTH** ABOUT **PROFITS** OR **PROGRESS?**

The Black community has many needs; another holiday isn't one of them.

BY WILLIAM C. RHODEN

CORPORATE AMERICA has discovered Juneteenth.

In an effort to placate Black consumers in the midst of a national uprising, corporations are giving their employees a day off.

No, thanks. I refuse to celebrate a holiday about freedom when we're still not free.

But this is the way it always works. An atrocity perpetrated against the Black community followed by outrage, protests, and promises of remediation. Invariably, individual Black people will benefit from white guilt, favors will be granted, and eventually things get back to normal.

When NFL commissioner Roger Goodell announced that the league would observe Juneteenth, at least six NFL teams quickly followed suit, announcing that they would permanently recognize Juneteenth. When the Washington football team, a franchise that then had the most racist name in professional sports, joined the parade, I said, "Stop."

At some point the gestures become so meaningless they neuter the very thing they are meant to honor.

There are different ways of hijacking a movement.

A movement can be co-opted before it realizes that it has been compromised. There was a poignant news story out of Seattle, for instance, where protesters continued to gather inside the so-called Capitol Hill Autonomous Zone.

A member of the African American Community Advisory Council, which works to foster relationships between Black residents and police in the city, accused the protesters of hijacking the message of Black Lives Matter in the city. The chairwoman of the group, Victoria Beach, said the so-called autonomous zone had the feel of a festival.

Corporations and leagues can mouth support and even throw money at a cause, as many are doing with Black Lives Matter. But when the culture of the corporation betrays its outfacing pronouncements, it can be accused of hijacking.

This is the problem when corporations become involved with social justice issues. So much of what they do is grandstanding, designed to stay on the right side of polling and the bottom line. During a time of major unrest, corporations are trying to find ways to convince Black consumers that the companies are worthy of their continued patronage.

Can you blame the corporations?

According to a 2018 Nielsen report, while African Americans

account for 14 percent of the population, we are responsible for $1.2 trillion in purchases annually. Corporations want to cater to us with words and platitudes. What they are far less eager to do is bring us into the C-suites, where lucrative contracts and compensation packages are hammered out, where business is doled out to friends and business associates.

Black employees at a corporation with no significant Black executive presence will look at gestures and grand pronouncements about Black Lives Matter with resentment.

Federal statistics show that African American employees in virtually every industry tend to be concentrated in the lowest-paying jobs with little if any power. According to the report, more than 80 percent of CEOs and more than 70 percent of all executives, leaders, and managers in the U.S. workforce are white.

For many of those who work inside these corporations and sit on their boards, the most tedious part of the job is placating white colleagues in positions of authority, especially those aspiring to–or purporting to–do good deeds.

In an analysis of white American viewpoints of African Americans, political scientist Andrew Hacker pointed out in his book *Two Nations: Black and White, Separate, Hostile, Unequal*: "To be black in America means reining in your opinions and emotions as no whites ever have to do. Not to mention the forced and false smiles you are expected to contrive, to assure white Americans that you harbor no grievances against them."

Writing in *Corporate Board Member* magazine, Gaurdie Banister said, "Directors must first get past the naiveté of believing that the systemic racism and injustice encountered by black Americans does not exist in their companies."

He added: "Many on boards believe that they have 'done enough' regarding racism and inequality in their company. They feel they have a meritocracy grounded in the 'best person for the job' mantra and that the various inclusion and diversity programs they have are working just fine. I submit that if that were all true, then thousands of people would not be in the streets protesting the system that produced Mr. Floyd's demise.

"Using words like 'diverse' or 'people of color' ignores the fact that Black people are treated differently than others," Banister writes. "Do we believe Ahmaud Arbery would have been tracked and shot if he were Asian?"

A movement can be hijacked with mountains of money.

Corporate support for Black lives is pouring in, with donations targeted for racial justice groups, bail funds, and Black-led advocacy organizations. But how much business are these gigantic corporations doing with Black businesses?

After initially telling employees they could not wear Black Lives Matter material, Starbucks quickly changed course and said they could wear Black Lives Matter shirts and pins. The coffee giant said it would provide 250,000 Starbucks-branded Black Lives Matter shirts for baristas and other employees who want them. But will a Black-owned company be chosen to make the shirts?

"These giant companies are spending billions and billions of dollars with their professional services firms, their investment banks, the law firms, the consulting firms, the advertising agencies. There's this whole ecosystem that we're left out of," said John Rogers Jr., the chairman, co-CEO, and chief investment officer at Ariel Investments.

Rogers has sat on more than a dozen boards over the years. He has been in the boardrooms when a company has announced a major transaction. "You have a special board meeting and all the advisers walk in and it'll be twelve white men walk in, the investment banker, the law firm, the consulting firm, the public relations firm, the government affairs firm," Rogers said.

"I've raised my hand and said, 'I have to acknowledge that this is not consistent with the values of this company to see only white men come in for this huge economic opportunity as we contemplate this transaction.'"

With daily protests and so many issues swirling around a far-flung Black community, it's easy to lose focus, and movements can be taken over as missions are blurred.

The prevailing impetus for African Americans must be closing the wealth and income gap. The gap has grown exponentially and continues to devour the hopes and aspirations of so many young African American lives.

Those lives matter.

With all due respect to the recent excitement around Juneteenth, corporations, including the NFL, should commemorate the series of massacres by whites across the United States in which Black communities that had begun to develop prosperity and independence were destroyed.

Corporations should develop a coordinated "Marshall Plan" to rebuild Black communities, just as the United States helped rebuild Europe following World War II. In this country, there is a war being waged against the Black community.

The *Washington Post* has documented the cases of more than 1,500 Black people who have been shot and killed by the police since January 2015. The devastation of the coronavirus made it clear that thousands of casualties result from limited access to medical care and healthy food. And there are the long-term casualties of those who lack access to top-notch education.

The African American community has so many needs.

What we don't need is another holiday.

Originally published June 19, 2020

AMERICA IS FACING A RECKONING OVER RACE, BUT WE'VE SEEN THIS BEFORE

Our history shows African Americans make gains, but are stopped short of full equality.

BY MICHAEL A. FLETCHER

WHAT KIND of country sees Black Lives Matter as a radical idea and Black suffering and death as unremarkable?

African Americans are dying at two and a half times the rate of white people from COVID-19, continuing a long history of unequal health outcomes that have seen Black people disproportionately stricken by diseases, including cancer, heart disease, and strokes. Black people are far more likely than white folks to fall victim to infant mortality, maternal mortality, and murder. Black men are six times as likely as white men to end up in prison and two and a half times as likely to be killed by police.

Until recently, most of America saw all that as no cause for alarm. It was just the way things were, and have been to a greater or lesser degree since the founding of the republic. Black lives, it seems, have always been expendable.

But since the world witnessed a Minneapolis police officer nonchalantly squeeze the life out of George Floyd by pressing his knee into his neck, there has been a seismic shift. Elected officials are moving to rein in police budgets and practices. New York and Virginia decreed Juneteenth a paid holiday for state employees. Congress is debating legislation to make it easier to prosecute bad cops. The Pentagon is considering rechristening army bases named after Confederate officers. The Quaker Oats Company has done away with the brand name Aunt Jemima, and food conglomerates Mars Inc. and Conagra Brands say Uncle Ben's and Mrs. Butterworth's are being reviewed.

"Something is fundamentally shifting," said the Reverend William J. Barber II, president of Repairers of the Breach, a coalition pressing for a national program to attack systemic racism and poverty. "There is a consciousness awakening and you cannot put it back in the box."

The nation has experienced startling racial watersheds before, of course, and each time African American gains were stifled long before full equality was achieved.

Reconstruction tried and failed to get the nation to recognize the humanity of African Americans. Following World War I, African Americans who had proven their valor in the trenches of Europe were returning home and hundreds of thousands of others were moving north to flee racial terrorism and abject poverty in the South. They found opportunity, but also murderous white hostility.

After World War II, as civil rights lawyers found once-unthinkable success chipping away at state-sanctioned segregation, the old order was maintained by redlining, massive resistance, and white flight. Even as the Black middle class grew, educational levels increased, and Black officials filled thousands of political offices, culminating in the election of Barack Obama as the nation's first Black president, those achievements did not erase racial disadvantages baked in over time. The nation's racial hierarchy is now perpetuated not by mobs, but by the way the criminal justice, education, and health care systems work, and the economic pie is shared.

That structure is now being challenged in unprecedented ways. But what will become of this moment?

A RECKONING

A poll conducted by SurveyMonkey for CNBC found a dramatic increase in the percentage of white people who agree that racism against Black folks is a major problem, a growing feeling that white people benefit from unfair advantages, and an increasing national consensus that the police do not provide equal treatment. It is as if Floyd's death removed the scales from the eyes of many Americans, allowing them to see how the country fosters and tolerates racial inequity, and even honors those who maintain it.

The demonstrations and reactions that followed Floyd's death are unlike anything the nation has experienced in a generation. A statue of Jefferson Davis, the president of the Confederacy, was toppled in Richmond, Virginia. A statue of Christopher Columbus was beheaded in Boston, another toppled in St. Paul, Minnesota, and a third submerged in a lake in Richmond. At Philadelphia's Italian Market, workers painted over a mural of the city's former mayor and police chief Frank Rizzo, who once urged residents to "vote white." After his statue was vandalized by protesters, it was also removed from the steps of the Municipal Services Building, where it had stood for twenty-one years.

"The statue represented bigotry, hatred, and oppression for too many people for too long. It is finally gone," tweeted Philadelphia mayor Jim Kenney.

The moment has also spurred uncomfortable racial conversations and confessions that might have been hard to imagine just weeks ago.

The top editor of *Bon Appétit* resigned in disgrace in early June after a picture surfaced of him and his wife dressing up as Puerto Ricans for Halloween. The old photo was only part of the story. Shortly afterward, *Business Insider* reported that the celebrated food magazine maintained a toxic culture that excluded and demeaned Black people and other staffers of color. Black folks received less pay, fewer privileges, and little of the respect accorded their white colleagues, the report said. In one particularly egregious example, the editor is accused of asking his Black assistant to clean his golf clubs.

The founding editor of *Refinery29* also resigned after employees took to social media to describe a culture of discrimination at the women's lifestyle publication. At the *Philadelphia Inquirer*, the executive editor resigned after a column headlined "Buildings Matter, Too" ignited a walkout by Black and other reporters at the paper.

The ongoing reckoning is reaching even the most buttoned-up corners of American society. The U.S. military, an organization often saluted for embracing diversity, has simultaneously marginalized African Americans. Just two of its top-ranking forty-one commanders are Black, and people are now speaking up.

Air-force chief master sergeant Kaleth O. Wright took to social media to urge his colleagues to acknowledge racism and do something about it.

"Who am I?" he asked. "I am a Black man who happens to be the Chief Master Sergeant of the Air Force. I am George Floyd . . . I am Philando Castile, I am Michael Brown, I am Alton Sterling, I am Tamir Rice."

Wright also called out what he referred to as "the Air Force's own demons," including a lack of diversity at the top and racial disparities in military justice.

After Floyd's death, the air-force chief of staff, General Charles Q. Brown Jr., also shared his long experience with racism. Brown, who was confirmed by the Senate to be the first African American to lead one of the branches of the U.S. Armed Services and the second to serve on the Joint Chiefs of Staff, after General Colin Powell, said in a video posted to YouTube: "I'm thinking about how full I am with emotion not just for George Floyd, but the many African Americans that have suffered the same fate as George Floyd."

Brown, a fighter pilot, said that over his thirty-six-year military career, he was "often the only African American in my squadron." At times, he said, his credentials were questioned when those of white pilots were not. He said he felt pressure to perform error-free to prove wrong those supervisors who expected less from him because he is Black.

In the realm of sports, where political and social statements were frowned upon in the past, almost nobody is saying "just shut up and play" anymore. Top college football and basketball coaches, mostly white men who make fortunes off the talents of Black men, have felt obligated to make public statements condemning racial injustice.

The schools have also been forced to listen to Black athletes posing pointed questions about the coaches they play for and the institutions they represent. At Clemson University, athletes are demanding that the names of buildings honoring white supremacists be changed.

Black athletes at the University of Texas are leading an effort to jettison the school song rooted in the era of minstrel shows, rename several campus buildings, and donate a portion of the university's athletic revenue to racial justice groups. And at the University of Iowa, the longtime strength and conditioning coach was let go after a large group of former players, many of them Black, voiced grievances about mistreatment in the program.

NASCAR banned the Confederate flag at its races. The NFL's hypocrisy over what is widely seen as its blackballing of former San Francisco 49ers quarterback Colin Kaepernick is being called out with renewed ferocity. And the long, contentious debate over the lack of Black coaching and front-office leadership in the predominantly Black league has taken on new urgency.

"We are definitely in a remarkable moment that has the potential to be a tipping point," said Tricia Rose, director of Brown University's Center for the Study of Race and Ethnicity in America.

There have been other remarkable moments in the past, but each time progress was halted long before the nation reached full equality.

CAUTIONARY TALES

In the years following Reconstruction, baseball was one of the most popular sports in the country, and by the 1880s, historians say maybe twenty Black players were in the professional leagues.

But that move toward integration was soon stopped with the help of professional baseball's first superstar, Adrian "Cap" Anson. Anson is most notable for two things: one being that he was the first player to reach three thousand career hits, and two being his determination to drum Black players out of the ranks of professional players.

In August 1883, Anson's Chicago White Stockings, the forerunner of the Chicago Cubs, played an exhibition game against the Toledo Blue Stockings, a squad featuring Moses Fleetwood "Fleet" Walker, who is often credited with being the first Black player in the majors. But Anson angrily refused to take the field if Walker played. Anson only relented when he was told that he would have to forfeit his share of the gate if he stuck by his decision.

Still, other players and managers took Anson's lead and similar incidents followed. In 1887, Anson refused to play an exhibition game in Newark, New Jersey, unless the local club removed its African American battery, catcher Walker and pitcher George Stovey. A few years later, white owners barred Black folks from professional baseball. The color line remained in place for nearly six decades until Jackie Robinson broke it in 1947.

Anson's racism did not prevent him from claiming an honored place in baseball history: He was enshrined in the Baseball Hall of Fame in 1939. Meanwhile, Walker, his lucrative sports career cut short, encountered ups and downs. He became a businessman and an inventor, worked at the post office, and did a year in prison. After his release, he edited a newspaper and wrote a forty-seven-page treatise, "Our Home Colony," which advocated for Black Americans to return to Africa.

Walker's ordeal mirrored the everyday horrors of Jim Crow. He and other African Americans lived through a new national consciousness that brought once-unfathomable gains—freedom from slavery, seats in Congress and state legislatures, civil service jobs, baseball celebrity—followed by a determined, soul-sapping retrenchment.

The promise of Reconstruction was to turn Black people from property into full Americans. But Black Americans were never allowed to claim and keep their citizenship because many white people could not see their humanity.

It is part of a cycle that has played out repeatedly in American race relations.

Following World War I, the nation again reached a racial turning point. Thousands of Black soldiers returned home from battling tyranny in Europe and were ready to claim their rightful place as full American citizens. At the same time, the first wave of the Great Migration was underway, with thousands upon thousands of Black people moving from Southern peonage to industrial jobs in the North.

But even as African Americans embraced new opportunities, they found themselves once again battling terrorism. With the nation in the grip of a flu pandemic in the summer and fall of 1919, race riots flared up across the country. Violence incited by white folks enveloped at least twenty-five cities and towns, leaving dozens of African Americans dead in Chicago and as many as two hundred killed in Elaine, Arkansas.

The wave of rioting was dubbed the "Red Summer" by civil rights activist James Weldon Johnson, and it coincided with a resurgence of the Ku Klux Klan and lynching across the country. Two years later, a white mob in Tulsa, Oklahoma, left more than three hundred Black people dead in a section of town known as Black Wall Street.

The violence was rationalized by the racist notion that Black people were a breed apart. Respected white scholars of the day theorized that African Americans were biologically inclined toward crime, even as white mobs carried out unspeakable assaults targeting their Black countrymen.

RESILIENCE

Congressman James E. Clyburn came of age in the decades following World War II as the nation's civil rights movement was slowly taking hold. He rose from legally segregated Sumter, South Carolina, to become the third-ranking Democrat in the U.S. House of Representatives. The events that occurred during his life are a testament to both the astounding success of the movement and the persistence of Black suffering.

Growing up, he loved baseball. He played second base at South Carolina State University, inspired by his hero, Robinson, who broke in with the then-Brooklyn Dodgers as a second baseman.

Clyburn saw that for all the racist abuse heaped on Robinson, his fate was different from Walker's. Robinson changed baseball forever, and his memory is widely revered. But Clyburn also remembers the searing events of the civil rights years–the murder of Medgar Evers in his own driveway; the bombing of the Sixteenth Street Baptist Church; the brutal police-led beating of peaceful marchers on the Edmund Pettus Bridge in Selma, Alabama; the assassination of Martin Luther King Jr.

Each of those moments shocked the nation's conscience, creating momentum for substantive change.

"Those events led to things like the Civil Rights Act of 1964, and the Voting Rights Act of 1965," Clyburn said. In 1968, the federal government outlawed housing discrimination.

The laws made a difference, moving the nation closer to its promise. But as always, there was backlash. By the late 1970s, affirmative action programs that helped Black businesses grow and fueled an increase in the number of Black college students were challenged in court as discrimination against white people, the start of a fight that still continues.

Through it all, the country continued to resist anything approaching true equality. Many white folks fled neighborhoods in cities when Black people started to move in. And when suburban neighborhoods attracted Black homeowners, they often fled those too. Across the country, white people resisted policies that required their children to attend schools with substantial numbers of Black students.

African Americans now had their citizenship, and their rights were guaranteed by federal law, but white people did not want to be their neighbors.

By the time Clyburn was elected to Congress in 1992, African Americans were once again being elected to political office in large numbers. At first, they relied largely on Black constituencies to elect mayors in majority-Black cities, and members of Congress in majority-Black districts.

But that shifted over time as more white folks felt comfortable voting for Black representatives. The tide grew slowly for decades until Obama was elected president in 2008, marking another racial turning point.

Many Americans saw Obama's election as proof that the country had finally overcome its racial demons. A country with an electorate that was just over three-quarters white had elected a Black president, so many white people saw the nation entering a "postracial" era.

The feeling did not last long. The first Black president was confronted with the nation's old problems. There were new cases of racial violence and police brutality, much of it captured on video. Also, the huge economic, health, and opportunity gaps separating Black and white people remained in place.

Life expectancy for African Americans is three years shorter than for white folks. Black people are 40 percent less likely to have a bachelor's degree than white people, and have just a dime for every dollar of white wealth.

"When George Floyd said, 'I can't breathe', I think it touched something much deeper in people who are also saying during this pandemic, 'I can't breathe,'" said Barber. "But it would be a terrible waste to have all this marching in the street and all we get is a piece of legislation that gets at the part of the issue around police violence and not deal with the violent public policy that affects Black life every day."

American history makes this much clear: America will find a way to continue tolerating and justifying disproportionate Black suffering. Whatever becomes of this hopeful moment, it will be followed by some type of backlash. The only question is how far things will roll back.

Originally published July 2, 2020

VICTIM NO. 79: AMERICA'S HOMICIDE **CRISIS** CLAIMED MY CHILDHOOD FRIEND

Eric Smith isn't just another statistic. He and my hometown were caught in this country's other pandemic.

BY DWAYNE BRAY

WHEN I was a kid in the late 1960s, I had a bunch of white friends. They were my neighbors in East Cleveland, Ohio. My family was the third Black household on Brightwood Avenue, a street with forty-eight well-built residential homes. Then, seemingly all at once, the white folks up and left. At the time, I didn't know what had happened, but our street was suddenly all Black.

I was just happy that Deon and Eric, two of my best friends, didn't go anywhere. Deon was a year younger than me, and Eric was two years behind his brother. We used to call Deon "Cat Eyes" because his eyes were hazel, an unusual thing for a Black kid. Eric was big for his age and had no problem running with us older boys. Deon and Eric, and the rest of the immediate family, lived with their grandparents on Brightwood off and on. My mom and I lived with my grandparents. Our families were good friends. Grandma used to send me to their house to "borrow" a cup of sugar or flour or a few eggs. As we grew up, I attended college, got married, had kids, and, as the years went by, would only occasionally see my friends from the old neighborhood.

In the summer of 2021, shortly before my annual trip home for the Fourth of July, I learned that Eric had died in a shooting at a notoriously violent street corner less than a half mile from where we grew up.

"This dude shot him in the back," a relative told me on a phone call. Reportedly, Eric turned to say how cowardly it was to shoot him when he wasn't looking and pulled out his own gun and the two men exchanged shots. Eric took a few steps, collapsed, and died, according to a 911 caller and Cleveland police.

Eric hadn't been living an easy life. He'd had a thirty-year narcotics addiction. (The medical examiner found that he had cocaine, PCP, and painkillers in his system at the time of his death.) He'd spent more than half of his adulthood cycling in and out of Ohio's prisons. He'd experienced homelessness. Earlier this year, a court-ordered psychological evaluation determined he suffered from mental illness. But it appears that diagnosis was long overdue and his illness may already have been a trigger for many of his previous issues with substance abuse and the law.

Now he is a statistic on a crime analyst's spreadsheet: gun-fatality victim no. 79 in Cleveland in 2021. The city is on pace for its most homicides in thirty years.

Some might say that Eric's demise started when he decided to take his first hit of crack cocaine in his twenties. He's not blameless, to be sure. But Eric's decline and the decline of my hometown are part of a wider system that deprives Black communities of adequate finances, indulges corrupt police, and treats drug addiction as a crime rather than an illness. And all these factors contribute to this country's pandemic of violence.

The numbers aren't lying: There is a homicide crisis in America, and like most unfavorable trends, it's hitting Black people the hardest. Homicides increased in the United States nearly 30 percent from 2019 to 2020, to 21,570, according to FBI figures.

The carnage is continuing, with the Council on Criminal Justice estimating the number of victims has increased an additional 16 percent in the first half of 2021.

Fifty-three percent of gun violence homicide victims in 2019 were Black men, even though they only make up about 7 percent of the U.S. population. The problem is particularly acute among Black men between the ages of fifteen and thirty-four. They're 37 percent of gun homicide victims but only 2 percent of the population, according to federal data analyzed by the Educational Fund to Stop Gun Violence and the Coalition to Stop Gun Violence.

Most experts attribute the rise in homicides to Americans arming themselves in wake of the coronavirus pandemic and social justice protests.

"We haven't seen these homicide [numbers] since the early '90s with the crack cocaine epidemic," said Saleh Awadallah, the assistant prosecutor who runs the Cuyahoga County Major Trial Homicide Unit in Cleveland. "People are more trigger-happy than they've ever been. Many of these homicides take place in a split second–being at the gas station, at different pumps, two guys have a look at each other, and we're having a shootout."

Nearly 40 million guns were bought legally in America in 2020, the most in a single year and a 60 percent jump from 2019. The trend continued in 2021. Through June, more than 22 million guns were purchased. A 2018 study estimated that there were 393 million civilian-owned guns in the U.S., which means the total number of guns may have increased by a staggering 15 percent in just a year and a half.

That increase in sales was especially notable among Black folks, according to the National Shooting Sports Foundation, which estimated purchases by African Americans increased by 56 percent in 2020 compared with 2019.

All these numbers mean one thing, gun violence experts say: We have more armed citizens, and with more people capable of pulling the trigger, we have more homicides.

Dan Flannery, director of the Begun Center for Violence Prevention Research and Education at Case Western Reserve University in Cleveland, said it's pretty simple: "When something happens and a firearm is available, it's more likely to be used."

Eric Donnell Smith was born on December 18, 1967, at the height of the civil rights movement. He would die fifty-three years later in the middle of a pandemic.

Eric's dad was a former navy seaman named Talbert Smith. Talbert, known as "Tee" to family and friends, was twenty when Eric was born. His first son, Talbert Deon Smith, had come nearly two years earlier.

Eric and Deon's mom, Arlaine Smith, had wanted to parlay her slim figure and pretty face into a career as a fashion model. She settled on being a cosmetologist. She and her twin sister sang Motown covers at local talent shows and often came away with the prize money.

Talbert had survived a catastrophic explosion off the coast of

North Vietnam just five months before Eric's birth. The navy said 134 men were lost that day on the USS *Forrestal*. Once out of the service, Talbert drove a truck for a vending machine company and got rave reviews for his performance. He was smart and knew how to get things done efficiently.

Soon Arlaine and Tee had four boys: Deon, Eric, Andre, and Trent. Talbert loved taking his sons down to Lake Erie, which is where the older ones learned to swim.

"Tee threw us in Lake Erie," Deon said. "He threw us in there. He said, 'Now, y'all get back to the edge.' I was the first one to get thrown in the water. . . . It was shocking."

Eric was a good swimmer from the jump and his dad recognized that his son had a special talent. Unlike a lot of Black kids of that day, Eric had no fear of the water. As he got a little older, Eric gained a reputation around Cleveland-area pools as a natural-born swimmer. That reputation took on mythical proportions when it came to a game known as the "greasy watermelon toss."

Lifeguards would slather a watermelon in cooking oil and drop it in the water. Frenzied swimmers would try to get it and hold on. But "it would start slipping everywhere," recalled Andre, one of Eric's younger brothers. "People were pushing it out of your hands like a football."

Eric had long arms and legs and a strong upper body. "Eric would cup it in his belly and just hold it," Andre said, "and it just always worked out for him."

But things weren't working out for Tee, who was experiencing flashbacks of the ship explosion. To deal with his post-traumatic stress disorder, he drank and did drugs. Arlaine and Tee separated.

On August 6, 1974, Talbert was at the lake with some friends. The day was sunny and a light breeze was blowing. "They were drinking, walking on the rocks, and he slipped and fell into the water and the undertow got him," Andre, now fifty-one, told me in an interview at his house in suburban Cleveland.

Andre was looking at his father's death certificate as we spoke. The document stated that Tee "drowned while swimming in lake." Some older relatives, though, suspect foul play was involved because Tee was an excellent swimmer who had been diving in Lake Erie since he arrived in Cleveland from Mississippi as a boy.

When he died, Tee was twenty-seven. Deon was eight; Eric, six; Andre, four; and Trent, one. All four boys got dressed up and went with their mom to Tee's funeral.

East Cleveland is only seven miles from downtown Cleveland, an easy commute that once attracted the wealthy and connected. Oil tycoon John D. Rockefeller had a 235-acre estate in the Forest Hill neighborhood of East Cleveland, one of his two homes in the area.

Eventually, his son donated the land to East Cleveland and the neighboring city of Cleveland Heights. John D. Rockefeller Jr. also donated land to East Cleveland for a public library, a hospital, and a junior high school.

After the Great Depression, working-class white people began moving in. They stayed until the 1960s, but once we Black folks arrived, they bounced.

Research by Mark Souther, a Cleveland State University professor, shows East Cleveland was 98 percent white in 1960 but 86 percent Black by 1980. That change took place even as the city's population dropped dramatically, from 39,600 in 1970 to 17,843 in 2010. It's now less than 14,000.

The transformation didn't happen by accident. Frank Ford, a senior policy adviser at the Western Reserve Land Conservancy outside of Cleveland, said real estate agents used integration to scare white folks into selling their homes at below-market prices. The concept is known as blockbusting.

And once those Black homeowners arrived, Ford said, they were penalized by a federal policy that dated back to the 1930s, years before any Black people had a chance to live in East Cleveland.

The Home Owners Loan Corporation (HOLC), a federal program designed to gauge the risk of making a home loan, began assessing what it called the "security" of neighborhoods. It generated color-coded maps that designated which communities HOLC deemed "most desirable" for lending and which were "least desirable." Areas with the lowest financial risk, and best chance for increased property values, were shaded green, followed by blue, yellow, and, the riskiest, red.

Once the white people moved out, East Cleveland–and other predominantly Black areas around the United States–were coded red, a system known as "redlining." "That went all the way through the 1970s and caused a lot of disinvestment" in Black communities, Ford said.

My family's two-story bungalow sat at 1824 Brightwood Avenue. It had three bedrooms, two baths, and a spacious, unfinished basement that was our play area on snowy winter days. We had to be careful not to get close to the furnace or we'd scald our hands, as my younger cousin once did. He had blisters for days.

Eric's grandparents lived next door at 1828 Brightwood Avenue in a slightly bigger brown bungalow. Our families were close and big. Eleven people were in our household. Eric's home had thirteen occupants, and that kept them in the crosshairs of the East Cleveland housing inspectors, who tried to keep the city just for "nuclear families" until the Supreme Court eventually told them to knock it off.

By 1977, the only white folks left on our block were three or four older adults. They were mostly shut-ins. We'd see them on the porch if the weather was nice, but that was it. There were no white families with young children, or even white working-age people.

Arlaine married postal carrier Johnny Howard soon after Tee's death, but she didn't always get along with her new husband, her children told me. So, she would bring her kids over to Brightwood to live with Talbert's parents.

That meant Eric and Deon were back in the neighborhood, which made me happy.

For several years in the 1970s, we did the Brightwood Block Club on Saturdays. Residents would band together to make sure the street was spic-and-span. The adults would cut grass, paint porches, and fix structures. The kids would pick up litter. Afterward, we'd munch on hamburgers and hot dogs from a grill.

We were proud of our street, our neighborhood, and our city—and showing whoever doubted us that we could take care of a neighborhood as well as anyone else.

When Eric was twelve, his family was living in another part of East Cleveland when his older brother Deon got caught up in a robbery and car theft with one of Arlaine's nephews. He would spend the next four years in juvenile detention.

Eric had to help Arlaine care for the younger siblings and deal with the strife in her marriage. Still, he was doing well in school and was focused on his swimming. In the tenth grade, he was selected to be on the Shaw High School varsity swim and dive team, his family said. They remembered he would wear a red-and-white T-shirt with the words "Swim" and "Dive" printed across the front.

Arlaine was receiving food stamps and subsidies from the

women, infants, and children's nutrition program back then. She would line the kids up at local charities so they could get free blocks of government cheese. "I still keep a can of beans in my locker at work to remember all the meals when it was sort of tough," said Trent, now forty-eight, as he nursed a pineapple upside-down cake beer at a restaurant in the Cleveland suburb of Independence.

But there were good memories associated with their kitchen too. "Eric was the best cook in the family back when we were kids," said Trent. Eric especially liked to heat up some Crisco and, after peeling and slicing the potatoes, make french fries from scratch.

By eleventh grade, Eric was done with organized swimming. He was running with a rough crowd. He drank and smoked marijuana, a few times stealing it from his stepdad. "Eric used to go into his drawers and sneak his weed," Andre said. "That's where the drug use started." Arlaine had had enough of her marriage and East Cleveland. She moved her kids, who numbered seven by now, to Cleveland Heights, just south of East Cleveland, a city with strong government and schools, all the things East Cleveland had hoped to have.

It was in Cleveland Heights where Eric would experience his first crush.

Her name was Daniza Embrose and she had smooth brown skin and a bright smile. She also had a mom and dad who didn't want their fourteen-year-old daughter dating a boy as old as Eric, who was seventeen.

"My parents were like, 'You can't have a boyfriend,'" Embrose said. But they relented, she said, because Eric "was just so endearing."

"Eric's best time was when he met Daniza," Andre said. "They did stuff together. They dressed alike. I felt like he was being a normal guy."

Neither had wheels, so they walked. Mostly they hung out at the

Coventry Village shopping district and did teenage stuff: "We'd go get pizza. We'd get sub sandwiches. And just kind of hang out."

Some days, Eric would slip on his old Shaw High swim shirt and people would ask if he was a swimmer. He loved the attention.

"Eric knew *everybody* on Coventry," Embrose told me. "Everybody loved him, respected him."

Her dad took Eric under his wing. He showed Eric around Cleveland's NBC news station, where he worked in video production.

"My parents tried to show him and guide him, not because I was his girlfriend, but they wanted to show him a different aspect of the world," said Embrose. "My mom took us to see Run-DMC at the Front Row [Theater]. We saw New Edition at the Front Row, too."

Eric was feeling the love of his girlfriend's family. What he wasn't feeling was school in his new community. He finished eleventh grade but didn't go back for his senior year. Instead, he worked at Lax & Mandel Bakery and hung around the Embroses, including tagging along when they vacationed in the Bahamas. "The first thing he did was jump into the ocean," Embrose recalled.

By 1989, when Eric was twenty-one and Embrose eighteen, the crush was over. She'd graduated and gotten a job. Eric had stopped working at the bakery and was spending more time in his old community of East Cleveland.

They were moving in different directions and broke up.

East Cleveland's tax base was dwindling even as the community's need increased. There were abandoned houses and apartment buildings. And by 1990, crack cocaine had taken over dozens of East Cleveland's street corners. Young men in oversized winter coats wearing multiple layers of clothing would hang out and sell the highly addictive substance.

My old street, Brightwood, was no longer a source of pride associated with the Block Club. The cops had given it a new name, one that indicated the amount of narcotics being trafficked there: the Million Dollar Block.

By then, I was working three hours away in Dayton, Ohio, as a crime reporter. Meanwhile, Eric was using crack and, in 1993, serving his first prison sentence for carrying a concealed weapon. It wouldn't be his last time behind bars.

Eric would spend nine of the next sixteen years behind prison walls for offenses ranging from felonious assault to robbery to auto theft. Every time he did time, he agreed to plead guilty without putting the system through the expense of a trial. But that changed with an arrest back on Brightwood in February 2009.

Around the city, the East Cleveland Police Department's street crime unit was known as the "Jump Out Boys" because officers had a reputation for jumping out of their cruisers and beating people they thought were selling drugs. It didn't matter if the person had no drugs on them or that the officers lacked probable cause to stop them.

I know they did these things because the detective who headed the street crime unit testified about it in state court.

Detective Randy Hicks said this under oath:

"If somebody mouths off to you, put them on the hood. Look for dope. You don't find any, make it inconvenient for them."

He also said this:

"We were told to strip them down in the middle of winter. Make it inconvenient for them to be on the corners."

Hicks admitted that he "beat up people all the time" and added, "That's the way we were taught. You ran from us, that's what happened."

—

Eric was forty-one in 2009 when he encountered Hicks and the street crime unit on Brightwood. It was a Sunday in February. Eric had been up to no good, selling weed when the cops rolled up. He bolted, but Hicks took him down and cuffed him. Eric had a rock of crack cocaine in his pocket.

Hicks told his partner that Eric had tried to get his gun. Eric denied it and, for the first time, demanded a jury trial instead of accepting the state's four-year plea deal. Hicks stuck to his version. The jury believed Hicks and Eric got ten years.

"They convicted him essentially on Hicks's testimony," Eric's defense attorney, Donald Butler, said when I called him recently. Eric was serving time in the Grafton Correctional Institute for that case on November 9, 2014, alongside Deon, who was doing four years for assault, when their mom died of cancer. The two of them watched Arlaine's funeral together via Skype.

Eric was still insisting Hicks had lied on him when Hicks showed up in court in 2016, accused in a civil suit of setting up another man in East Cleveland.

This incident had happened on April 28, 2012. Arnold Black, a landscaper, testified that Hicks stopped his truck without justification and then punched him while he was sitting handcuffed on his car bumper. Black also claimed that the East Cleveland police took him to the station and locked him in a storage room for four days without food, water, toilet facilities, or medical attention to his head, which was swollen after being punched by Hicks.

Officer Jonathan O'Leary confirmed Black's story, telling supervisors that an informant had told Hicks about a car with a kilogram of cocaine stored in a door panel. When they stopped Black and failed to find any drugs, Hicks had indeed struck Black while he was handcuffed, O'Leary said. Black required surgery to stop bleeding in his brain, his attorney, Bobby DiCello, said in an interview.

The case had to be retried because of a technicality, but a second jury awarded Black $50 million in compensatory and punitive damages from Hicks and the city of East Cleveland, among others.

Eric thought the Black case proved Hicks, who had resigned from the police force by then, had lied about him too. He wanted a new trial, but never got one.

"Randy testified to a department-wide practice," said Eric Foster, a local attorney. "Then why wouldn't we be looking into every case coming out of East Cleveland? All the stuff that every defendant said in every courtroom that this officer made this up and took this from me, [Hicks] *said* they did it." Hicks has never been charged. But other East Cleveland officers have faced charges for a variety of misconduct. One was found to have kicked a handcuffed man in the head. He was fired—until the policemen's union successfully appealed because it had taken too long to discover what the officer had done.

Not long ago, two East Cleveland officers were arrested for allegedly stealing $5,000 from a man during a traffic stop. The money, the man said, was to help pay for his mother's funeral.

Police chief Scott Gardner declined to be interviewed. But police captain Ken Lundy said all the complaints of misconduct have left the department stained.

"It definitely makes the job tough on officers who are trying to do the right thing when they see two officers arrested for theft," Lundy said. I asked Lundy about Hicks. He said, "We don't want those people in the department. We are going to call officers out when they're doing wrong and that includes all the way up to prosecution."

Part of the problem is that East Cleveland can't afford to pay well and often has to settle for problematic candidates for its fifty-person force. "A lot of these officers have gotten reprimanded or had an opportunity to resign from another police force and decide that they are going to come to East Cleveland and take a pay cut to re-prove themselves," said city councilor at large Timothy Austin.

Bad cops and the inability of the justice system to root them out quickly has multiple add-on effects. People are more likely to see the police as corrupt and be unwilling to cooperate in investigations. If arrest rates are depressed, there's less deterrence of serious crime. And acceptance of bad practices means that low-level criminals like Eric can spend more time in jail on questionable charges and come out even less prepared to live on their own or find gainful employment.

After nine years in prison, Eric was released on January 25, 2018. But this last stint had changed him. On most days, he was good, friends and family say. But on others, he could appear lost, talking like he was disconnected from reality.

His old girlfriend, Embrose, said she saw him one day and he didn't know who she was.

Eighteen months later, he was back behind bars, charged with burglary and menacing. He spent five months in the county jail. After being released, he missed an appointment with his probation officer and was picked up again. His public defender, noting that he had been previously diagnosed with depression, PTSD, and bipolar disorder, asked that Eric be given a psychological exam to see if he was competent to stand trial. It showed Eric had a severe mental illness.

He'd been telling his brothers that helicopters were following him around.

"I said, 'Eric, come on, bro. You been getting high,'" Deon said. "He'd tell me if he was or not. But he wasn't."

Christine Montross, an associate professor of psychiatry and human behavior at Brown University, performs mental competency evaluations in criminal cases. There are about 356,000 seriously mentally ill inmates in America's jails and prisons, she said.

"I see people all the time with severe mental illnesses who are in punitive facilities when they ought to be in therapeutic ones," said Montross, who explored the issue in her 2020 book, *Waiting for an Echo: The Madness of American Incarceration.* "Incarceration routinely makes mentally ill people worse and it also renders psychiatrically stable people less well."

In the spring, Eric had become a resident at the Y-Haven Transitional Housing and Treatment Center, which provides shelter to homeless men, among others. Y-Haven operates out of the Carl B. Stokes Building, named for the man who was elected the city's first Black mayor in 1967, a month before Eric was born. But in early June, Eric left Y-Haven and didn't return. He called his counselor and told her he'd relapsed, his brother Andre said. Executive director Ed Gemerchak said Y-Haven's routine is to follow former residents for a year, but Eric's counselor could never reach him. "In Eric's case, we did have someone pursuing him," Gemerchak said. "He had a great relationship with his counselor."

Eric was out in the streets, and no one knew what he was doing. What is known is that he returned to familiar ground–East Cleveland and the adjacent Cleveland neighborhood of Glenville.

On June 7, he phoned his brother Andre around 5:30 a.m. Andre was working his early-morning shift.

"That's when I was begging and pleading with him to get off those streets," Andre said. "'You had no reason to be in that area,' I said. 'How long is this going to keep going?'"

Andre talked to him again on June 15 and they had a similar

conversation. A few days later, Deon met up with Eric, who told his brother that someone was out to kill him. He was preoccupied with a chopper that was flying around Cleveland.

"I'd say, 'What is it about you, Eric, that these helicopters are following you?' Is there something pertinent about you? Why are they following *you*? And he kept saying someone is trying to kill him."

On June 25, Eric called Andre again: "He told me he loved me ten times in a row and he asked me to pay his cellphone bill," Andre recalled.

The next day, according to Cleveland police and three of Eric's brothers, Eric and a woman he knew had an argument at a bus stop at the corner of East 125th Street and Superior Avenue in Glenville. That location is only a half mile from Brightwood Avenue. The relatives told me the woman made a call on her cellphone and that two men showed up in a car. One of the men and Eric allegedly talked about issues Eric and the woman were having. According to Eric's family members, who say they know some people who knew witnesses to the shooting, Eric was leaving the corner. The man Eric had spoken with was also leaving, but the second man who came to the bus stop reportedly opened fire, shooting Eric in the back. The autopsy report said he'd been shot twice in the back and once in the chest.

"Somebody got to shooting and he tried to shoot back and he's not moving," the first of several women who called 911 said. That caller said the injured man wandered over to a vacant lot and fell next to a yellow truck.

"He's right there by it," she said, referring to the truck. "He's dead. He's not moving."

Deon said someone called to tell him his brother had been shot, but he couldn't go to the hospital to identify the body because he was under house arrest. So he called Andre with the news: Eric was dead.

—

In Cuyahoga County, which includes Cleveland and its suburbs, the total number of homicides went from 190 in 2019 to 257 in 2020, the county's medical examiner, Dr. Thomas Gilson, said.

"I've been trying to ring the bell that gun violence is significantly worse in the last year or two," Gilson said.

Prosecutors here say that 85 percent of the homicide investigations they end up charging involve a Black male victim. "Guns are a symptom of something bigger," Gilson said.

Those who have spent their lives working to reduce violence say the driving force behind people shooting each other is no mystery. "The root cause of gun violence is literally poverty," said Bindu Kalesan, a researcher at Boston University's School of Public Health. "There is a saying within the public health community: When there is a new disease, look for it in the place where there is the least wealth."

Eric's family was poor and he lost his father at an early age. Experts say those two factors alone explain a lot about how his life developed. East Cleveland has one of the highest poverty rates in the state of Ohio at 37.5 percent. The child poverty rate in the city is close to 54 percent.

The numbers aren't that different in the adjoining Cleveland neighborhoods. Glenville, where Eric was killed, has a 36 percent poverty rate, with nearly 53 percent of children living below the poverty line, according to data from the Center for Community Solutions, a think tank trying to better socioeconomic conditions for the poor.

"A greater share of children live in poverty than any other age group," said Emily Campbell, associate director of research for the center. "Children don't choose to be poor. We ask people to pick themselves up by their bootstraps. We can't ask that of children. And we can't punish children for the circumstances that their parents are in."

Cleveland is the poorest big city in the nation, surpassing Detroit, census data shows. So while city officials are partnering with the business community to bring in prestigious events such as political conventions and the 2022 NBA All-Star Game, the communities with the least continue to struggle and vulnerable citizens like Eric die in the streets.

"We lost our brother Eric Smith, man, and there are other men and women who we are losing," said Cleveland councilman Basheer Jones, whose ward includes several high-poverty neighborhoods. "But this is a symptom of a bigger problem."

It cost the state of Ohio roughly half a million dollars to keep Eric in prison over the course of his life. Jones said it would cost taxpayers less to start investing in poor kids' lives early on. "What people have to understand is you pay now or you pay later, but you're going to pay," he said. "Whether you're paying for the jail cells. Whether you're paying for the extra police. You're paying in some way, so we might as well pay and be preventive rather than have to pay and be reactive."

Frank Jackson, Cleveland's mayor for the last sixteen years, didn't run for reelection. Ten days before Eric's death, he was one of twenty-seven big-city mayors requesting President Joe Biden's assistance to help reduce gun violence, saying local communities were overwhelmed.

On a September evening when Cleveland's football stadium hosted its first sold-out Browns game in nearly two years, a result of the pandemic, Jackson could be seen on the local news alongside Chief of Police Calvin Williams, pacing back and forth at a shooting scene in the city's Garden Valley housing development. Jackson's twenty-four-year-old grandson, Frank Q. Jackson, who had multiple brushes with the law over the past two years, had been killed.

As with Eric's shooting, no arrests have been made in the death of the younger Jackson.

Art McKoy, the head of antiviolence group Black on Black Crime Inc., calls the corner where Eric was killed in Glenville "a hot spot." He said Eric was at least the tenth person killed in that area in the past decade.

McKoy, a short man with a thick mustache, has been trying to bring awareness to this issue for years. But not that long ago he got a new perspective on violence.

In 2018, McKoy was working at his barbershop in East Cleveland when a nineteen-year-old accused him of not giving him a good haircut. The young man punched McKoy in the face, breaking his nose and eye socket. It took him six months to recover.

The nineteen-year-old later called McKoy to ask for forgiveness. He said he didn't realize he had hit a man who was well known in the community for decades of work on antiviolence.

"He said, 'Mr. McKoy, I'm sorry. I didn't know that was you. I'm so sorry, man.'"

McKoy told the young man to give him time to heal.

"I realized one thing," he said. "There has to be a stop-the-pain movement in our communities because pain is inflicted on one another at the bat of an eye for no reason.

"I'm talking about, I get mad with you and I'm knocking you out. I'm talking about getting mad with you and breaking your nose. I'm talking about getting mad with you and stomping on your spine and paralyze you. Why? Because a young man said that I messed up his ten-dollar line, and he's willing to kill me."

Councilman Jones echoed a similar sentiment about poor Black children being in pain and, as a result, defaulting to violence over any little thing.

"People are walking around unhealed, man, and we're not dealing with the problem," Jones said. "That's somebody's father, somebody's uncle. There's a pain that the family has to go through. That continues to spread, that continues to be regurgitated in a sense, unhealed wounds."

Yet amid the poverty and pain, these poor communities have islands of hope.

I stopped in at the East Cleveland Public Library to look at some old Shaw High yearbooks. I spent some time in the building back when I was a student in the public school system, but not nearly enough.

To help close the digital divide between poorer and richer communities, in 2018 the library became one of the first in the county to allow patrons to check out Wi-Fi hot spot units. "Before the pandemic, this time of day, this place would be packed," said Elmer Turner, who is the executive assistant to the director, Carlos Latimer, who went to Shaw High with me. "Since the shutdown, people have been trickling back in."

Farther east down Euclid Avenue, I found a former drug dealer who was trying to turn his life and his neighborhood around. His name is John Lastery and he was cutting hair inside his business, BossFitt Barber Lounge.

Lastery started his shop not long after his release from prison on a weapons offense. He said he wants to set a positive example for youths because gangbanging and drug dealing aren't the way to go.

"I could still be on the streets selling drugs, wasting my talents," he said as he lined a customer's hair.

Lastery's biceps flexed each time he moved a straight razor around a man's head. He's about five-feet-nine and says he can bench 350.

"How can I be BossFitt, if I ain't fit?" he said. "I sculpted myself into the king I'm supposed to be."

He's also bullish on the area.

"If this is the Mistake on the Lake, I don't see it," Lastery said. "You had the Rockefellers in East Cleveland. He wouldn't have come here for no reason."

Seti Richardson is an ex-offender who works with a segment of society that's most susceptible to gun violence: other ex-offenders. He runs the Re-entry Alumni Association, which aims to keep those who have been in prison from going back and from hurting anyone or being hurt themselves. I watched as he led a midweek meeting for ten people, which he said is down from the dozens of regular attendees before the pandemic. On this day, Richardson welcomed a twenty-seven-year-old man who recently came home after four years in prison. A judge had asked Richardson to take the man on.

Also in the room were a grandfather and grandson. Aside from me, the young man was the only non-offender in the room. His granddad opened up.

"I wasn't there for my son. Why?" the sixty-four-year-old said. "Because I was in the penitentiary."

Richardson turned his focus to the twenty-seven-year-old, who was tatted, wore Ohio State Buckeye sweats, and had the powerful build of an NFL linebacker. Richardson asked him a question all the others in the room, except for the boy and me, could relate to.

"How many fights you had in the penitentiary?"

"Too many to count," he finally answered.

One light-skinned man, who was fifty-six, spoke next.

"I ain't bragging, but I got six numbers," he said, referring to the times he's been locked away. "When I was growing up, I was in the streets. I was a heroin addict. Didn't care nothing about going to no jail.

"I hate to say this, but I was a true sucker," he continued. "I thought I was a true player."

"Brother, stay out of the penitentiary," a man in his sixties told the twenty-seven-year-old. "Stay with us. We're going to love you. We're going to nurture you."

Ten miles away in the Collinwood area of town, I caught up with Ted Ginn Sr., a legendary football and track coach and founder of a boys' school that enrolls students from impoverished areas.

Ginn Academy opened in 2007 and has a 95 percent graduation rate, Ginn told me with pride.

He wore a red sweatsuit with a matching red hat bearing a letter G for Glenville High, the Cleveland public school where he's the football coach. (Ginn Academy students play sports at Glenville and other Cleveland public schools.) Glenville, the neighborhood where Eric was killed, is famous both for its intractable poverty and for producing athletes such as Ted Ginn Jr., Troy Smith, Cardale Jones, and the agent representing LeBron James, Rich Paul.

Ginn Sr. played center for Glenville in the 1970s. He's sixty-five now, and after a bout with pancreatic cancer in 2012, he looks more like a receiver, which is the position his son held down in the NFL for fourteen years.

We sat at a table in the conference room off his office at the 375-student Ginn Academy. He was aware that although I'm employed by a sports network, I didn't come to talk football. I was there to gain insight into how community leaders are coping with the rise in gun violence, something Ginn knows all too intimately. His nineteen-year-old nephew, Diamond Russell, was a Ginn

Academy student when he was shot and killed in 2016 at a Shell gas station in East Cleveland.

"Diamond got in the car with his friends," Ginn said softly. "He was four days from graduation. They went over there by the gas station and dude just started shooting."

The shooter, Alonzo Patterson, eighteen, didn't know Russell. He was convicted of manslaughter and sentenced to twenty-five years in prison. An accomplice got six years for involuntary manslaughter.

"That could have been me, you, anybody," Ginn said. "I talked to the chief of police. I said, 'Do you know the mentality of a kid thirteen to twenty-five? You don't know it. With no direction, and he's got a gun, he's going to shoot it every day. I don't care if he shoots in the air. I don't care if you shoot a cat, or a dog, or something or somebody, because nobody has given him values about guns.'" Ginn knows that many young people in hard-hit neighborhoods are growing up without a father and some without a mother too. He was raised by his mom–she died at age thirty-eight when he was nineteen–and his grandmother. The family would eat together nightly and he learned many lessons during those meals.

"We have forgotten all the core values of raising young people," Ginn said. "We see that the kids today, if they don't see their future, they don't think they have one. Where are they going to find love and understanding? We're moving too fast. Nobody's sitting at the table anymore with our children. And these are the results right here, because nobody's raising our kids."

So Ginn has doubled down on his educational proposition, spending more time than ever with his students.

"I'm working harder now than I've worked in thirty years because I have to stay with the kids to try to take up their whole day," Ginn said. "So you try to keep them busy and try to keep the outside influences out. I got something to do with them every day. And then you still might miss."

In some ways, Deon said, neither he nor Eric recovered from seeing their old man in his casket.

"Oh, that killed us; that crushed us," Deon, now fifty-five, said. "We didn't need to see him like that for our last time. It destroyed us. It woke Andre all the way up. Me and Eric, it hurt us more than anything because we were used to him."

Everyone I talked to agrees that Arlaine was a good mom—always making sure her children had a roof over their heads and food in their bellies under difficult circumstances. But Arlaine had a blind spot when it came to Deon and Eric.

Her two oldest boys loved their mom, but they also loved their addictions, and it drove her crazy as they cycled in and out of prison. When they were home, they took whatever she had. They didn't do it out of maliciousness. They did it out of desperation.

"They done stole my car and crashed it and now I can't get to work," she'd tell others.

Andre used the phrase "eternal hope" to describe his mother's attitude toward his older brothers. Hope that one day they'd mature and be men. But they were never taught manhood skills. Deon was locked up at fourteen. Eric romanticized street life. Andre said his mom didn't want to hear the truth about her older sons and would get upset if anyone tried to call her on her permissiveness.

"Why do you hate your brothers so much?" she would say to him.

"I don't hate them. I don't like what they're doing," Andre told her.

"She just never wanted to believe it," he said. "And I was pleading with them: 'Look at your mom. Look what you're doing to her.'"

And what did they say in response?

"They used to tell me I don't understand," Andre said.

"I'd say, 'Hold on. I grew up in the same house at the same time with the same problems. When you didn't eat, I didn't eat. So how do I not understand?'

"Deon used to call me 'Mr. Know-It-All' because I would read and I would try to make the good grades, because our house was so full of turmoil that I would take solace at school because that's the time I could be normal."

Today, Andre and Trent have middle-class jobs as supervisors at Cleveland-Cliffs Inc., a steel manufacturer. They're both married with families and houses in the burbs.

Even though the brother's trajectories diverged, all of Arlaine's children remain a close, loving family.

For nearly two weeks, Andre had been racking his brain for the right words to use for Eric's eulogy.

Finally, it was time. More than one hundred of us filed into the sanctuary of the Imani Temple Ministries in Cleveland Heights.

Arlaine's six kids sat together in the first pew to the left of Eric's gray casket–the three remaining Smith boys, Deon, Andre, and Trent, and the three Howard siblings, Johnny Ray Howard Jr., Daren Howard, and Shemika Smith. Eric's stepfather was there too and so were three of Arlaine's sisters, including her twin, Elaine, who had come up from Alabama.

As a selection of "Hallelujah, Salvation, and Glory" played, Andre, who had been stoic since his brother's death, experienced a fit of emotion. He rose from his seat and languished in front of Eric's coffin.

He'd been doing so much in the fourteen days since Eric was killed. Trying to find out what the cops knew. Taking the lead in planning the funeral. Responding to every text and call about what had happened. He was operating on fumes and it was catching up to him.

He hurt for his family. For himself. And for Eric. Eric had had so much promise. He was a smart and wonderful brother, but he could never pull it together. Andre wanted things to be different. His eyes weren't fixed on anything or anyone. Finally, a pastor politely led him back to his seat.

When it came time for the eulogy, Andre decided not to refer to the notes he'd been compiling for two weeks. Standing at the pulpit high above the casket, he spoke from the heart.

Eric taught him to ride his bike and then stole his bike, he said.

Eric enjoyed being "in the back as a leader, not front," until Deon went away in the early 1980s and Eric had to be out front.

He mentioned Eric's propensity for showing up at your door unexpectedly. And that despite being such a tough guy, Eric was unafraid to tell his brothers and others that he loved them.

"I feel like it is such a waste for this to happen like that," Andre told mourners. "This is the toughest, because there was so much potential there . . . but he wasn't seeking it."

Eric fathered one son, and Andre spotted "Little E," who is in his thirties, in the church.

"He loved you, man. He just didn't know how to love you because we didn't have that growing up."

Andre said he wanted to leave everyone with one thought.

"He wasn't some random dude out there wandering the streets," Andre said. "He had a family. . . . Many nights I cried about him. Many nights I prayed. Many nights I went looking for him."

At that point, Deon, Andre, and Trent, Talbert's three living sons, huddled over their deceased brother.

Racquel Hubbard, a local performer, was singing the words from Mary J. Blige's "Hourglass."

A trickle of family members joined the three brothers at the casket. Then more family approached.

So many people were hugging in front of the gray casket, you could no longer see Eric Donnell Smith, the seventy-ninth homicide victim that year in Cleveland.

Originally published October 18, 2021

THE **"COMMA EFFECT"** ON BIAS AND **BLACK LIVES**

That grammatical pause helps explain how racism thrives.

BY DOUG GLANVILLE

THE COMMA EFFECT.

It shapes the nuance of bias in America. A person is described and we look at the qualifiers that follow the comma: the victim of vigilante justice, *who smoked weed in junior high*. The man who shot up a movie theater, *but was an altar boy at his church.*

That comma wields great power. It can humanize, it can demonize, and although it takes a short breath to bring it to life, it can make a the loss of a life seem inevitable or, most cruelly, necessary. It is justice working in hindsight, hinting to us in code whether that grave outcome is deserved or if we should be sympathetic. Yet what comes after that comma often drips with bias in explaining what happened or what should happen.

That grammatical pause helps explain how racism can grow, even thrive, generations after slavery ended. It is the jump ball where the referee throws the ball slightly to one side, sometimes intentionally. It is the fastball on the edge of the strike zone where the right call is blurred so completely that bias is all that is left to decide whether it is a ball or strike.

But in this game of race in America, the stakes are truly life and death. The rules state that three strikes and you are out, but power is the true determinant of how those rules are enforced. And power is selective. Some get more than three strikes, others strike out before they even walk up to the plate. And maybe worst of all, some get up to bat and every pitch is called a strike no matter where it crosses the zone.

In that case, you better start swinging. Assuming you even have a bat.

Consider Doug Glanville, comma, the ballplayer.

Draft day changed my status in 1991 from a twenty-year-old college baseball player to a professional. "Ballplayer" now carried weight and elevated my station in life. Once that comma pointed to becoming a professional, it might as well have been an exclamation point.

The phone rang only fifteen minutes after the draft started. This was a good sign. The earlier the phone rings on draft day, the higher you are on the draft board. I picked up the receiver in my parents' home in Teaneck, New Jersey, and in glancing at the clock on the wall, I knew I had to be the top selection for the team on the other line. The Chicago Cubs had chosen me twelfth overall. My stock had risen even with the ballplayer label about to adorn my placard. Now I had become:

Doug Glanville, the first-round pick.

As a Black man in America, despite the ennobling narrative that is often told, Major League Baseball wasn't saving me. In fact, part of the ensuing negotiation emphasized my return to college after the baseball season on their dime so I could complete my senior year at the University of Pennsylvania. My parents, both first-generation college graduates, insisted on this outcome, and so did I. I wanted to honor the sacrifices they'd made to make it possible, and I was only one semester away from an engineering degree that had required significant work. I also hoped that a new comma could save me from certain indignities in life:

Doug Glanville, Ivy League engineering graduate.

But I was already suspicious of these labels. They can stoke elitism. They were still only a veneer when it came to color, even if someone holding the cards decided certain achievements made me a better person, that I was one of the "good" ones. But assessing the character of anyone, without that first impression in which race and all of the biases that come with it is front and center, is a tall order. An Ivy League degree doesn't help us know the core of a person. But in the American game, checking certain boxes is sold as a grant of immunity or equal access, pushing the content of our character or at least the accoutrements of achievement to the front of the discussion so that no racial identity comma would be needed.

Despite growing up in a town that voluntarily desegregated in the mid-60s, I had enough experiences before the phone call on draft day to know my college degree would not be enough to counter the first adjective that the world sees when I enter the room:

Doug Glanville, Black man.

My parents made this a source of pride. My mother was our in-house activist. Setting up cottage parties and opening up Saturday schools to teach Black history and SAT prep. She was a unifier too, bringing people in our diverse town together to forge understanding, while always whispering to me about the subtleties of racism. As a young boy, I knew about unfairness well before I connected the dots to race. I remember being detained on a field trip while in New York City after getting separated from my class and being accused of breaking into the museum we were visiting. I remember a summer camp coach nastily kicking me off of the tennis court for wearing jeans, while the next day he let a blond-haired girl play in jeans right in front of me. It was less painful to chalk these up as favoritism, or security concerns, and much harder to dig deeper and see how race is always in play.

Still, I quickly learned about the explicit acts of racism that eliminated all ambiguity about intent. Walking home from elementary school in my idyllic hometown, I went by a house that I passed every single day. But this time, a young white man was outside on the porch. He flipped open his switchblade and dared me, the "N-word," to come over to him. I kept walking and thankfully, he never got out of his chair. Would this guy have killed me, a fourth grader, because I was Black?

Even with knowledge and awareness, I still hoped that my baseball comma would make me less threatening or less at risk in my own life. Maybe my fame would grant me more bandwidth. My parents knew better. They were skeptical from the first day pro scouts came calling. My mom's aunts and uncles mostly settled in Philadelphia. They were big baseball fans, but also held a long-standing grudge against the Phillies for how they treated Jackie Robinson. My family was happy on draft day, but they also issued a number of warnings about the "good ol' boy" system that props up baseball. I understood that, but I also loved the game and hoped that would be enough to endure whatever came my way.

We negotiated with the Cubs for weeks, and finally, after I signed and reported to minor league baseball, my career began in earnest. I did not get the royal first-round treatment, maybe because of my tough negotiations. Instead of heading to Chicago to meet the city, I was sent to Niagara Falls, New York, to meet the minor league team on the road. Not long after the road trip ended, I was called into the office.

I could feel the strangeness in the air as I sat down.

There were four baseballs lined up on my coach's desk. And the conversation went something like this. . . .

"Are these your baseballs?"

"Yes."

"Well, we don't appreciate you stealing our baseballs."

"Stealing?"

"We found them in your locker and all baseballs are property of this team and the Chicago Cubs."

My mind was racing. *Why are they talking about "stealing"? Why would I steal these baseballs and then leave them in my locker in plain view? I guess they had a problem with people taking baseballs home—in the minors there is a limited supply—but why the dramatic tribunal?*

I had to figure out a way to call them out while respecting my coaches and not fully embarrassing them or expressing my pure outrage. So I played detective.

"Once again, those are *my* baseballs, and if I were stealing them, why would I leave them on the top shelf of my locker so that you could see that I was stealing them?"

That did not go over well.

Then I got specific.

"Let's look at the labels on these baseballs."

None were from this minor league or the Cubs. There was an

NCAA ball, a Cape Cod ball, a ball from home, and a typical one you would buy in a store. All with my initials on them. Their first reaction was that I "could have just written my initials on their baseballs too."

The comma effect exacerbates the doubt that comes with being Black in America. It is reinforced in the faux-gray area that is still black and white under scrutiny. The kind of scrutiny that reveals that this neutral zone is never truly neutral. That for a Black person, it can turn a simple issue around a shortage of baseballs into a hearing, not a conversation.

Well, cross off Doug Glanville, the ballplayer, as a way to get the benefit of the doubt during a criminal inquiry. That was clearly not enough. Maybe when I become a big leaguer . . .

Off the field, being Black is a form of omnipresence, the inability to be invisible. It is the inability to just focus on your job, the inability to just "stick to sports" because you still have to play them in a black uniform, one that does not come off when you put the grass-stained uniform in the laundry. It is also a source of pride and unity, a shared experience in the world that can create solidarity. But this comes with a simplistic way to be categorized, perpetually and dangerously fitting the generic "description" of a suspect or the worst-case imaginations of white society.

It took me time in my professional path to know how to embrace the Black man after that comma. It required patience to be able to celebrate being both individual and part of a collective body, even when your American individuality is always absorbed into the collective with or without your consent. A reminder of the constant fight to define yourself beyond the racialization of society's scapegoating. I found I did have some say in what came next.

One of the biggest commas ever written in the Black experience was added in the codification of the Thirteenth Amendment, which abolished slavery. On the heels of the Emancipation Proclamation, which strategically abolished slavery in only the Southern states in rebellion, President Abraham Lincoln and Congress sought a pragmatic approach to end slavery and unite the nation after the bitter Civil War. The comma was part of the compromise.

The amendment reads:

Section 1. *Neither slavery nor involuntary servitude, except as a punishment for crime whereof the party shall have been duly convicted, shall exist within the United States, or any place subject to their jurisdiction.*

That comma before "except" was used to rebuild the white South, a concession for the inconvenience of stripping them of their unpaid labor force. It sat in the hands of the enforcers of the law who decided what was a crime and what was not. We know enforcement of the law was used to essentially reenslave Black people with impunity, through Black Codes and inescapable cycles of sharecropping.

We see this in the retroactive justification in a whole host of situations. We were jogging, renting, walking, mowing the lawn, shoveling snow, or getting a cab. But we were "suspicious." And that suspicion introduces the most powerful comma of all. The postmortem comma, used to justify a deadly use of force. This punctuation is weaponized, unleashed retroactively to avoid intro-spection and accountability. It has the effect of making our deaths appear like an afterthought, or even mandatory, out of a need for law and order.

And death is only one result. For the living, it fans indignity and invites other forms of nonlethal subjugation and pain.

But Doug Glanville, the major leaguer, would change that, right?

My professional baseball career worked out pretty well. I added all kinds of commas that in theory would place me in a bubble of racial bliss: 1,100 hits, millionaire, nice neighborhood. I played almost fifteen seasons until I retired in 2005. There were many examples of moments when that comma absorbed entire communities under the same banner–Phillies and Cubs fans, Ivy League alumni and baseball lovers, entire cities in playoff moments. I saw the beauty of sport and its potential to unify and teach society about the power of team.

In the right circumstances, that pinstripe uniform was a refuge, even as I knew it couldn't protect me from all racial animus. It couldn't explain what life was like when I headed home and wasn't recognized as a big leaguer, facing the Lexus dealer who would not let me test-drive a car because he had "lost the keys."

When I retired on June 25, 2005, I was already engaged to be married and unsure of what was next in my professional life. Philadelphia offered a lot from my baseball career, and my alma mater was nearby. But I was not sure how the world would view me when I took off that uniform. Now I was sure:

Doug Glanville, the retired ballplayer.

But still I had some sway, some insulation, right? An ability to get the benefit of the doubt?

On a snowy day, I went out to shovel my driveway. The temperature was hovering around zero degrees, notable because in these circumstances I know I am zero degrees of separation from the Black man in the mug shot, the man embedded in America's fear of itself.

I look up and see a police SUV pull up across the street. It is from the bordering town, not the city where I live, an unusual phenomenon in an area that is so provincial. The officer gets out of his cruiser. He's a young white man, and he strolls across the street toward me as I stand up tall in my driveway. I tensely await the engagement. Is he lost? I have no ID, I haven't shaved in days, so concern is rising, but I would find out as soon as he finishes crossing the street. Without introduction or explanation, his first words were . . .

"So, trying to make a few extra bucks shoveling people's driveways around here?"

Of course. Still Doug Glanville, Black man.

Retirement is over. Now I'm adding a new comma.

Doug Glanville, writer.

Originally published June 29, 2020

LYNCHING
MEMORIAL
+++ AND +++
TERRORISM

ALI-FRAZIER

BLESSING & A CURSE

A CAN

G NEGRO LEAGUES
K TWITTER ##

DRY

THE **WACO** HORROR

What does it mean to share a name with the victim of one of the most infamous lynchings in American history?

BY JESSE WASHINGTON

BEHIND THE COURTHOUSE

START AT the back door of the magnificent stone courthouse, where a wave of white men dragged Jesse Washington into the alley, tearing his clothes off as they went. Walk sixty-five steps over the red alley bricks to North Fifth Street, where the swelling mob paused to cinch a chain around Jesse's neck. Cross Fifth, turn right, and take the short walk to Washington Avenue. Thousands of people massed here to partake of the killing of the seventeen-year-old farmhand. As Jesse was pulled down the wide street that cruelly shares his last name, they attacked him with knives, bricks, shovels, and clubs. Blood covered Jesse's dark skin.

It was almost noon on May 15, 1916. With the Texas heat climbing into the eighties, the Waco Horror had begun.

I can feel the boiling bloodlust of the mob on a cool night in April as I retrace the final steps of Jesse Washington's life. I've come to Waco to explore the meaning of this century-old atrocity, to probe beneath the eerie coincidence of sharing a name with the victim of one of the most famous lynchings in U.S. history.

I first saw a photo of Jesse's remains nearly twenty years ago and delved into the story from afar. After being convicted of the rape and murder of Lucy Fryer, a white farmer's wife, he was dismembered, hanged, and burned as more than ten thousand people watched, including the police chief and mayor. Then he was dragged behind a horse until his head flew off. No one was prosecuted for those crimes. But international publicity of such public brutality helped galvanize the antilynching movement and solidify the influence of the recently formed NAACP.

A decade ago, I watched indignantly as efforts to commemorate Jesse's lynching were stymied by the white power structure in Waco. More recently, I pondered the parallels with recent killings of unarmed Black males that exploded into national prominence. Above all, I yearned to confront the city in person.

Now I stand on the corner of Washington and Fifth, nighttime spotlights illuminating the courthouse's stained white walls, deserted streets cutting through acres of empty parking lots, and I feel the weight of history and hate.

MONUMENTS AND MARKERS

Mayor Malcolm Duncan Jr. meets me in a trendy coffee shop near the courthouse. Half of the storefronts flanking the shop are vacant; downtown Waco has been hollowed out by suburban sprawl and misguided 1980s development strategies. Looming over the block is the twenty-two-story ALICO Building, once the tallest structure west of the Mississippi, a relic of the time when Waco's culture, commerce, and cotton wealth made it the "Athens of Texas."

Duncan, sixty-three, is a white former truck dealer whose father and grandfather also were Waco mayors. He has pushed programs to address poverty, jobs for released prisoners, and health care for low-income residents. Waco's poverty rate is almost 30 percent, much of it concentrated in the Black community. About 21 percent of its 128,000 residents are Black.

Duncan supports efforts to memorialize the lynching. He wants his children to know about it. He worries that his grand-father, who was in his twenties at the time, may have watched it happen. Other members of Waco's white elite–Greater Waco Chamber of Commerce president Matthew Meadors and county commissioners Will Jones, Kelly Snell, and Ben Perry–didn't respond to my messages.

I like Duncan. I ask to see the spot where Jesse was killed, but Duncan is uncertain of the exact location. I ask him about the 1905 lynching of Sank Majors from the steel bridge at the end of Washington Avenue, one block from where we stand. Duncan has never heard of Sank Majors.

Throughout downtown Waco there are monuments, memorials, and markers filled with names–for slain law enforcement officers, Vietnam veterans, a fatal 1897 duel between a newspaper editor and a judge, the 114 people killed by the tornado of 1953. A wide plaza called Heritage Square features handsome benches, gurgling fountains, two long L-shaped trellises supported by graceful columns, and hundreds of bricks bearing names of donors. I observe aloud that Jesse Washington's name is nowhere to be found downtown.

"Is that denial?" asks Duncan.

You tell me, I reply.

"I'm just trying to understand it," Duncan says. "I can't explain it."

Scheherazade Perkins can explain it. "We've been so focused on trying to cover it up, hide it, ignore it, say it didn't happen, say it's not our fault, we didn't have anything to do with it, that it was them, not us," she says.

Perkins is a member of the Community Race Relations Coalition, which for more than a decade has been trying to foster some sort of healing around Jesse's lynching. I meet Perkins, a Black woman with a résumé ranging from chemist to consultant, at the spacious ranch home of coalition chair Jo Welter in China Springs, a twenty-five-minute drive north of Waco.

Welter, a white mother and homemaker who has dedicated herself to social justice issues, recounts their 2006 efforts to commemorate the ninetieth anniversary of the lynching through a memorial service and official resolutions from local authorities. White members of the McLennan County Commissioners Court, which runs much of Waco, "acted like we didn't exist," Welter says. They refused to respond to messages or to meet with her, even when she showed up at their offices.

Lester Gibson, the sole Black commissioner, did propose a resolution that included such terms as "regret," "atonement," and "travesty of justice." The white commissioners didn't say a word in response and moved on to the next order of business.

Driving back downtown from Welter's home, I wonder if white citizens are as burdened by this history as Black folks. I stop along a beaten-down commercial strip of North Nineteenth Street, but none of the people I meet there know about the lynching. When I describe the event to Paula McCommas, a Mexican American pawnshop proprietor, she's opposed to the idea of a historical marker. "It's been so many years ago. All we can do is pray," she says. "Sometimes you just gotta say, if God is in control of all our lives, we all pay our debts."

I get back in my rental car and drive to the courthouse where the mob seized Jesse, hoping that God has come to collect.

THE HOUSE OF JUSTICE

Built in 1901 by renowned architect James Riley Gordon, the McLennan County Courthouse is a grandiose, three-story neoclassical structure of limestone, marble, and red Texas granite. Thirty-two wide steps lead to a front entrance flanked by six Corinthian columns. From afar, the stone walls gleam white beneath the cloudless blue sky. Up close, they are yellowed by age, weather, and what I imagine are the sins that occurred within.

Atop the central dome of the courthouse stands an eighteen-foot-tall statue of Themis, the Greek goddess of moral order and justice. Circling the building, I notice something awry with the statue. Two years ago, a sixty-five-mile-per-hour storm ripped off Themis's left arm, along with the scales of justice she held aloft. The scales were found hanging in a nearby magnolia tree. What remains of the arm is a bent, blackened rod that reminds me of Jesse's charred limbs.

Through the entrance and past the metal detector is a circular lobby, three stories high, with wide hallways heading north, south, east, and west. High above, the dome beneath Themis's feet glitters with blue and red stained glass. Six painted murals circle the ground-floor lobby, depicting Waco's history starting from its 1837 founding as Fort Fisher, a temporary Texas Ranger station. Painted on one panel is a circular piece of rope suspended from a bushy green tree outside the courthouse.

"Hanging tree with noose," the caption reads, below a list of educational and cultural landmarks and the headline "Athens of Texas."

I'd been aggravated by the noose for years, since reading about an unsuccessful attempt to have it painted over. But then I see something even more disturbing.

Beneath the mural, mounted on a small wooden stand, is the resolution ultimately passed by the county commissioners after they refused to say a word in response to the proposal by Gibson, the lone Black commissioner.

The document begins by saying lynching was "a widely documented and accepted practice in the United States, the State of Texas, and McLennan County from the early 1800s to the 1920s." The second paragraph says "lynching affected people of all colors and races." The resolution concludes three vague paragraphs later, without mentioning the specific lynching that was so barbaric it immediately made international headlines.

The name Jesse Washington is not there.

Somehow, after years of studying this story, I had missed this brazen refusal to acknowledge even the basic facts of Waco's horrifically racist crime. To see the document displayed in what's supposed to be a house of justice feels like a backhand to the face. Reading it again, I'm pulled into other powerless moments. I feel the despair of seeing the Cleveland officers who killed twelve-year-old Tamir Rice escape responsibility. The anger resulting from the acquittal of the Los Angeles cops who beat Rodney King. The sickness of learning that segregationist South Carolina senator Strom Thurmond fathered a daughter at age twenty-two with his sixteen-year-old Black maid.

"Hello, Judge," I hear the deputy manning the metal detector say.

The judge, a white man with white hair and a blue blazer, makes small talk with the deputy. The judge enters the elevator. I hurry in after him and the door closes on the two of us.

"My name is Jesse Washington," I say. "Does that name mean anything to you? Are you familiar with the history of the name here in Waco?"

"No, I'm not," he responds. He looks uncomfortable–he probably thinks he sent me to prison years ago and I'm back for revenge. The elevator door opens on the third floor. "I have to go," the judge says. I don't ask him his name.

Confronting the courthouse, this symbol of the white power structure, gives me a small measure of satisfaction, and a large portion of determination. The burial of my name is starting to feel like a twisted sort of validation. If my name and what it stands for weren't so potent, the people here wouldn't be so scared of it. But I'm not going to let them ignore it.

The building contains six courtrooms. I don't know which one, if any, is where Jesse sat in chains while the jury took four minutes to determine his guilt. Outside several of the courtrooms are dockets of names and cases pinned to bulletin boards. They make me think about the machinery of mass incarceration, the way laws passed and enforced over the past fifty years in a racially biased fashion have wrecked the Black community. I think about how Ferguson, Missouri, funded the city government by targeting Black residents with petty fines and court fees that often led to arrest warrants, jail terms, and lost jobs. I think how likely it is that much injustice has been done in this building.

On the second floor, an older white man with a judge's black robe over his arm is walking down the marble-floored hallway. "My name is Jesse Washington," I tell Justice Al Scoggins. He's never heard of the lynching. I tell him the briefest version of the story and ask if he has any thoughts. "No," he says. "I'm not from McLennan County."

A wooden door opens on the darkened, empty Tenth Court of Appeals. The only light comes through three stained-glass ceiling windows. Marble columns circle the room, giving the sense of prison bars. The walls are lined with twenty-two photographs of judges going back to 1923. Twenty-two white men.

Back in the lobby, I see a Black sheriff's deputy. We shake hands and I introduce myself. His grip tightens.

"That's a powerful name," the cop says.

INTO BLACK WACO

I exit the courthouse and turn left on Washington Avenue. It's three blocks to the graceful crescent moon of the Washington Avenue Bridge, built of steel in 1901, and the site of Sank Majors's lynching, eleven years before Jesse's. I cross the Brazos River into East Waco. Black Waco.

Eight blocks past the bridge is the Kelly-Napier Justice Center, which handles noncriminal legal matters such as small claims and traffic violations. This small building feels much different from the courthouse across the bridge. Portraits of Black officials hang on the walls, including one of Lester Gibson, who was elected to the board of commissioners from this district. Matters are adjudicated by a Black justice of the peace, Judge James E. Lee Jr.

Lee knows exactly who Jesse Washington was. His parents told him the story as a child. Lee has told it to his four children, and shown them the frightful pictures. "Future generations need to know what happened," Lee says.

In a nearby barbershop, the lynching is common knowledge. "Even today, you get caught up in the wrong place in Texas, you gone," says Keith Pullens, thirty-four, the shop owner. A conversation ensues about towns and counties to be avoided, lest a brother end up dying like James Byrd Jr., dragged behind a pickup truck by white supremacists in Jasper, 220 miles to the east, in 1998.

All of the customers bring up the legend of the tornado of

1953, which killed 114 people and destroyed downtown. The tornado, they say, traveled the exact path along which Jesse's corpse was dragged.

I drive past a boxy old Chevy Caprice parked in door-high weeds and a large lot planted with neat rows of vegetables to visit the home of Linda Lewis, a longtime activist in local politics. Lewis was valedictorian of Waco's segregated George Washington Carver High School in 1965 and attended the state's flagship university, the University of Texas–Austin, which had just admitted Black students.

"But I grew up in Waco, so I was ready," Lewis says.

Her parents told her about Jesse and Sank Majors as a warning. She was not allowed to cross the Washington Avenue Bridge. "When you grow up in the recent shadow of a lynching, you learn that life is not fair, that you have to work twice as hard, be twice as smart, don't cause any problems, don't cause any undue attention to yourself, study real hard," Lewis says.

"I have lived long enough now to know that the things that are written and taught in history are not true," she says. "I'm not surprised that non-African-descended Wacoans don't know about Jesse Washington. It's not significant to them in their lives or worldview."

On Elm is a gift shop filled with kente cloth, books, jewelry, greeting cards, dozens of church hats and dresses, and shirts that say "Real Men Pray Every Day." When I introduce myself to the proprietor of twenty-six years, Marilyn Banks, her eyes flicker.

"You have a meaningful name," Banks says.

Her shop is filled with Black memorabilia, but she doesn't like the idea of a historical marker for Jesse. "It's painful," she says. "It brings too much sadness for now. I know it's part of our history, but I'm not willing to relive it every day and make a big issue out of it. I prayed about it, put closure to it, then put it away."

A NAME'S BITTER PAST

My own name comes from pain and shame.

My great-grandmother Mary White was born in Bamberg, South Carolina, in the early 1900s, in rural conditions not far removed from those of slavery. Mom White, as she was known to all of us, worked as a sharecropper and gave birth to her first child, a girl named Curlean, when she was in her early teens. Nobody still alive knows who Curlean's father was.

Mom White moved to North Philadelphia amid the Great Migration. She got married and had four more children. From a very young age, Curlean was sexually assaulted by the brother of Mom White's husband. The abuse became apparent when, at fourteen, Curlean turned up pregnant. Mom White, who kept a pistol in her nightstand, swore she would shoot the rapist dead if she ever set eyes on him again. He disappeared.

In 1937, fourteen-year-old Curlean gave birth to a boy named McCleary. Everyone called him "Bunch." As he was growing up, nobody would tell Bunch who his father was. Curlean eventually moved to another state and left Bunch to be raised by Mom White and Curlean's younger sisters, who were so close to Bunch's age he considered them more siblings than aunts. Bunch was a born artist, sensitive and observant, deeply damaged by his family's dysfunction and the repressive racial atmosphere of Philadelphia. Bunch also was extremely intelligent, so of course he discovered his father's identity.

As soon as he could, Bunch fled Philly for New York City, where he met Judith, a young white social worker. They had a son in 1969. Bunch named his firstborn after his mother's rapist. He told family members that he wanted "to turn something horrible into something beautiful."

I am Bunch's son. The child molester's name was Jesse Washington.

Bunch was never told how long his mother was abused, but he knew there was something he did not know. A lifetime of trying to scratch this unreachable itch is part of what eventually pushed Bunch into mental illness, drug abuse, and death as a seventy-one-year-old homeless man on a New York City park bench.

This is my name. To discard it would mean being defeated by the past. To reject it would betray my father's determination to confront his identity and history, as horrific as they might be.

THE LYNCHING OF JESSE WASHINGTON

Jesse Washington worked and lived on the farm of George and Lucy Fryer in the town of Robinson, just south of Waco. Jesse was illiterate and possibly mentally disabled, according to an NAACP investigator who visited Waco soon after the lynching. At about sunset on May 8, 1916, twenty-one-year-old Ruby Fryer found her mother, Lucy, fifty-three, with her skull bashed in. Jesse was plowing a nearby cotton field. Three hours later, the seventeen-year-old farmhand was arrested in his yard while whittling a piece of wood. He had blood on his clothes, a deputy later testified.

A mob was already forming, so Jesse was taken about a hundred miles to the Dallas County Jail, where he signed a detailed confession with an X, police said. The written document said that Lucy Fryer was "fussing with me about whipping the mules" when Jesse hit Fryer in the head several times with a hammer, raped her, then struck her twice more with the hammer.

The trial was set for Monday, May 15. "All day Sunday and into Monday morning, people poured into Waco" from miles away, Patricia Bernstein wrote in her 2006 book, *The First Waco Horror: The Lynching of Jesse Washington and the Rise of the NAACP.*

Spectators jammed the courtroom for the trial, which began at about ten a.m. and lasted slightly more than an hour. Witnesses testified that Jesse told authorities where to find the murder weapon. There was no testimony about rape. Jesse's court-appointed attorneys asked just one question: "Who were present when the hammer was found?"

The verdict and death sentence were barely spoken when the mob surged forward, carried Jesse out the back door of the courthouse, and dragged him to the square outside city hall. The chain around his neck was flung over a tree. He was dangled above a large dry-goods box filled with wood, which had been prepared earlier that morning.

While Jesse was still alive, "fingers, ears, pieces of clothing, toes and other parts of the negro's body were cut off by members of the mob," the *Waco Times-Herald* reported. Someone castrated Jesse, according to the NAACP investigation, and carried his penis around in a handkerchief, showing it off as a souvenir.

The killers yanked Jesse into the air, then lowered him into the woodpile and poured coal oil over him. About ten thousand people crowded the area, according to the *Waco Times-Herald*, hanging from nearby windows and perched atop buildings and trees. "As the negro's body commenced to burn," the paper reported, "shouts of delight went up from the thousands of throats."

Jesse burned for two hours, leaving just a skull, torso, and limb stumps. A horseman lassoed the body and dragged it through town until the head popped off. Some boys extracted Jesse's teeth and sold them for five dollars each. The headless mess was dragged behind a car to Robinson and hung in a sack outside a blacksmith's shop, until a constable took it away that evening. Jesse was buried in an unmarked grave.

Jesse was one of 2,842 Black men known to have been lynched between 1885 and June 1, 1916, according to the NAACP magazine, the *Crisis*. Yet Jesse's demise was so extraordinarily barbaric, *Crisis* editor W.E.B. DuBois documented the crime in an eight-page supplement to the July 1916 issue, which he titled "The Waco Horror." The NAACP's focus on Jesse's lynching gave the new organization prominence as a civil rights advocate, and helped make the fight against lynching a national issue.

The *Crisis* account includes a photo of Jesse lying on a pile of burning wood. His short hair is still visible, his facial features not yet charcoaled. It's the most life I've ever seen in Jesse.

"Hang there," reads an antilynching poem by activist Leila Amos Pendleton in the June 1916 issue of the *Crisis*, "until their eyes are unsealed and they behold themselves as they are."

100 YEARS OF GRIEF

Jesse had several siblings. One of them had a daughter named Caldonia Majors. Caldonia had a daughter named Maddie Ervin. Maddie Ervin had children named Mary Pearson, Shirley Bush, Denise Mitchell, Maddie Brawley and Howard Majors Jr.

I'm sitting with Mary, Shirley, and Denise, plus Shirley's daughter Yolanda, listening to them talk about their cousin Jesse.

"My mom was always telling us what had happened, my grandma, my grandfather, my aunties, my uncles, and all of them," says Pearson, sixty-seven. "They always said this here, that one day justice was going to be done. They always said that. They said, we may not be here when it happens, but it will happen."

For Jesse's family, justice would be a historical marker at the spot of the lynching and an official apology. Even though both seem within reach, the decades of resistance have made the family bitter.

"It's something I just can't shake. I look at the pictures . . . it just makes me want to go get me a machine gun," Pearson says. "You lose rest. You can't sleep."

I suspect living in Waco hasn't helped. Waiting to meet the

sisters and Yolanda in the lobby of one of Waco's nicest hotels, I count sixty-three white patrons, one Black, and one white man with a mixed-race daughter. Pearson calls ahead and asks, "Should we come in the front door?" A benign question, or perhaps an unconscious reflex from her younger years, when she would have had to enter through the back.

The four women believe Jesse was innocent. They get riled up during the conversation, their observations piling on top of each other into a mountain of righteous consternation.

"What really gets me is how could you have a heart to do another soul like that? I mean, you can see a chicken, a hog that have no soul. . . . How could you sit up there and go and get pieces of his body and save it as a souvenir? . . . How they drug him in his flesh, flesh was falling off the bone. . . . Seventeen years old? Seventeen? That takes a whole lot out of me. I've tried to keep from getting angry, but I can't help it. That's the reason why I had to go up under the doctor to get me some medicine. . . ."

The more they grieve, the more my heart swells. I've chosen this journey; they were saddled with it. I think of Zora Neale Hurston writing that the Black woman is the mule of the earth. Their pain grows into demands for a statue of Jesse like the Martin Luther King Jr. memorial in D.C., a movie like *The Ten Commandments*, a documentary, reparations.

Finally, I ask them, "How do you think it would feel not to be angry?"

The possibility doesn't seem to register. Pearson brings up the historical marker again. She calls it a "monument."

"This is where we have to accept justice," Pearson says. "We can't accept it no other way. We don't have the ones that did it."

When the women hug me good-bye, it feels like they're family.

Bush says, "Thank you, Jesse Washington."

A WOMAN WAS MURDERED

Ruby Fryer, who found her mother's bludgeoned body, had a daughter named Mildred Wollitz Saffle. Mildred had a daughter named Charlotte Morris. I'm sitting with Morris in the home of her son Coy Morris, listening to her talk about her great-grandmother Lucy Fryer.

I've been dreading this moment. I found Morris through an email she sent to organizers of a Baylor University march in Jesse's memory. "To have you start this in our hometown is disgusting," she wrote. "You want to commemorate the last lynching, then fine, but don't immortalize Mr. Washington in grace and glory. What the mob did to him was wrong, I don't disagree, but what he did to my great-grandmother was also wrong."

I have a responsibility to explore their side of the story, but I worry that Morris and her son, like others I encountered in Waco, will be ignorant of and resistant to historical truth. I fear any exploration of Jesse's guilt will lessen the lesson of his lynching. I fear my heart will close to them.

Morris rocks nervously in a recliner in the living room of her son's comfortable two-story brick home. Unlike people in Black Waco, Morris did not grow up knowing about the lynching. Her grandma Ruby always said Lucy Fryer was killed, but went no further. Morris only discovered Jesse's fate as an adult after Ruby, aging and gripped by dementia, ran away from her nursing home because she was scared of her Black caretakers.

It's an article of faith for Morris that Jesse smashed open her great-grandmother's skull with a hammer. Jesse had blood on his clothes, he confessed, there was a trial, he was convicted by a jury–Jesse was guilty.

"Do they even know what they're marching for?" Morris says of those who commemorate the lynching. "Do they just think that this man was picked out of the cotton field and hung for no reason?"

Morris is equally certain that "it's never been about race to us, it's about a man murdering a woman." She repeats this theme several times. I think it's because Morris is a product of her time and place. She recalls swimming in a pool where Black people weren't allowed, and her father ran a gas station where Black customers used the back door. Yet she says, "I never remember in Robinson there being a difference" between whites and Blacks.

I remind myself that her family has suffered. I try to extend the same understanding to her as I did to Jesse's cousins when they said Jesse deserved a statue like Martin Luther King Jr.'s.

It's not easy. Not when she says things like, "I don't understand how people today can apologize for something that happened a hundred years ago. . . . That's like us asking [Jesse's kin] to apologize for Jesse killing our great-grandmother."

I might not have been able to extend that understanding if it wasn't for Coy.

He's thirty, studied history in college. Grew up in Robinson and loves his town, but also spent time in integrated Waco neighborhoods with his dad's family. Coy shares his mother's dismay that Lucy Fryer is often referred to as just "a white woman" in accounts of the Waco Horror.

"Look," Coy says, sitting next to me on the couch, "she has a name. Just say her name."

He volunteers that the lynching "is something that Waco has tried to sweep under the rug and is still continuing to."

He states unequivocally that Jesse killed his great-great-grandmother with that hammer, but then doubles back to leave some wiggle room. He questions how an illiterate teen could dictate such a detailed confession. He knows the verdict and the lynching were preordained, "that innocent or guilty, his fate was sealed from the get-go."

Later, when he mentions that the good thing about American history is you can see the documents for yourself, I interrupt. I have to give Coy my personal litmus test.

Documents written by the secessionist states clearly state that the cause of the Civil War was slavery. I'm unbothered by anyone's opinions about politics, affirmative action, or gay marriage, but my heart reflexively slams shut on those who refuse to face plain facts about why the Southern states rebelled.

"What do you think caused the Civil War?" I ask.

"The South didn't want to give up the slave labor," Coy replies.

I extend a hand across the couch. Coy shakes it. Our connection makes it easier to confront my biggest fear.

There is a widespread belief in white America that Black people are primarily responsible for the ills plaguing the Black community, that the problems created by 350 years of slavery, lynching, and segregation have somehow been solved in the last few decades. This leads to the claim that the recent killings of unarmed Black people were in part the fault of the victims. Each was responsible for his own demise, according to this false narrative.

So I have to ask the great-granddaughter of Lucy Fryer, do you believe Jesse was in any way responsible for his lynching?

"He bears responsibility for the murder," Morris says. "He does not bear the responsibility for a mob coming in and getting him and burning him and cutting him up and dragging him to another town."

"He doesn't have to bear responsibility for that at all," she says. "Nobody does."

I feel a brief wave of relief; then my optimism is deflated by her final two words. Nobody bears responsibility? What about

Waco, the city, the leadership of the hypocritical Athens of Texas, which sent a Black boy's burned head rolling down its oh-so-civilized streets and has refused to admit guilt for the last hundred years?

Maybe I have to accept that every one of the thousands of culprits, those who yanked the chain or lit the match or watched approvingly, has escaped responsibility in this world. Maybe I need to seek solace in God's admonition to forgive. This is the modern African American dilemma, after all, between uplifting ourselves and relying on white people to have a change of heart.

I start looking for a way to show Morris my truth.

I tell her I'm sorry her relative was killed. She's thankful. I gently tell her that the destruction of Jesse Washington is not more important than the murder of Lucy Fryer; a life is a life. But Jesse's name has more meaning, especially since the racist roots of the Horror linger on.

She agrees. "More significant in history, but not more important."

Coy says, "A man confessed, a man was tried and convicted and sentenced to hang and so our family got that justice. The man that murdered her in our eyes was brought to justice, so if anything else we always have that."

That's painful to hear. What happened to Jesse, with the consent and approval of Waco's government, was the definition of injustice. And injustice still strikes Black America, through mass incarceration and the killings of Trayvon, Tamir, and all those killed in anonymity before the internet let us say their names.

Jesse's family—by now, I count myself among them—says justice would be a historical marker. Charlotte and Coy Morris accept that view, as long as it includes Lucy Fryer's name.

I suppose that's fair. Neither Black nor white can solve America's race problem alone. We all must release some suspicion, bias, or bitterness. So when the historical marker is finally bolted to the scene of Waco's crime, I can accept Lucy Fryer's name next to Jesse's.

"I hope," Coy says, "that it heals whatever they need healed."

SAY MY NAME

The spot where Jesse burned is now a little-used parking lot near city hall, within sight of the courthouse topped by a statue of justice with a broken arm. Birds chirp in nearby trees amid a misty midday rain. When I close my eyes, it's easy to imagine the mob closing in on Jesse, the agony, the flames.

I'm suddenly flooded with gratitude that I was born in a different century. That I can walk these streets proud and unbothered, question the mayor, sit on a couch with Lucy Fryer's family, stalk white judges in the courthouse.

As much as the spot of the lynching itself resonates with me, I'm also powerfully drawn to Heritage Square, forty paces away. It's all the names on the bricks. Each inscription is another arrow to the heart, evidence of Waco's refusal to say my name. How many names are there? I must count them.

Ten names, a hundred, two hundred. Ellen North Taylor. Nell and Jim Hawkins. Murray Watson Jr. Three hundred, four hundred, and still no end in sight.

Names are hiding everywhere, names of schools, citizens, mayors, businesses, and civic organizations. Lehigh White Cement Company. George Washington. United Daughters of the Confederacy, Waco Chapter 2381. We Are One Family–the Human Family–the Bahai faith.

One hour, ninety minutes, two hours. I'm going to miss my flight, but I can't stop counting the names. The thousandth one rolls by. The count finally ends at 1,312.

I feel soiled, vengeful . . . then triumphant. Empowered. The one name missing from Heritage Square symbolizes Waco's attempt to deny its full heritage and to pave over the sins of the past. Yet here I stand, living proof of the power of that past. Jesse is an ancestor of today's victims of injustice, the names we never would have known save for the world-changing power of camera phones and social media. A large part of America tried to discredit these names, to say they did not matter. They failed, and unwittingly unleashed their power. By trying to deny the reality of these names, they burned them into history:

Trayvon Martin.

Tamir Rice.

Eric Garner.

Freddie Gray.

Walter Scott.

Jesse Washington.

Originally published May 17, 2016

ALI-FRAZIER WAS MORE THAN A FIGHT, IT WAS PART OF MY AWAKENING AS A BLACK MAN

As a college student, I was fighting to find my place in a changing world.

BY WILLIAM C. RHODEN

MARCH 8, 2021, marked the fiftieth anniversary of one of the most important events in boxing history. The fight also coincided with a period of personal growth for me as I confronted the harrowing reality of being an African American in the United States of oppression.

On that date in 1971, Muhammad Ali and Joe Frazier met for the first time at New York's Madison Square Garden. An overwhelmingly white sports media called this bout between two Black champions "the fight of the century."

There have been hundreds of great heavyweight title fights, but only three in U.S. history can be classified as a fight of the century.

Jack Johnson, the first Black heavyweight champion, defeated Jim Jeffries, the Great White Hope, in 1910. Jeffries was forced out of retirement to "save" white manhood and protect white supremacy from what journalist Charles Dana called "a Black rise against white supremacy."

The second fight of the century took place in New York in June 1938 when Joe Louis defeated the German Max Schmeling, becoming the United States' first Black hero.

The third fight of the century was Ali–Frazier I.

Where I was on the night of the big event? It would have been great to have had a story to tell. Truth is, the specific details of my whereabouts are hazy.

I was an evolving, nineteen-year-old sophomore at Morgan State University, a historically Black university (HBCU) in Baltimore. In all likelihood, I was off somewhere licking my wounds, trying to rebuild my confidence after a disastrous football season. The 1969 season was my first year as a starting defensive back. The irrepressible coach Brutus Wilson reminded me that I'd given up more touchdowns in one season than the entire Bears defense had given up in two years. So, I was dealing with that.

Then there was the ever-present fear of the military draft. At nineteen, I was a prime candidate for it. As an African American, I would almost certainly be sent to Vietnam. Two of my high school classmates–a promising quarter-miler and a former starting quarterback–lost their legs in combat. Though registered for the draft, I prayed every night that the war would end before my number was called.

Four years before his 1971 fight with Frazier, Ali refused to be drafted on religious grounds. He was convicted of draft evasion, and stripped of his title and his license. For three years, Ali was unable to fight. In those years, he became a hero of the antiwar movement, the embodiment of Black power, and the precursor of future generations of Black athletes who would use their visibility to fight against injustice.

This was the essence of his significance in 1971, not as a boxer but as a patron saint of resistance.

Seven years earlier, in 1964, on the other hand, it was all about Ali's boxing skills and his audacity. I may not have been able to remember where I was on March 8, 1971, but I knew exactly where I was on February 25, 1964, when Ali–then Cassius Clay–upset Sonny Liston to become heavyweight champion.

I was at home in Phoenix, Illinois, listening to a radio broadcast of the fight with my father. Traditional, knock-'em-out, old-school fight fans like my father predicted that Liston would annihilate Clay. Just before the broadcast began, my father got up from his chair, put on his hat and coat, and headed toward the door leading to our backyard.

"Where are you going?" I asked, taking the bait.

"I'm going to catch Clay," he said.

We laughed. The idea that Liston would knock Clay from Miami, where the fight was being held, to our backyard in Phoenix, was hilarious.

We listened as Clay defeated Liston in the upset of the century. After the fight, Clay announced he was a Muslim and had changed his name to Muhammad Ali. The cultural and political implications of the announcement went over my head.

I took in the Liston–Clay fight as a naive thirteen-year-old-Black boy. By March 8, 1971, I was a different cat. A soul brother. A proud HBCUer.

Between February 1964 and March 1971, my understanding of

the United States' destructiveness, white oppression, and Black people who facilitated that oppression had deepened. In large part, that insight was brought about by fellow Black athletes.

In 1967, former Cleveland Browns great Jim Brown convened a meeting of Black athletes to support Ali. In 1968, Tommie Smith and John Carlos staged a human rights demonstration on the victory stand at the Mexico City Olympic games. After the 1969 Major League Baseball season, St. Louis Cardinals player Curt Flood defied the baseball establishment by refusing a trade.

Perhaps what completely woke me up was the slaying of Fred Hampton in my hometown.

One year and three months before the Ali–Frazier fight, Hampton, chairman of the Illinois chapter of the Black Panther Party, was slain in his bed during a predawn raid by Chicago police. The police had been given the apartment floor plan by a Black FBI informant. Frazier, unfairly or not, was cast by Ali as belonging in the sphere of Black informants, Uncle Toms, the white man's Negroes and Head Negroes-in-Charge whose mission was to keep white people informed and in control.

As for the Ali–Frazier fight, Frazier defeated Ali that night in 1971. But while the victory would be the highlight of Frazier's career, it was simply another chapter in the legend of Ali as a global cultural icon.

Frazier lost his heavyweight title to George Foreman in 1973. A year later, in an upset perhaps as great as his victory over Liston, Ali snatched the title from Foreman. Ali and Frazier met two more times, with Ali winning both fights, including the spectacular Thrilla in Manila.

I was in Atlanta covering the 1996 Olympic games when Ali reached yet another pinnacle. Suffering from the ravages of Parkinson's disease, Ali lit the Olympic flame. Many of those who resented Ali for his antiwar stance embraced him that night as a hero.

Writer Scoop Jackson pointed out that in the lead-up to the 1971 Ali–Frazier fight, Ali could have been better, Frazier could have been better. These two Black men could have treated each other better.

They were gladiators who needed each other. And Black folks need each other.

I'm not sure where I was on the night of March 8, 1971, but I certainly know where I am today: in the midst of an ongoing struggle, an existential boxing match.

Ali helped point the way.

Originally published March 8, 2021

A **BLESSING** AND A **CURSE**: THE RICH **HISTORY** BEHIND **"BLACK TWITTER"**

From Black Voices to MySpace to Instagram, Black creativity has defined social media from the start.

BY DAVID DENNIS JR.

SAMUEL TAYLOR Coleridge's "Rime of the Ancient Mariner" is an epic poem from 1798 about a disastrous sea voyage. In the poem, an albatross, a symbol of good luck, leads a ship out of icy waters. But when a sailor kills the bird, the crew's luck turns bad and the shipmates punish the sailor by tying the bird around his neck.

Today, there's a digital bird representing the duality of curses and blessings: Twitter. The social media platform has blessed careers, jump-started social justice movements, and created cultural trends. This has been especially true for Black users who have used Twitter to circumvent traditional channels in order to get their voices heard.

Simply put, Black folk have found a way to use social media to change the world. Shiggy dance crazes. Phrases such as "on fleek." Providing platforms for artists such as Drake and Gucci Mane to thrive. Civil rights movements. Surviving R. Kelly. #MeToo. #OscarsSoWhite. These are all Black people loving, creating, thinking, rebelling on social media.

From presidential elections to reactions to TV shows, it's all there at our fingertips. Countries have been toppled, careers have started and ended, thanks to what happens on Twitter, Facebook, Instagram, and other social media platforms. And at the heart of these moments are Black people–the leading purveyors of American culture and the harbingers of cool.

Social media is also full of anti-Black trolling and trauma for minorities, even as we populate these spaces with our ingenuity and fanatic participation. As a result, some Black people are seeking refuge in more controlled spaces, such as the GroupMe messaging app and private Facebook subgroups, or even cutting themselves off from social media altogether. Now, while the country is in the throes of a pandemic and social distancing, social media is as vital as its ever been and an even bigger factor in our everyday lives.

How did we get here? How did these spaces become so toxic for Black Americans? And why did we flock to them in the first place?

It all started in a newsroom a few miles from Walt Disney World.

BLACK VOICES
Founder: Barry Cooper

Barry Cooper was a sports reporter for the *Orlando Sentinel* during Shaquille O'Neal's rookie year in 1992–93. The newspaper's parent, the Tribune Company, had a partnership with AOL and was publishing articles on the upstart online provider. During the early '90s, media companies were figuring out who used the World Wide Web and the ways they consumed news content, so analytics were critical. Cooper, who had taken an interest in digital media, realized something about his sports coverage online.

"We . . . noticed that a lot of the traffic was coming from Black readers," said Cooper, who now works as a digital media consultant. "So [the Tribune Company] launched a site in 1995 that catered directly to the African American community, and called it Black Voices."

Cooper and his small team of reporters were reporting national news relevant to Black communities, often focused on happenings at historically Black colleges and universities. Almost immediately, the site was leading traffic across AOL-owned properties.

The surge in popularity was accompanied by a community of now-legendary chat rooms that helped set the blueprint for current African American social media use. They covered topics from politics and sports to relationships and current events. The Black Voices chat rooms provided a place for African Americans to find community with like-minded people, as well as discover new perspectives on Blackness they wouldn't necessarily find in the mainstream media.

The big hit? The BBW room, as in beautiful Black women. As is often the case in social media, Black women were holding the conversations and generating the traffic that made Black Voices so popular–and everyone else followed.

"They'd talk all night about everything from TV shows to random relationship topics," Cooper said. "The rooms provided that sense of community, where you can reach people like you from all over the country who have the same challenges and perspectives. That made the whole digital thing attractive to Black people."

During this time, AOL users were charged based on how much time they spent online, and the results were lucrative. "People were spending four hundred to five hundred dollars a month on AOL and a large part of the time was spent on Black Voices," Cooper said. "Black consumers, when they're passionate about something, they spend what it takes to get it."

The Tribune Company saw the site overperforming and put $5 million toward making Black Voices an entity unto itself. The site had offices in Chicago, Los Angeles, and New York that produced news and videos with the taste and concerns of Black consumers in mind, covering everything from the O. J. Simpson trial to *All Eyez on Me*.

"When we look back on Black Voices . . . we were doing a lot of things before they were done in the mainstream," Cooper said. "We had original content and would go out on the street and interview Black people about things going on in the culture. We were doing some YouTube stuff before YouTube got in the game. We think now about how well Facebook has done and all of it was built on community. We were building that same type of community."

Black Voices was sold to AOL/Time Warner in 2004 and then became part of the Huffington Post brand. Gone are its message boards. The new Black Voices is more focused on editorial, offering op-eds and news about everything from Black Lives Matter to who rocked the best looks at the Oscars. Though the site came under fire a few years ago for having a staff that didn't necessarily reflect the "Black" in Black Voices, the legacy of the chat rooms looms large.

THE MESSAGE BOARDS

AllHipHop

SOHH

Lipstick Alley

As internet use expanded exponentially over the '90s and early 2000s, Black communities began forming spontaneously on the opinionated and rapid-fire message boards that accompanied rap music sites such as the still-popular AllHipHop, founded by Greg Watkins and Chuck Creekmur in 1998, and SOHH (Support Online Hip Hop), created by Felicia Palmer and Steven Samuel in 1996. These boards provided space for passionate rap fans to discuss their favorite artists—and even hold rap battles, in written form.

Lipstick Alley, which began in the early 2000s as an offshoot message board on former Tennessee Titan Eddie George's personal website, of all places, is one of the internet's most influential African American forums. It features news, sports, celebrity gossip, fashion and hair care from an African American perspective and is also a hub for unverified VIP tales. The message boards there are raw, but can be the birthplace of mainstream breaking news.

Black users could be themselves in these safe spaces before safe spaces were a thing. Here, they didn't have to worry about bots or trolls or egg avatars that would use racial slurs.

Two of the most impactful and lasting communities are Okayplayer and NikeTalk. Here, Black people have shared information on everything from retro Jordans to the newest Nike tech gear, and both coddled and critiqued up-and-coming artists such as Wale, J. Cole, and Desus.

OKAYPLAYER

Founders: Questlove and Angela Nissel

"I got a call from Questlove," said Angela Nissel, recalling the conversation she had with the Roots drummer that led to the formation of Okayplayer in February 1999.

Now a bestselling author and producer of shows such as *mixed-ish*, *The Last O.G.*, and *Scrubs*, Nissel, back then, was a recent graduate of the University of Pennsylvania who was working at a sleep clinic while building websites on the side. "He said, 'We have a little bit of a problem.' He put Okayplayer.com on the [1999 *Things Fall Apart*] album, but he didn't actually have a website. Plus, he was about to go on tour, so he needed me to put something together."

Nissel, who met Questlove while they were working tele-marketing jobs in Philadelphia, had to put together a site for Roots fans quickly. She started with the idea that fans would want to get closer to the group and learn about aspects of their lives not seen in music videos or during their rare TV appearances.

"I'm like a kid sister to a lot of those guys and it gave me access that most people didn't have," she said. "I was their first introduction to the internet. They'd trust me to put their words out there."

Nissel would dig around Questlove's house and find a piece of memorabilia—receipts, drumsticks, clothing—and ask him to tell a story about it; then she would put that story on the site. "I knew that if you went in someone's house and saw their record collection and if you have a lot of that music in common, then you're going to be friends," Nissel said.

The Roots won a Grammy for the *Things Fall Apart* single "You Got Me" and had put together a community of artists such as Common, Erykah Badu, and D'Angelo, who recorded together and amassed a passionate fan base. Okayplayer allowed those fans to almost touch their favorite artists through their computer screens.

"OKP was the first place where you could talk to other Black people from all over the country who shared your experiences and interests," said rapper Phonte Coleman, who was a mainstay on the message boards even after his career took off as one-third of the rap group Little Brother. "OKP removed the stigma of talking to strangers on the internet because we had the shared bond of music. If you were a Prince fan, you could be on a forum of other Prince fans. OKP is where you can find bigger music nerds than me. And I'm a big music nerd."

The message boards were divided into rooms similar to the AOL Black Voices chat rooms. "The Lesson" was for deep crate diggers who wanted to compare notes on their favorite artists. "Pass the Popcorn" was for movie lovers. There was a freestyle forum for rappers to write out bars and see who could rhyme better. And "General Discussion" was no holds barred or "f– Iraq," as Coleman explained it.

Just as with Black Voices, Black women were the engine driving Okayplayer. "So many of us go about our lives hoping to see other Black people," said Nissel. "For Black women, the world could be exhausting to us. We just want to sit down with a glass of wine and beer and not have to comfort anybody else. This was the first space where we felt not alone."

Little Brother, consisting of MC Phonte, rapper Big Pooh, and producer 9th Wonder, got their start posting music on the Okayplayer boards for immediate feedback. "It helped spread the word. I can't overstate the importance those message boards had on our careers. OKP was like a baby version of SoundCloud."

Coleman isn't the only person whose career took off from the OKP boards. Desus and Mero, the late-night TV hosts, used to crack jokes on the boards as well. The Okayplayer message boards were the beginnings of what is now known as Black Twitter, where conversations about Blackness and Black influence really started to take shape.

NIKETALK
Founder: Nelson Cabral

As Okayplayer was setting the tone for Black subcultures, NikeTalk was paving the way for Black influence in the corporate and fashion world.

NikeTalk, which has no official affiliation with the shoe brand, was formed in 1999 as a spot for sneaker enthusiasts to come together to speculate about upcoming shoes, show off their newest finds, and pine for classic shoes they'd missed out on in previous years. If you've ever scoured the internet for a sold-out sneaker, then chances are you've ended up on NikeTalk. A sneaker wasn't hot until it got the NikeTalk seal of approval (as well as recognition from places such as the Sole Collector message boards, which are no longer in existence). And of course, the community was heavily occupied by Black commenters.

"NikeTalk was definitely one of my main entry points into the internet," said John Gotty, a veteran of the message board who went on to launch the now-defunct hip-hop site the Smoking Section. "I learned about downloading music. I learned about different shoe trends across the country. I made friends on that site."

Much of sneaker culture as we know it—companies knowing which shoes to reissue, which features are popular, and who should be the new signature athletes—came in part from perusing the NikeTalk message boards. The site also went beyond shoe talk, as fans of brands from Gucci to Champion compared notes. Designers such as Heron Preston Johnson, who started the Been

Trill clothing company, were first seen soaking in the opinions of passionate wearers on NikeTalk.

Much like Okayplayer, NikeTalk also became a place for upcoming musical artists who wanted to test out their material and get immediate feedback. A young Wale could often be found in the message boards posting music, debating with fans, and posting about his love for SB Dunks. J. Cole would also post his music looking for feedback.

"I knew that if an artist like Kendrick Lamar was getting posted across different regions like the Midwest and South, then it was clear he would be the next big thing," said Gotty.

NikeTalk, which still flourishes as a place for sneaker fans, is more than a cultural meeting place–it's a lucrative spot for those entering the shoe resale market. "NikeTalk was my first experience running a business," said Gotty. "We ran a reselling site called NDemand Conceptz. We'd go buy shoes in bulk and resell them before a lot of people were doing that. If there was a shoe sold-out a lot of places and we had access to them, we'd buy them in bulk, turn around, and sell them online. All that started through meeting people on NikeTalk. It taught me that you can eat off of the internet."

Both Okayplayer and NikeTalk are still active, vibrant communities. But they aren't as populated as they were during their heyday, thanks to the mass exodus to Twitter and Facebook.

MYSPACE
Founders: Chris DeWolfe, Tom Anderson, Jon Hart

BLACKPLANET
Founder: Omar Wasow

In 2003, a brave new world began in Beverly Hills, California: MySpace. Histories of the internet often skip from the message boards to Facebook and Twitter. But that overlooks the monster that was MySpace. It was the largest social media site in the world from 2005 to early 2008, and in 2006 had more visitors than Google in the United States.

In its prime, MySpace gave users the ability to create their own pages and profiles with customizable pictures, friends lists, and backgrounds. News of Facebook allowing personal information to be used without permission, and Twitter's failure to protect users from abuse, has prompted some nostalgia for the days when MySpace ruled the digital world.

But Black users didn't run to MySpace out of the blue. Many were already using BlackPlanet, which had upward of 15 million users. BlackPlanet became the prototype for MySpace, as founder Omar Wasow told Complex in 2011: "The guys who started MySpace . . . looked at BlackPlanet as a model for MySpace and thought there was an opportunity to do a general market version of what BlackPlanet was."

MySpace, though, appealed to a wider (i.e., not just Black) audience. Black users flocked to MySpace and BlackPlanet as a means for pushing their profiles beyond what they could do on message boards–customizing pages with selfies in tall tees and bling, while Soulja Boy boomed from computer speakers as soon as a page was opened.

And MySpace's Top 8? The space on a page where users could pick their eight closest friends and significant others? That was the home of real-life high school and college drama that would last for days.

"You got to pour a little liquor out for MySpace," Coleman said. "Everyone on OKP went straight to MySpace even though we were still on the boards too." Coleman was an example of someone who used the site to boost his profile and bring fans closer to his everyday life. While posting music on message boards and debuting songs on his MySpace page, he would also post hilarious blog entries on his MySpace profile about everything from liner notes and backstories to Little Brother albums to takes on white people's reactions to him wearing fitted hats.

"We were never a big group in terms of a big record label machine behind us. We had to use every tool in that toolbox," Coleman said. "I didn't think anybody is going to read these posts. We saw more people are reading this than we realize. I was just using every tool that we had for us to get out there."

MySpace's and BlackPlanet's lasting impact on the Black community came from the fact that they allowed users to teach themselves a skill that's invaluable on today's internet: coding. Once users discovered what a little lightweight hacking could achieve, it was just a matter of digging through the internet for HTML and CSS codes to transform their pages.

"I started off literally just starting with the basic stuff," said Paola Mendoza-Yu, a user experience designer in L.A. "I learned you could hijack the whole page. I made a new design every week. I was obsessed. . . . Years later I realized what I was doing was coding."

The customizable MySpace and BlackPlanet pages encouraged creativity and self-expression (as evidenced by a BlackPlanet page of a high-school-aged Kevin Durant that resurfaced in 2019), something African Americans are often discouraged from exhibiting in the real world.

"I was writing custom CSS and JavaScript and manipulating the layout and color palette and the page," said Mina Markham, a senior engineer for Slack who designed the user interface for Hillary Clinton's campaign site Pantsuit. "Coding on MySpace allowed me to do more things like that on the internet. It showed me I could make stuff that truly reflects who I am."

MySpace and BlackPlanet helped create a generation of Black kids who were coders without ever taking a class in coding, developing a skill that allowed some of them to enter a space that was overwhelmingly white.

"I think that learning how to code empowers young Black people and young Black girls that they really can do and be anything," said Markham, who teaches with Black Girls Code. "Tech has a way of lifting people out, allowing them to make a decent amount of money, and it doesn't take years and years of training and upfront money like being a doctor would. The idea of being able to create something from beginning to end, it's just really powerful."

Like the message boards, MySpace fell victim to the popularity of Facebook. But there may be another reason for the shift too. In the 2011 anthology *Race After the Internet*, Microsoft researcher Danah Boyd argued that a form of white flight was occurring among teens, driven by the perception that MySpace was becoming Black. All the customized Black pages on the platform led white users to leave for the more "elite" Facebook, which had previously only accepted college students. One notable exchange from Boyd's work sticks out:

> I met Kat, a white fourteen-year-old from a comfortable background. We were talking about the social media practices of her classmates when I asked her why most of her friends were moving from MySpace to Facebook. Kat grew noticeably uncomfortable. She began simply, noting that "MySpace is just old now and it's boring." But then she paused, looked down at the table, and continued. "It's not really racist, but I guess you could say that. I'm not really into racism, but I think that MySpace now is more like ghetto or whatever."

The divide between the two sites was backed up by demographic research. In 2009, marketing firm Nielsen Claritas found that wealthy individuals were 25 percent more likely to use Facebook while less affluent individuals were 37 percent more likely to be on MySpace. Intentionally or not, MySpace was the social media site for those who filled their pages with hip-hop, selfies, and flamboyant page designs, while Facebook was for white and Asian users.

MySpace lost half of its subscribers in 2010 alone. By 2011, the company's staff of 1,600 had dwindled to 200. By 2013, MySpace was 215th in total web traffic.

For years afterward, MySpace would be treated as a joke–a graveyard of old pages where selfies taken on flip phones, poor fashion choices, and embarrassing childhood decisions reigned supreme. But the site once was much more. It was a home for Black people to customize their experiences in ways that we haven't seen on social media since.

"I don't think there's anything currently that allows you to express yourself like we were doing back then in MySpace," said Mendoza-Yu. "We were exploiting a flaw in MySpace's system. Facebook figured out [how] to get around that flaw. If I were sixteen or seventeen, I don't know where I would go to have the freedom online I had with MySpace."

Added Markham: "The big social networks have stripped away the power from the user. You can't customize the Facebook page. They've stripped away the personalization. . . . Even if kids are really aware of coding, it might not feel attainable."

(It should also be mentioned that Tumblr, once a space for Black creatives to share interests and ideas–and explore images of sexuality not found on mainstream adult sites–ended in 2018 by getting rid of its sexually explicit content. As a result, the space has become a haven for far-right users, making it less welcoming to the

Black users who helped popularize the site. Images of sexuality are banned, but no such ban exists for swastikas, for instance.)

Black creativity was the driving force of MySpace and BlackPlanet. Now social media is largely run by the big two–Facebook and Twitter–for better or worse.

FACEBOOK

Founder: Mark Zuckerberg

INSTAGRAM

Founders: Kevin Systrom and Mike Krieger

Facebook is used heavily by African Americans, especially in relation to the total population. In 2018, Mark Luckie, a Facebook employee, posted a farewell memo that summarized the data on Black usage, as well as the problems that Black users and employees faced at the company:

"African Americans are more likely to use Facebook to communicate with family and friends daily, according to research commissioned by Facebook. Sixty-three percent use Facebook to communicate with family, and 60 percent use it to communicate with friends at least once a day, compared to 53 percent and 54 percent of the total population. Seventy percent of black U.S. adults use Facebook and 43 percent use Instagram, according to the Pew Research Center. Fifty-five percent of black millennials report spending at least one hour a day on social networking sites, 6 percent higher than all millennials, while 29 percent say they spend at least three hours a day, 9 percent higher than all millennials, Nielsen surveys found. Black people are driving the kind of meaningful social interactions Facebook is striving to facilitate."

Especially since the 2016 presidential election, though, Facebook has developed a reputation as a breeding ground for false information, tampering, and anti-Black sentiment. Black users are more likely to be flagged for their posts than others. The site has developed a reputation for being a place where Black freedom of speech is quelled. Beyond that, Facebook has had to fight off one scandal after another revolving around user privacy.

Despite all of these problems, Facebook has maintained its hold on Black users. "I used to waste so much time on message boards, but now it's my safe space from the internet," Nissel said. "I'm in so many Black women groups on Facebook. A lot of people are finding smaller communities within the bigger communities."

Zuckerberg's company, now in its third decade of existence, is one of the most recognized brands in the world, comparable to McDonald's or Walmart. Facebook is also the site known for connecting families, where users can leave comments for aunts and uncles and share pics with grandparents. These safe spaces, and the time people have invested on the site, have made Facebook such a part of Black life that it's hard to imagine us turning away from it.

In 2012, Facebook bought Instagram, which was known as a place to post pictures and captions. Since then, it has become a culture changer and one that is being jet-streamed by Black creatives. (Instagram has successfully positioned itself as an alternative to Facebook–only 29 percent of Americans know the platform is even owned by Facebook.)

Black teens make up the largest block of users on Instagram. One of the reasons for this is the type of technological access Black Americans have compared with their white peers. Instagram (like Snapchat) is a mobile-only app, and for many Black kids, their phones are their only connections to the internet. As a result, Instagram is the site they often flock to. And the places where Black teens congregate often become spaces for innovation and the birth of new trends.

Celebrities have also flocked to Instagram. When Beyoncé announces a pregnancy, she does it on Instagram. When Durant announces he's leaving the Golden State Warriors, he does so on Instagram. When LeBron James wants you to know what album he's listening to while he drinks a bottle of red wine, he does it on Instagram.

Instagram is also a place for Black entrepreneurs and influencers to launch businesses and feed their families. For instance, Alexis Felder's popular LexiWithTheCurls brand, highlighting travel and Black hair products, has allowed her to flourish as a businessperson and name.

Felder gravitated to Instagram because of the community she built with other Black women pushing and supporting one another. "Instagram is like a sorority for women of color," she said. "It has helped me understand the power of collaboration. Three influencers are stronger than one. We have grown together and now we make money together.

"Some of my influencer friends and I were amongst the first to tap into the travel market and work with tourism boards and travel-based companies," she said. "I have gotten comped hotel stays in hotels and resorts all over the world. I have made money from beauty and lifestyle brands through my Instagram."

Instagram is also a space for Black media to tell stories outside of traditional newsrooms. Sites such as the Shade Room, with more than 18 million followers, and Baller Alert (more than 5 million) have taken their online communities directly to Instagram, posting news and celebrity stories on their social media pages. The Shade Room, especially, is a social media version of Lipstick Alley, pushed by its ravenous fans and nonstop comments on every post.

"The one thing I don't like about Instagram is that it's super-oversaturated now with influencers," Felder said. "You have to go over and beyond to get attention or to get that next gig. I know one thing, if IG ever crashes or ends, a lot of people will lose a huge chunk of their income."

TWITTER

Founders: Jack Dorsey, Noah Glass, Biz Stone, and Evan Williams

VINE

Founders: Dom Hofmann, Rus Yusupov, and Colin Kroll

It's important to differentiate between the early days of Twitter and the social media giant we see now. When I joined in 2009, Twitter felt like a whole new world, where message boards and the comment sections of websites and communities that I'd formed online could converge in one place. Jokes would fly, drama would ensue, and celebrities would interact with fans without much fear of repercussions or "dragging." It was a place where Rihanna and Ciara had a public argument like they were one of us.

The content on the message boards, which previously had stayed in the undercurrent of American pop culture, now became a public spectacle. Okayplayer and NikeTalk users flocked to Twitter to expand their communities and talk about Prince albums or Foamposites with more people than before. MySpace users traded customization for an ability to use hilarious hashtags or the wittiest jokes to show off their creativity.

The rest of the world watched Black users on Twitter and wanted to be a part of the culture. Articles popped up across the internet about "Black Twitter" and what these people of color were talking about online. Hashtags such as #IfSantaWasBlack would turn into hours-long roasting sessions in the tradition of playing the dozens, with pictorial references to classic Black TV or movie moments populating the timeline. It was like one gigantic barbershop or salon joke marathon. But unlike an OKP message board or Black Voices page, the world was able to watch.

"Black people–specifically, young black people–do seem to use Twitter differently from everyone else on the service," Farhad Manjoo wrote in *Slate* in 2010. "They form tighter clusters on the network–they follow one another more readily, they retweet each other more often, and more of their posts are @-replies–posts directed at other users. It's this behavior, intentional or not, that gives black people–and in particular, black teenagers–the means to dominate the conversation on Twitter."

Some called the article "voyeuristic" and others said its lead image–a black Twitter bird with a fitted cap–was offensive. But it revealed a truth: Black people had found their voice on Twitter and others were fumbling to understand that voice.

In October 2009, the Pew Research Center released the first study of Black people overindexing on Twitter. It found that 26 percent of African Americans were using the platform online compared with 19 percent of whites. The impact of Black Twitter was undeniable, especially combined with Vine, the social media site that allowed people to share eight-second clips. Many of these would go viral thanks to Black users on Twitter.

While there was no access to the coding that would allow customization, Vine was a space for Black creatives to test the limits of their imaginations. The site launched household slogans such as the "LeBron James kid" or "Yeet" vine. Comedians such as King Bach parlayed online celebrity to movie and comedy show deals.

Even as Twitter became a space for Black creativity, it never experienced the white flight that had plagued MySpace, and it's not totally clear why. Maybe enough white celebrities stuck around on Twitter to make it feel safe. MySpace required more searching to find the newest trends, while Twitter had widespread virality that allowed everyone to feel they were a part of the conversation. Maybe the trends started by Black users were more easily co-opted and followed by white users who could then feel they were an early part of the trends instead of latecomers or outsiders. Whatever the case, Twitter's Blackness isn't the albatross that MySpace's was seen as being.

At first, even with Twitter's popularity and the research studies, it was hard to quantify the economic potential of Black people on Twitter.

Then *Scandal* came out.

Shonda Rhimes's 2012 show starred Kerry Washington in the first prime-time TV show lead for a Black woman in thirty-seven years. The show was given a midseason premiere and received mediocre reviews—marks of a show that typically wouldn't make it to a second season. However, Black users—Black women in particular—found a character they could relate to online in the form of Washington's no-nonsense fixer with incredible style.

"Without Twitter to boost its profile and then its ratings, *Scandal* probably would have been canceled," observed the *Los Angeles Times* in 2013. By the second season, though, the show was outperforming *American Idol* on Twitter and raking in 9 million viewers.

Scandal allowed the entertainment industry to measure the impact of Black social media support. The power of Black users on Twitter led Nielsen, the company that measures TV viewership, to invent a rating to measure the social impact of TV shows. *Scandal* topped the ratings in the system's inaugural week. It became clear that companies needed to pay attention to the buying power and impact of Black social media users. TV shows with Black leads such as *black-ish* and *How to Get Away with Murder* would follow, and there's a direct line from the popularity of *Scandal* to the creation of the blockbuster movie *Black Panther.*

But "Black Twitter" would show power beyond pop culture. Soon everyone would see how Black mobilization on the internet could change the world.

TWITTER IN 2014 AND BEYOND

Eighteen-year-old Michael Brown was gunned down by police officer Darren Wilson on August 9, 2014, in Ferguson, Missouri. Although Brown's body lay on the ground for four hours, there was no mainstream media coverage of the event. Instead, pictures of Brown's body flooded Twitter timelines and Black people demanded answers. Within hours, hundreds of folks were headed to Ferguson's streets to find out what happened and why Brown's life was taken.

"I remember seeing it all on Twitter and all these Black people talking about what had happened," said civil rights activist DeRay Mckesson. He was so moved that he drove from Minneapolis to Ferguson. Meeting there with other activists, Mckesson decided that the best use of his skills would be to chronicle what was happening on the streets, and he used Twitter to achieve that goal.

"Twitter is the friend who is always awake," Mckesson said. "There are people who are gifted in leading action and lead the action, but I could streamline the flow of information, and used Twitter to do that. I tried to tweet in a way that was clear, concise. Reporters had to follow me to know what they were going to get next."

Twitter became a conduit for Black folks to talk about police violence and social justice movements across the country. #BlackLivesMatter reached the mainstream thanks to Twitter in 2014. A new Black liberation movement was formed, in large part by people putting their feet to the ground on American streets, but also thanks to people tweeting. Twitter magnified the moments when Black people were victims of police violence and inequality. The world witnessed something similar in 2011 when the Arab Spring uprising was enacted through Facebook posts, Twitter posts, and YouTube videos. As *Middle East Eye* wrote in 2015, Black Lives Matter is America's Arab Spring.

"We don't have to wait for mainstream media to tell the story anymore," Mckesson said. "The protest shifted the power dynamic."

Twitter (and for a time, live video apps such as Periscope) became a Black liberation tool, whether that was the site's intention or not.

As Black folks tried to get free, however, anti-Blackness became a part of the social media experience. Mckesson and other activists who had become public figures post-Ferguson were subjected to death threats, harassment, and hacking attempts. Bot accounts started to appear, often with stolen avatars, that were designed to intimidate, harass, and spread false information. Russia sought to amplify racial anger by buying Facebook ads about Ferguson in the lead-up to the 2016 presidential election.

It seems like any person of color who pushes against societal norms and racism winds up in the crosshairs of traumatizing attacks from a digital mob. Actress Anna Diop endured harassment by racists over being cast as Starfire–an orange alien–in the *Titans* TV series. Vietnamese American actress Kelly Marie Tran deleted her Instagram account after attacks from racists who were upset over her role in *Star Wars*. Leslie Jones did the same on Twitter after the abuse directed at her for being in the *Ghostbusters* reboot in 2016.

Twitter has tried to address online abuse but has failed to do so in a way that eliminates much of the hate speech on the site. It eventually deleted the account of Alex Jones, the commentator who argued that the Sandy Hook shooting was a hoax. But far too many such tweets slip by. I've reported hate speech to Twitter, including the use of racial slurs, only to have the company respond that there was insufficient evidence for it to take action.

WHAT'S NEXT?

TikTok, a video-sharing app, has emerged as the new Vine. Just as with MySpace, Twitter, and Instagram, the site is where Black trends become international trends. Take, for instance, the "Renegade" dance. The craze was started by Jalaiah Harmon, a teenage girl from Atlanta who posted the original version on Instagram. The dance was then widely adopted by TikTok users and landed Jalaiah on the court at the NBA All-Star Game showing the world the moves. Meanwhile, Roddy Ricch's "The Box" beat out Justin Bieber for the top spot on Billboard charts, powered by teens playing the song on TikTok.

It's only natural that COVID-19-imposed social distancing would cause people to gravitate toward social media, and TikTok is at the heart of this new world. Dance crazes come fast and furious. The "Don't Rush" challenge, featuring people changing from their loungewear to fancy getups, was adopted by everyone from nurses to WNBA stars. Drake developed his own dance catering to TikTok fans as the "Toosie Slide" earned him another No. 1 hit.

The social media platform has become a means of family bonding, as videos are made with mothers, grandmothers, and babies embracing the shared creativity that isolation can bring. LeBron James, Ciara, and Shaquille O'Neal, among others, have joined in on crazes with their entire families dancing along.

Overall, Black social media users have used this trying time to create art and share just how creative we can be. Instagram is a club every weekend, with people such as DJ D-Nice spinning sets that attract hundreds of thousands of viewers on Instagram Live. Swizz Beatz and Timbaland launched a "Verzuz" series in which hitmakers pit their biggest songs against one another every weekend. Moments like these turned social media into a means of temporary relief while the world seemed to be at its saddest. This is a testament to the power of Black brilliance as it intersects with the technology that can bring us together.

Still, the question remains: With social media as toxic and divisive as ever, why do Black people still use it? From personal experience, I can say I still use Twitter because it's a massive resource for spreading my work. There are still communities of wrestling and basketball fans I like to talk with, as long as I ignore my mentions. But if I ever get to the point where I don't *need* Twitter, I'm gone and not looking back.

For Mckesson, Twitter still represents a space to speak the truth to the masses. "The people who dismiss social media don't see the full extent of the way it impacts these movements. Twitter helped us organize in ways we couldn't have otherwise."

Going back to private spaces where every word isn't subject to harassment might be the future of Black social media. Black millennials are flocking to GroupMe, a mobile app owned by Microsoft, where groups of friends can communicate with one another privately. I'm in several: Black travel groups, a group of about ten wrestling fans, a group for Black writers. A lot of the toxicity of social media is absent in these spaces, and I feel like I can be my unfiltered self in the same ways I used to be on message boards and comment sections without worrying that bots will pull up my statements months later.

So where does that leave social media for the future? Something wholly new may come along that will make these concerns obsolete.

"The kids communicate through Fortnite now," Coleman said. "Which is good, because we've reached peak social media. Black people are just tired."

That fatigue has manifested itself in a constant balancing act: using social media for its benefits while also finding ways to protect ourselves from trauma.

Will there ever be a social media platform that is safe for Black people? Social media is a digital reflection of the real world, and any hope for a digital utopia is as strong as our hope for a real utopia. For a space where racism doesn't weigh us down like an albatross around our necks.

Originally published May 19, 2020

THE **GUT-WRENCHING** HISTORY OF **BLACK BABIES** AND **ALLIGATORS**

It's not a myth: babies were used to lure gators and crocodiles for hunting.

BY DOMONIQUE FOXWORTH

IN THE summer of 2016, two-year-old Lane Graves was attacked and killed by an alligator in central Florida. We should all mourn the death of this innocent child. And empathize with a family whose grief will no doubt be punishing and eternal. As a father, it hurts to even imagine. My thoughts are with that family.

Soon after the attack, Florida officials euthanized five alligators and planned to eliminate more. Obviously, killing those alligators will not bring back Lane and offers no real solace to the family. But it hammers home one important American belief: Animals' lives are less significant than that of a human child.

That same year, a gorilla was killed at the Cincinnati Zoo after it injured a three-year-old boy after the boy fell into the animal's enclosure. It was tragic that the gorilla was killed, but the zoo officials did the right thing because a child's life is sacred.

Can you imagine an America when that was not true? Can you imagine an America when a child's life was so insignificant that he was intentionally put into the pen of a dangerous zoo animal? An America when a child was intentionally placed at the edge of alligator-infested waters to lure the ferocious beast for hunters?

"Baits Alligators with Pickaninnies,"reads a *Washington Times* headline from June 3, 1908. The article continues, "Zoo Specimens Coaxed to Summer Quarters by Plump Little Africans."

The New York Zoological Garden's zookeeper sent two Black children into an enclosure that housed more than twenty-five crocodiles and alligators. The children were chased by the hungry reptiles, entertaining zoo patrons while leading the alligators and crocodiles out of the reptile house, where they spent the winter, into a tank where they could be viewed during the summer.

According to the newspaper article, "two small colored children happened to drift through the reptile house." The zookeeper "pressed them into service." He believed that alligators and crocodiles had an "epicurean fondness for the black man." He also believed, along with all the people who allowed it to happen, that the lives of those children were nearly valueless. There is no mention of punishment for the zookeeper in the 166-word article. It offers not one adjective that would imply that the actions of the zookeeper were despicable, unthinkable, or even reckless.

Was using Black children as gator bait unacceptable? No. Unbelievably no.

The idea that Black children are acceptable gator bait was not born in the head of one zookeeper; it was a practice in the American Everglades that inspired lore and occasioned memorabilia.

In 1923, *Time* magazine reported that "colored babies were being used for alligator bait" in Chipley, Florida. "The infants are allowed to play in the shallow water while expert riflemen watch from concealment nearby. When a saurian approaches this prey, he is shot by the riflemen."

This tactic was more humane than the one described in a *Miami New Times* article. Alligator hunters would sit crying Black babies who were too young to walk at the water's edge. With rope around their necks and waists, the babies would splash and cry until a crocodile snapped on one of them. The hunters would then kill the alligator only after the baby was in its jaws, trading one child's life for one alligator's skin. They made postcards, pictures, and trinkets to commemorate the practice.

In October 1919, the *Richmond Times Dispatch* printed what appears to have been a joke titled "Game Protection." It reads, "We understand the Florida authorities are going to prohibit the use of live pickaninnies as alligator bait. They say they've got to do something to check the rapid disappearance of the alligator through indigestion."

A Minnesota paper, the *New Ulm Review*, printed an article in January 1922 previewing the attractions at the Brown County Fair. In the section about fireworks, the article boasted that "there will also be a big colored alligator pursuing a fleeing pickaninny, and many other beautiful designs."

In October 1902, the *St. Louis Republic* described all of the floats in the city's Veiled Prophet Parade. A secret society founded by a former Confederate soldier, the Veiled Prophet Organization held a parade to tell the history of the Louisiana Purchase. Float No. 15 was called "Plantation Life in Louisiana." It displayed a "monstrous alligator swallowing a fat pickaninny."

Some believe the abundance of memorabilia, jokes, and celebrations were inspired by fiction, not actual events. But this distinction almost doesn't matter. These events are but a droplet in the swamp that is the Maafa. Derived from the Swahili term meaning "great disaster," in English Maafa has come to represent a history of offenses and ongoing effects of horrors inflicted on African people. Beginning with the transporting of Africans to America to enslave them, the American Maafa is rife with dehumanizing violence.

Crammed in a ship's hull for months, African people lay shoulder to shoulder in excrement. The people who died of illness were thrown overboard and attacked by sharks that had learned to follow the ships for an easy meal. Destined for a fate as cruel, the Africans who survived the journey endured further physical and psychological destruction: separated from their families, branded, dismembered, castrated, and raped.

These are wrongs that cannot be righted, brutalities never grieved, atrocities ignored and mockingly memorialized, as recently as the 1960s, by a pencil pusher depicting a Black baby in the mouth of an alligator.

The Christian people responsible for centuries of Maafa justified their sins by convincing themselves that Blacks were an inferior race. In 1905, professor William Smith published *The Color Line: A Brief in Behalf of the Unborn*. In the book's foreword, Smith answers the question that is the title of chapter 2, "Is the Negro Inferior?" by writing, "Inferiority of both the Negro and the Negroid is argued at length, and proved by a great variety of considerations." That belief was accepted as fact, infecting the ideology of all and influencing laws and opinions that shape our present.

I know this is dark stuff that we don't want to think about, but we should face it. We should be reminded of it and the ways our dark chapters inform our biases, our politics, and the ways we feel about one another. We should feel sadness for Lane Graves and for the nameless children whose deaths were not accidental. But sadness is not action. Empathy and understanding are characteristics that prompt actions. Actions that give birth to progress.

Without all of us acknowledging the vile germs of our history and their contribution to the dysfunction that is present-day American injustice, we cannot expect a cure. Confronting the submerged shameful actions of our past is the only way to understand their enduring societal effects and begin to address them.

Originally published June 22, 2016

MLB ELEVATING THE STATUS OF **NEGRO LEAGUES** IS THE **PROBLEM,** NOT THE **SOLUTION**

Black baseball is not less than.
And never will be.

BY CLINTON YATES

THERE'S A phrase, likely coined by some old white guy, that goes "winners write the history books." In the case of Major League Baseball, not only do they write the history books, but apparently they decide when everyone else's histories are legitimate too.

At the end of 2020, MLB announced that the records and statistics from the seven operations that we now classify as the Negro Leagues will be recognized as part of Major League Baseball's history, presumably paving the way for the posthumous enshrinement of various players in the Hall of Fame in Cooperstown, New York.

"The perceived deficiencies of the Negro Leagues structure and scheduling were born of MLBs exclusionary practices," John Thorn, the Official Historian for Major League Baseball, said in a press release. "And denying them Major League status has been a double penalty, much like that exacted of Hall of Fame candidates prior to Satchel Paige's induction in 1971. Granting MLB status to the Negro Leagues a century after their founding is profoundly gratifying."

Of all the nonsense that the most duplicitously conservative sports league in the history of the United States of America has ever pulled, this might be the most ridiculous piece of soft supremacy we've ever seen. This announcement says, in effect, "Be grateful, we now view you as whole." News flash: That's the problem. Not the solution.

The first time I met Bob Kendrick, it was a hot summer day in my mother's hometown of Kansas City, Missouri, where she grew up watching the Monarchs play. Like many before and after me, I was lucky enough to catch the president of the Negro Leagues Museum on a day when he could give me a personal tour. It was easily the most emotional baseball experience of my life that didn't involve being on the field. Not once did I think about some random town in upstate New York while I was there.

The work that Kendrick has done over the years to champion, document, highlight, and grow the the Negro Leagues and its history is unparalleled in sports. It's impossible to overstate how important he is to the sport, never mind Black baseball, and for him, today, I'm happy. But overall, there is a fundamental misunderstanding of a basic fact that needs to be recalled while everyone in Midtown New York City is patting themselves on the back.

"Negro" does not mean less than. And never will.

So while the names of generations of players will finally be recognized by people who seem to think that statistics are what make baseball, the entire notion of "recognition" being solely acknowledged through the lens of a league that suspended a Black person for saying "n———a" on a ballfield is absurd. The goal here is not to be more like MLB. The goal is for MLB to get on board with the rest of the world.

"The Negro Leagues Baseball Museum is thrilled to see this well-deserved recognition of the Negro Leagues," Kendrick said in a statement. "In the minds of baseball fans worldwide, this serves as historical validation for those who had been shunned from the Major Leagues and had the foresight and courage to create their own league that helped change the game and our country too. This acknowledgment is a meritorious nod to the courageous owners and players who helped build this exceptional enterprise and shines a welcomed spotlight on the immense talent that called the Negro Leagues home."

I'll say what Bob is too classy to say or perhaps feel: It's about time y'all white folks acknowledged us, so thanks. But again, if you are the kind of person who genuinely ever viewed Major League Baseball as the summit of what the sport could and should be, then you were never paying attention to begin with. It's the top flight of the most economically abusive sport in this country. Baseball is the sharecropping of American sports.

Branch Rickey, the guy who is famously credited with integrating the game by signing Jackie Robinson to the Brooklyn Dodgers, is the same guy who effectively created the system we used to know as Minor League Baseball, until the bigs basically crushed the soul out of that too. Reminder: Minor leaguers have never made a living wage.

For many years, MLB has celebrated itself as inclusive, riding the coattails of Robinson's strength for generations. Meanwhile, Kendrick is trying to figure out how to keep the lights on in Kansas City, because it's not like MLB is paying the museum's bills. And there are people roaming the earth who think the Negro Leagues were just one autonomous thing that we just sorta decided to do because that was the way of the world.

Black folks taught Japanese people how to like baseball. Black folks started playing night games because it was the only time white folks would let us use their stadiums. Black folks let women *actually* play on the field, rather than just sticking them in skirts and making a movie years later about it to much fanfare. Those contributions to baseball have nothing to do with numbers in a book and never will. But they won't be understood or recognized as vital because so-called seamheads are too busy worrying about how Black ballplayers match up against their childhood heroes.

It's well known that the reason the Negro Leagues failed is because of MLB's meddlesome approach. Once they started stealing the talent, the draw lessened. If you want to get hard-core, you could argue that Robinson going to Major League Baseball was a death knell for Black baseball, not the other way around. Why? Because all the systems of development and expertise that came along with us being us were tossed aside to appeal to the concept of being the apple of the white league's eye. If Major League Baseball had simply allowed a handful of teams to operate their businesses within their framework, aka joining the league, we wouldn't be where we are today with less than 10 percent of players in the bigs being Black.

Today, sure, it's great that MLB has decided that Black folks are worthy of their gaze. But don't forget about all the guys who are still fighting for what they consider to be fair pensions because the bigs enjoy paying lip service more than they do actual dollars.

I'm happy for Bob. He's the most brilliant and charismatic person in baseball. He deserves everything he wants, and if this action today puts him closer to his goals, I'm all for it. (He also happens to be the best-dressed man in the game, by a gazillion miles.)

But miss me with this "made whole" nonsense. Major League Baseball is one league in one country. At this late date, joining the globe in recognizing that Black folks are real people without whom you could never survive is not a reason to say "you're welcome." It's a reason to say "sorry."

Originally published December 16, 2020

A NATIONAL **LYNCHING MEMORIAL** RECOGNIZES THE **DOMESTIC TERRORISM** THAT KILLED MY **GREAT-GREAT-GRANDFATHER**

My family came to mourn his death and proclaim our history.

BY KARIN D. BERRY

I MOURN the man I never met.

Charles Brown, my maternal great-great-grandfather, who died seventy-eight years before I was born, was taken from the cellar of his employer's house and hanged by a white mob in southwestern Mississippi in September 1879.

What I imagine about his slaying is vivid, painful, and sometimes difficult to talk about because I struggle not to cry. I think of his terror at being forced into the woods, knowing he was about to die. I am certain he felt betrayed and angry as he looked at his killers, whom he almost certainly knew or may have worked for as a carpenter.

I can't forget the final words of the *East Feliciana* (Louisiana) *Watchman* article written about the lynching: "Brown . . . when called for Friday morning was found near Mount Pleasant, unable to respond–his head in a halter–his feet reaching vainly for terra firma–dead."

For years, ugly newspaper reports and half-remembered family stories were the only evidence of my ancestor's murder. That changed recently, when the nation's first memorial to the more than 4,400 people who were lynched in the United States between 1877 and 1950 opened in Montgomery, Alabama. For my family and thousands of others, the National Memorial for Peace and Justice is a chance at long last to see our loss publicly recognized, to tell the stories of the victims and prove that, despite everything, we have endured.

"OUTRAGE AND RETRIBUTION"

I first learned about the lynching of Charles Brown in 1988. His grandson Theodore, my grandfather, told me about the killing when I asked him about our family's history. He told me his grandfather, a carpenter, had built a house for a white man who then refused to pay him. Brown told his wife, "I'm going to get my money" and left home. His family never saw him alive again.

I spent decades struggling to confirm this story. So many seemingly simple facts weren't known and may be unknowable: What really happened before the mob seized him? Where, exactly, did the lynching happen? Where was he buried? I switched to other questions about my family history and tried to solve them. Then I'd remember the story of Charles Brown's lynching, and puzzle over it again.

My experience researching my family matches that of many African Americans: equally fascinating and frustrating. I've traveled to five states and visited libraries, state archives, cemeteries, and museums. I found freedmen who migrated to Ohio in 1843, a private in the U.S. Colored Troops during the Civil War, and a great-great-uncle who married an Irish immigrant around 1870. But most of what I need doesn't exist. Descendants of enslaved Africans face the challenges of tracing a slave owner, slaves who are identified with only a first name and scarce records. Sometimes we are forced to ignore conventional genealogical research, work from family myths and stories, and rely on historical context.

When I first went down south on a research trip, the few facts my grandfather gave me had already fallen into place. An 1870 U.S. Census record in Louisiana showed that Charles Brown, a carpenter, lived in East Feliciana Parish, Louisiana, with his wife, Amanda, and four children. I found a parish death record from the U.S. Mortality Census dated June 1880. The column for the cause of death for Charles Brown, age thirty-nine, stated "hung" in "Sept. 1879." The 1880 U.S. Census said that his wife, my great-great-grandmother Amanda, was a widow.

In 2006, I found what I believe is the first newspaper account of my great-great-grandfather's lynching. Headlined "Outrage and Retribution," it had been published in the *Woodville Republican* in Wilkinson County, Mississippi, the area where he was slain. The article stated that Brown had argued with Mary Phares, wife of the white homeowner, Wilbur Phares, and threatened her with a hatchet. Mary Phares ran screaming from the house, it said, as her husband and a Black employee,

Louis Swift, were returning from working in the fields. They got Brown under control and brought him to the sheriff. Neighbors heard about the confrontation, came to the house, and took Brown away. He was found hanged the next morning.

It's hard to know how much of this story to believe. There are reasons to doubt significant portions of it. But what is undoubtedly true is that Charles Brown's murder matches the context of the times. The slaves of the Deep South had been freed only fourteen years earlier, and the white backlash against Reconstruction and the empowerment of Southern Blacks was in full force. Lynching, along with Jim Crow laws and racial segregation, were tools for maintaining control over all African Americans, not simply devices for punishing individuals. According to research by the Equal Justice Initiative, the organization behind the lynching memorial, Mississippi had the highest number of African American lynching victims, followed by Georgia and Louisiana. Brown lived in Louisiana and his slaying occurred in Mississippi. And pieces of the story mirror common features of "terror lynchings": a fear of interracial sex, especially between Black men and white women, and allegations of violence. According to the *Woodville Republican*, Brown reportedly picked up a hatchet and was going to commit "a nameless outrage" (a euphemism for rape) on a white woman. Those whiffs of sex and violence are likely why the story of a carpenter's killing in rural Mississippi was picked up by at least ten newspapers from New Orleans to Bloomington, Indiana.

IT'S STILL MISSISSIPPI

That terror of the Deep South has stayed with my family for generations. One of my trips, to the Mississippi Department of Archives and History in Jackson, alarmed two cousins from Ohio, who demanded that I call them as soon as I got to Mississippi and again as soon as I (safely) left.

Well . . . it was Mississippi, known for its white citizens' murderous brutality toward Black people. One doesn't have to search hard for reasons to worry. In Woodville, the county seat, Clifton Earl Walker was attacked and killed by a white mob in 1964. The murder remains unsolved.

Mississippi got too close to my mother, Mattie Berry, when she and a cousin accompanied me on one of my trips. I wanted to find out whether Brown's lynching resulted in a court case. I did not believe anyone had been arrested or charged in his death, but I had to rule out the possibility. I found crumbling records of five or six criminal court cases dating to the 1800s at the courthouse in Woodville, but nothing about a prosecution for a lynching.

On the way back to Baton Rouge, Louisiana, our rental car got a flat tire. I pulled over and parked at the end of a driveway that led to a majestic old house. I could not get cellphone service to summon help, and as I walked up and down the quiet rural road hoping to get a signal, a white man walked out of the house, followed by three dogs. He offered to change the tire. We started chatting, and he told me that his family had lived in Wilkinson County for generations. They were descendants of Confederate officers and he had retired to Mississippi and moved into his family home. I asked him if he had heard of Mount Pleasant. "Why, yes," he said, and pointed in the direction we had come from. I blurted, "That's where my great-great-grandfather was lynched." Looking stunned, he took a step back and said something about that being terrible.

When he finished installing the tire, my mother offered to pay him. He said no to the money and responded with a request: pray for his wife, who had lung cancer. When I settled back into the car, my mother hissed from the back seat, "Why did you say that? You don't know him. Something could happen. You don't know." I laughed it off—someone who wishes you harm does not change your tire and ask for a prayer in return. But for Mom, it still was Mississippi.

"A RATHER GOOD DARKY"

We don't know much about Charles Brown's daily life. Where was he born? Who were his parents? Did he have brothers and sisters? How did he learn his carpentry skills? My grandfather said his father told him that Brown was never a slave and that he was from Virginia. His slaying occurred at the height of the Exodusters movement in late 1879, when African Americans fled the South to escape new Jim Crow segregation laws. As many as forty thousand people settled in Kansas, Oklahoma, and Colorado—twenty thousand of them bought land in Kansas. Did he and Amanda long to leave the repression in Louisiana and Mississippi?

I found a complaint filed with the Freedmen's Bureau in Baton Rouge by a Charles Brown who said that he wasn't paid for whitewashing a fence in 1868. I don't know if this was my great-great-grandfather. But if it was, it shows that, like many newly freed people, he was used to fighting to make a living.

However, he seemed to have been in demand for his skills as a carpenter, and he may have been viewed as good-natured. The *East Feliciana Watchman* reported that before Brown was killed he "heretofore had been regarded as a rather good darky." Of course, that sentiment was no protection from a violent, undeserved death at the hands of some of the same people who found him such a valuable worker. His value stopped at the labor he provided to them.

Until now, the only versions of the circumstances of his hanging survived in newspaper accounts that spoke from his killers' perspective. The *East Feliciana Watchman* reported: "The news spread, and by nightfall an incensed crowd of citizen neighbors neared the place and quietly took possession of Brown." The *Memphis Daily Appeal* declared, "A Black Rapist Lynched." The *Cincinnati Daily Star* said, "Brown's Body Forms a Dangling Decoration on a Mississippi Tree." The headline in the *East Feliciana Watchman* called the hanging "Lynching of a Ravisher." The *Woodville Republican* went further, saying, "Of his crime there is no doubt, of his fate, we have only to say, served him right. . . . We feel that in such cases there is but one course to be pursued, no matter whether the guilty wretch be black or white."

SUNKEN GRAVES

I decided to go back down south with my sister, Stephanie Berry, to trace Brown's steps from his home in East Feliciana Parish, Louisiana, to the area where we believe he was hanged.

On this trip, the road into Mississippi seemed familiar. Woodville was very, very quiet. The town has only 986 residents. The county had 9,233 people in December 2017, 71 percent of them African Americans. Many county residents are descended from slaves brought to cultivate cotton in the early nineteenth century and who later became sharecroppers. The longtime sheriff, Reginald "Pip" Jackson, is Black.

Wilkinson County is well known for its fine plantation mansions. The Woodville Civic Club has published several books about the plantations and Confederate history. The club has not published any books about slavery–the word doesn't even appear on its website–but it does run the local African American Museum, which features exhibits about famous people born in Wilkinson County, including composer and conductor William Grant Still (1895–1978) and civil rights activist Anne Moody (1940–2015).

Main Street in downtown Woodville becomes Route 24 east of town and runs past the Rosemont Plantation, which is the boyhood home of Jefferson Davis, the only president of the Confederate States of America. The civic club praises Davis on its website as someone "still recognized by almost all historians as one of the most remarkable and accomplished figures of nineteenth century American life."

We drove along Route 24 to search for whatever we could find of the Phares family. Newspaper articles about the lynching reported that Wilbur Phares lived in one of two neighborhoods: Whitestown, also called Whitesville (neither name appears on modern maps of the county) or Mount Pleasant. Wilbur was the nephew of David Lewis Phares, a prominent Mississippi physician who founded two schools in the county, both of which had closed by the end of the Civil War. Wilbur Phares grew up in his uncle's home, probably beginning after his father died in 1845. Wilbur Phares's home, the one my great-great-grandfather was building, was likely located somewhere between Woodville, the county seat, and Centreville, the county's largest town. (I was able to find one Phares descendent, Stephanie Kirchner of Chicago, who is Wilbur Phares's great-great-granddaughter. But her mother left Woodville for the North as a child, and Kirchner said she wasn't aware of anyone in the family who knew the story of the lynching.)

As I drove, I kept thinking that somewhere along this fourteen-mile stretch, a mob hanged my great-great-grandfather. Exactly where, I would never know. I only have hints, including a newspaper article that said his body was found three miles from Phares's house.

In my research, I've been able to find descendants of three of my great-great-grandparents' eight children: my great-grand-father, Charles; his brother Thomas "Tom" Brown; and their only sister, Estelle (Brown) Nickerson. The next day, Stephanie and I went looking for their graves. Charles is buried in Hope Cemetery, a small, gated graveyard located next to a strip mall in Baton Rouge. Many grave markers were faded or missing, as was the case with Charles's grave. Several graves had sunk belowground, leaving only an outline in the grass.

We headed to Norwood Cemetery in East Feliciana Parish, where Estelle Nickerson is buried. The cemetery was located in a large clearing in the woods. Similar to Hope Cemetery, many graves had no identification and others had simply sunk far underground, leaving only a casket-shaped outline. We did not find Estelle.

We checked Ebenezer Baptist Church Cemetery in the small town of Slaughter, where relatives said Tom Brown and his wife, Emma, were buried. Again, I stared at the outlines of collapsed graves, wondering if they held Tom or Emma Brown.

OUR FAMILY STORY

Like many of those 4,400 people whose names are etched–or, sadly, only identified as "unknown"–on the lynching memorials columns, no one knows Charles Brown's burial place. No one knows where he was hanged. No one knows the names of his killers. The memorial is the only place where we can pay our respects to him.

My family has kept the memory of a father and husband alive for 139 years, beginning with his name. His son, my great-grandfather, was Charles Brown. In my grandparents' generation, the oldest son, my great-uncle (we called him "Uncle Buddy") was named Charles. My mother's brother is named Charles Brown. My grandfather's sister, Savannah Hudson, named one of her sons James Charles.

The lynching is etched in family memory too, passed down by mothers, fathers, and grandparents. But like a game of Telephone, the story has acquired layers over the years: One cousin says she was told Charles raped a white woman and was dragged behind a horse till he died. Another says she heard this episode was a setup by Mary Phares to get him killed. And one cousin declared that Charles was actually born in Brazil and never lived in Mississippi or Louisiana.

My mother's two sisters don't remember hearing about a lynching. Neither did her younger brother. Mom vaguely remembers talk about a hanging. However, my mother's cousin Thomas Hudson said his mother told him about the lynching when he was ten or twelve. "We would sit on the porch," he recalled. "We could get her to talk about other family members. . . . I remember he had worked all week and when it came time to get paid, he didn't want to pay. They came to the house sometime during the night and lynched him." His older sister Lois Sanders remembered her mother telling her that "my grandfather's daddy was lynched, but I don't remember no details."

I added my research to our family story, helping make the story of my great-great-grandfather more complete: He was a thirty-nine-year-old father and husband. He was determined, a hard worker who provided for his family. He would not let anyone cheat him out of payment for his work. He was brave–he had to be to challenge Phares, a white man from a prominent family, for his rightful payment. If he was actually a free man from Virginia, as my grandfather said, then he was a survivor. Many free African Americans starved to death when they could not find work after the Civil War.

His widow, Amanda, was only twenty-eight when he died. She had to manage the family farm alone and raise eight children. When the U.S. Census taker came to the Brown home in June 1880, the summer after the lynching, he listed two of them as stepsons. James, fifteen, and George, thirteen; and William, ten; Freeman, eight; Thomas, six; Estelle, five Charles, three; and Abram, ten months. Abram would have been a newborn or Amanda may still have been pregnant when Charles was killed on September 11, 1879.

A SACRED SPACE

My journey continued when I joined my mother, sister, and cousins in Montgomery to see Charles Brown's name on the first national memorial dedicated to victims of lynchings. I was excited, but the sorrow I always feel about my great-great-grandfather remained.

Opening day was rainy, windy, and cool, somber weather for a somber day. Signs at the entrance and posted throughout requested lowered voices and reminded all that it is "a sacred space for the dead." I went by myself, and the few visitors in the early morning numbered in the dozens, with whites slightly outnumbering African Americans. Most of the crowd was middle-aged to elderly.

The ground gradually declined until the columns were no longer at eye level but overhead. Lining the walls in the lower area were dozens of plaques that briefly described the circumstances of dozens of lynchings: A man was lynched because he failed to call a white man "mister"; a man was lynched because he owned a prosperous farm; a woman was lynched because she fussed at white children for throwing rocks at her.

The rust-colored column with Charles Brown's name is close to the entrance. Directly beneath the heading "Wilkinson County Mississippi," my great-great-grandfather's name is at the top of a list of nine victims. To finally view his name felt like a confirmation of his death, part of the process of researching his lynching for all these years.

The next day, I returned with my mother and sister. I led them to the column that bore Charles Brown's name. My sister and I watched as our mother strode to the column and smoothed her hand across her great-grandfather's name. "Here it is," I said.

My mother began to cry. "No, no," she said. "It's all good. It's all good. . . . I made it. By the grace of God, I made it. He allowed me. Oh, my God.

"Bless you, Karin, you found it all," she said, sobbing. "Oh. It was all true, wasn't made up. . . . Can you believe it really happened?"

Twenty-one Brown descendants went to Alabama for the opening of the memorial. They came from Atlanta, St. Louis, Baton Rouge, and a couple of cities in Texas. My first cousins Gail Delaney and Felicia Powell came with Felicia's son, William; his wife, Dominique; and their sixteen-month-old daughter, Ari. Felicia said they stood in a circle around the column holding hands while William said a prayer. And they cried a little, she said.

"My granddaughter will be able to tell her granddaughter, and the memory will go on forever," my cousin told me.

Mom's first cousin Thomas Hudson visited the memorial with his wife, Julia; daughter Carol Hudson; and grandson Julian Hudson-Love. They drove in from Fort Worth. "To me, it's the equivalent of attending his funeral," he said. "They don't know where he's buried, any of that . . . so you know your final resting place, my great-grandfather's final resting place."

Our visit to the memorial wasn't the end of my journey or my great-great-grandfather's story. I am still searching for the descendants of Charles and Amanda's five other children. One of my cousins has proposed a family reunion.

But Charles Brown's family was there: Mattie Berry, Stephanie Berry, Gail Delaney, Felicia Powell, William Powell, Dominique Powell, Ari Powell, Norma Reed, Mariea Dunn, Patricia Dunn,

Jimmie Brown, Tommie L. Gauthia, John Henry Brown Jr., Thomas Hudson, Julia Hudson, Carol Hudson, Julian Hudson-Love, Tina George, and Ina Hatch. They are witnesses to his legacy.

And I was there. I too am a witness.

Originally published May 15, 2018

IF YOU **TRULY KNEW** WHAT THE **N-WORD** MEANT TO OUR ANCESTORS, **YOU'D NEVER USE IT**

It was used and still can be used to make us hate ourselves.

BY BRANDO SIMEO STARKEY

A FEW years ago, I read slave narratives in order to explore the lives of Black agricultural workers after the end of the Civil War. The narratives came from the Federal Writers' Project of the Works Progress Administration, a program that employed researchers from 1936 to 1938 to interview former enslaved people, producing more than 2,300 narratives.

Those whom the law defined as property recounted various unique human experiences–their daily horrors and monotonies, how they freed themselves or learned of their emancipation, the surge of exhilaration upon securing freedom, and how they endured life on the edges of a white supremacist society in the decades thereafter.

As I pored over the narratives, I was struck less by their experiences, as heartrending as they were, than by how their experiences sculpted their self-perceptions. The best explanation of what I gleaned, what social scientists call "internalized oppression," describes the psychological trauma that ensues when a person from a stigmatized group believes those negative stigmas.

White folk indoctrinated them into accepting their supposed inferiority. These narratives illustrate the success of this campaign of mental terrorism, and no word conveyed the depth of this internalized oppression more than "nigger." Now, whenever I hear the epithet, a visual and emotional representation of the heinous process by which a people—my people—were induced to think they were less than trespasses into my thoughts. After years of habitual use of "nigger," I banished it from my speech to honor the humanity that many never saw in themselves.

The internalized oppression revealed itself in various ways. Sometimes the former enslaved people clearly, perhaps subconsciously, considered themselves subhuman, just like how their former owners regarded them. Jim Allen, for example, dubbed himself his master's "pet nigger boy" and a "stray" and thought himself privileged because he could sleep on the floor beside his master's bed. That he likened himself to a fortunate mangy mutt or frisky feline crushed me. The word laid bare a worldview that held Black folk as a lower order of being, as when Irene Robertson claimed her former master, Mr. Sanders, was mean, in part, because "he beat his wife like he beat a nigger woman."

"Nigger" also signaled antipathy toward fellow Black folk. After the end of slavery, Mattie Mooreman went north to Wisconsin with a white family for whom she worked. Members of the family wanted her to go to the circus to watch a Black boy's performance. She told her interviewer, "Guess they thought it would be a treat to me to see another niggah. I told 'em, 'Law, don't you think I see lots, lots more than I wants, every day when I is at home?'" But read how she talks about the family's baby, whom she constantly watched over, fearing, irrationally, someone would kidnap him: "No matter what time they come home they'd find me there. 'Why don't you go in your bedroom and lie down?' they'd ask me. 'No,' I'd tell 'em, 'somebody might come in, and they would have to get that baby over my dead body.'" Her eyes fixated on the white baby, but she saw too many niggers.

A barrage of dispiriting uses of the word bloodied me as I combed through the narratives. "The Ku Klux kept the niggers scared." "The Ku Klux did a whole lot to keep the niggers away from the polls. . . ." Slaves owned by "nice" masters are repeatedly called "free niggers." "Niggers ain't got no sense. Put 'em in authority and they gits so uppity." "I'se just a poor old nigger waitin' for Jesus to come and take me to heaven." Slave traders are called "nigger traders." Defiant enslaved people required the service of a "niggerbreaker." "Nigger dogs" aided the recapture of those who escaped.

Perhaps more depressing, ironically, was that circumstances sometimes led them to opt against calling a Black person a nigger. William Porter stated that "some of the Tennessee niggers was called free niggers. There was a colored man in Pulaski, Tennessee, who owned slaves." A Black man who kept others in bondage—he's a "colored man," yet those who were owned were "niggers."I instantly thought of a moment from the *O. J.: Made in America* documentary when a white woman who saw Black people talking to Simpson uttered, "Look at those niggers sitting with O. J."

Simpson delights in hearing this because she "knew I wasn't Black. She saw me as O. J." Porter's outlook matched that of both the racist white woman and the unspeakably racially deranged O. J.

Since reading those narratives, I've noticed this mindset when perusing the remarks of freed people in other contexts. For example, before the trial of Rufus Martin, a Black man who stood accused of the 1903 murder of Charles Swackhammer, a woman whom the *Fort Worth Star-Telegram* referred to as an "old negress who occupied a front seat in the court room" bellowed:

> It's the white people that is to blame. They know that they got to make niggahs work or they ain't no good and they know as long as they 'low niggah men to loaf aroun' low down saloons they ain't goin' to work. This man come from a good niggah family—one of the best I knows of, but the p'lice 'lowed him to loaf around without workin', and to drink and gamble, till he just got to be no good and thought he didn't have to work. The police ought to raid them low down niggah saloons every day and every night till they make every blessed one of the niggah toughs go to work or else send 'em all to the county road. Them saloons is what makes bad niggahs and the white folks is to blame for it, 'cause they let 'em run.

That Martin sported a reddish mustache, light hair, and skin so bright he could pass for white almost certainly colored her perception that Martin came from a "good niggah family."

Black folk rescued the word from the smoldering debris of a virulently racist land, reclaimed it, and renovated the slur into a celebration of Black camaraderie—defenders of contemporary usage of "nigger" repeat this. When this tale collides with reality, however, it shatters as a misreading of history–the current use of the word is owed less to white folk calling Black folk "nigger" and more to Black folk who thought they were niggers and said so. Black people have hurled the infamous word for nearly as long as white folk have. It exists within Black speech now because it existed within Black speech then. The uncomfortable truth must be confronted: Absent the internalized oppression of those who called white men and women their masters, "nigger" would probably not be a part of Black folks lexicon. We Black folk are reclaiming it not from bigoted white folk but from our ancestors, who, sadly, deemed their Blackness a badge of inferiority.

I seek not to usher the word to the gallows. I harbor no aims to kill it. I can still bump a Young Thug track or chortle at a Dave Chappelle routine. "Nigger" does not bar my enjoyment of popular culture. My soul, though, winces whenever I hear it. The decision for Black people to include it in their vocabulary, nonetheless, remains personal, and I reject the criticism of Black folk who continue to wield it.

I write only to summon the words of former enslaved people from beyond the grave to express that "nigger" is haunted by the ghosts of hate and the more spiritually chilling ghosts of self-hate.

Originally published May 18, 2017

AR

'SCHOOL DAZE' IS STILL RELEVANT

UNCLE PHIL

CAN A BLACK HEROINE FIX 'KING KONG'?

THE UNBEARABLE WH

CULTU

'GAME, BLOUSES'

WHAT MICHAEL K. WILLIAM

TS

DIDDY'S
WHITE
PARTY

TONI MORRISON

O & BOUJEE BLACK GIRL STYLE

EVERY
MAN

THE LOW KEY COOL OF 'JAKE FROM STATE FARM'

✳
✳
✳
✳

SHOCK G

MADE ROOM ON THE DANCE FLOOR

✳
✳
✳

ESS OF 'OKLAHOMA!'

RE

UGHT ME ABOUT BEING A MAN

THE **LOW-KEY COOL** OF "JAKE, FROM **STATE FARM**"

Jake is the regular, stand-up everyman that Black people see in our communities all the time–but rarely on TV.

BY LONNAE O'NEAL

IN THE past couple of years, "Jake, from State Farm" actor Kevin Miles has catapulted to fame. On TV, he's spreading the word about insurance rates to everybody from delivery drivers to NFL MVPs. In the streets, he's posing with fans clamoring for pictures and autographs.

As spokesman for a national ad campaign with back-to-back Super Bowl spots and his face on multiple platforms, it's not his fame that surprises. It's the lane in which it's happening. Miles, in the role of Jake, is the kind of regular, stand-up everyman that Black people see in our families and communities all the time. We just seldom see him on television, or historically in America, as a good neighbor.

In a popular culture conditioned to understand young Black men as athletes or entertainers, or on one side or another of the criminal justice system, Jake represents a departure. The character offers a window into the racial architecture of fame.

Often, "you've either got to be wacky, or you've got to be dangerous" to land jobs as a Black actor, said Miles.

He moved from the South Side of Chicago to Los Angeles to pursue a career in acting, and had already done some commercials when he auditioned for the role of Jake. Many other insurance spokespeople are comedic talents. They're witty and quirky.

"I knew if I tried to do something wacky or crazy, it probably wouldn't have fit me or my frame," he said. "I just wanted to come with something that felt like truth. Felt like a best friend that's next to you."

"Jake is like the guy next door, the boy next door that grew up," said Henry C. Boyd, a marketing professor at the University of Maryland. "The perception is there that, man, you went out of your way, Jake. You gave me the inside deal."

Insurance can be dull and ads for insurance companies can take antics and hyperbole in order to stand out. But Boyd calls Jake's charisma, charm, and conventional good looks something that can win for State Farm. "He's become a franchise success," said Boyd. That success marks a universal, all-American appeal. But don't misunderstand. Without the slightest patina of performative ethnicity, he still feels authentically Black.

It's all that low-key cool.

"Who was the most extraordinary, low-key person we've seen in the last twenty years?" asked Mark Anthony Neal, chair of the department of African and African American studies at Duke

University. With Jake, "you also hear that Barack cadence," Neal said. "He speaks in small bunches. And then it's kind of an accent, then he speaks in a couple of more bunches. So it's never too fast, but it's stylistically Black."

The nature of the commercials also help reinforce Jake's chill. "Especially the ones with [Phoenix Suns star] Chris Paul, all kinds of crazy stuff is about to happen, but with Jake, there's never any drama," Neal said. "It's always, 'No, we're good.'"

"Think about Dennis Haysbert, who also did these auto insurance commercials after playing the president of the United States on [the Fox series] 24," Neal said. "There's just something about his coolness under pressure that white folks are drawn to."

Alexis Williamson and DeWayne Carter were both students in Neal's Black popular culture and history of hip-hop class. They say the face of a company impacts their buying decisions. Williamson says her family uses Allstate because her mom likes Haysbert. But "it's not top of dome anymore because Dennis Haysbert isn't their guy, and Jake is State Farm's guy," she said. The Jake campaign, "I definitely would say, gives me a different idea about the corporation."

The nuance here matters. It's not simply that Jake is Black. It is that "he doesn't have to be a rapper, or he doesn't have to be a star quarterback, basketball player, whatever it may be," said Carter, who was a defensive tackle for Duke's football team. It makes Jake's popularity a hundred times more powerful, Carter says. "He can just exist. He can just be himself."

"It's so authentic and that's what is appealing to me," said Williamson. "It feels like there's somebody Black on that [State Farm creative] team and they're allowing them to create in a really significant way."

Patty Morris, assistant vice president of marketing for State Farm, says the relaunch of the Jake campaign and leaning into the "like a good neighbor" slogan "has probably been the most rewarding thing I've worked on." It's the affection people have for the character and "a culmination of things that have happened" with COVID-19 and the racial justice movement that make him the right character and message for the times.

In 2019, when State Farm was seeking a brand refresh, the Marketing Arm ad agency encouraged the company to lean into Jake. They cast their net widely to find a professional actor to carry the campaign and replace the actual State Farm employee who gained a cult following as the original Jake in the 2011–16 campaign. They relaunched Jake sitting at his cubicle during the Super Bowl pregame in 2020.

In a Super Bowl commercial with NFL MVP quarterbacks Patrick Mahomes and Aaron Rodgers, Drake played Jake's stand-in. The campaign helped make State Farm one of *Ad Age* magazine's top ten marketers of 2020. And it was part of a brand overhaul that helped the ninety-eight-year-old insurer grow its auto policies by 1.5 million.

This meant reaching younger, more diverse audiences, and putting Jake in gaming and music and sports. Jake is also in situations that reflect changes in identity and demographics.

"That's why the pizza commercial is so striking," said Neal, referring to the spot where a young delivery driver insists on giving Jake free pizza and a tub of ranch dressing as thanks for giving her that special "Parker" rate. "Here you have a young, non-traditional white woman, who is representative of a certain kind of constituency, and Jake. And they connect. They vibe on some sort of level, because it's going to be their world going forward. It's going to be–her world is going to be Jake's world and all kinds of non-traditional figures."

"We set out to say, 'All right, if we're going to extend this character and really scale this into a full-fledged campaign, we need this humanization of the brand to be relatable and likable.' Of course we said those things," Morris said. "We didn't go into that casting saying, 'We need to cast a young, energetic, super-charismatic African American man.' We said, 'We need to cast the person that best embodies our brand ethos.' And that certainly includes authenticity, it includes being honest and helpful, and those are all part of State Farm's brand value set, and that's what we were looking for. And the best person to fit that role was Kevin and he was African American, and that was great with us."

Williamson, who was pursuing a certificate in management and marketing, said the ad campaign demonstrates cultural literacy, a standard by which her generation judges the companies that are asking for their money.

We're "in a space where we still have to explain that Black people exist in the world just as anybody else. Just like white people. We are not juxtapositions to white people. We are just people," she said. "I think Jake does a really good job of just being out in the world and existing as he is, and he is Black. And so that comes with different mannerisms and tendencies that other communities may not have, but at the end of the day, he's still a super-relatable guy."

It's a simple thing that Black people have been preaching forever, Carter says. "Representation matters. Not only representation—authentic representation, not performative action."

Not the people companies hire "just so they can say we're diverse," Carter said. "Authentic representation matters because it's authentic, it's real, it's beautiful in my opinion." And it sells. That's the lesson to take from Jake. "Especially in this day and age, people love to see diversity, especially at a corporate level," Carter said. "That's a big thing that corporations can take away."

Miles, who eventually wants to go on to bigger roles, hopes

his portrayal of Jake helps casting agents understand that Black people have more to give than the single dimension that's often asked of them.

He quotes a line from the Drake song "6PM in New York" about ambition and who belongs on the throne. "All the great actors that I love are just phenomenal at playing in the middle, sometimes, and I just wanted to be close to that too," Miles said. "I just wanted to see where my everyman was.

"It's great that at the core of what I'm trying to do, it's resonating and being seen," said Miles. "I hope that it opens a door where that can be a norm." One that shows a regular brother, with a low-key chill, can also be a superstar.

Originally published June 21, 2021

FOR **SHOCK G,** THE MAN WHO MADE ROOM FOR EVERYONE ON THE **DANCE FLOOR**

"The Humpty Dance" helped fat girls feel entitled to pleasure, even as we debated the latest unauthorized bikini pic of a Kardashian.

BY MINDA HONEY

I'M ONLY 17 percent ashamed to admit that the first thing I did after hearing about the bikini pic Khloe Kardashian didn't want the world to see was to go search for said pic. It was super easy to find. Kardashian is in a two-piece assembled from animal print fabric strung together on black thread. Her legs are slightly crossed at the thighs, she's wearing no makeup, and she has the soft smile you make when a grandma who cherishes you wants to take your photo.

In other words, Kardashian looks really, really normal.

It's not that I lack empathy for Kardashian. I'm a woman who's had terrible photos of herself slapped on the internet. But this is not that. She looks pretty and soft and happy—just not staged and prepped for the consumption that keeps capitalism churning. For years, the Kardashians have cashed in on their contributions to the unattainable beauty standards set by pop culture that paradoxically persuade young women that this level of beauty *is* attainable in real life with the right purchases. (Belly-vanishing tea and lip goop are the starter pack.) Social media is a looking glass that reflects what and who's allowed to be desirable. Thin waist, thin features. Get you a filter that can do both.

This casual photo of Kardashian popping up online is a *Wizard of Oz*, behind-the-curtain moment. A friend on Twitter questions this latest Kardashian drama, wondering why they think we, the general public, don't know the family business is a multi-billion-dollar enterprise built on a fantasy made possible by the best lighting, photoshopping, excessive dieting and exercising, plastic surgery, and other methods I'm not wealthy enough to know about. I hop into the thread to point out that sometimes the cage is one of our own making; even a beautiful lie is still a lie, and keeping up with your own image ain't always easy.

By comparison, Cardi B remains unbothered by paparazzi out to catch her off the clock, because the woman has remained real with her audience from day one about what she looks like when she's not done up. We've seen her without makeup, in her bonnet, and in all manner of around-the-house clothes. I don't know what's at the core of Cardi B's confidence. But recently, I came to understand that mine, in part, comes from some lyrics in a song whose best-known bars are about getting busy in a Burger King bathroom.

That song "The Humpty Dance" was performed by Shock G

and the Digital Underground. I hadn't thought about the group in years, but I was definitely in my feelings when I learned that Shock died in April 2021 at the age of fifty-seven. Maybe it was the white wine I'd been sipping that evening, but the news of Shock G's death catapulted me to the past.

Digital Underground released "The Humpty Dance" in 1990 when I was five years old. The music video lost the award for best rap video at that year's MTV Video Music Awards to MC Hammer's "U Can't Touch This." I had an MC Hammer doll in purple glitter genie pants and I doubt Shock G's self-esteem anthem disguised as a party rocker was really on my radar like that. But the song likely dominated the radio at the time, the lyrics seeping into my young subconscious on car rides around town.

You can't always put much weight behind song lyrics. Sometimes they're dashed off hastily or the performer is simply putting on a persona, and Humpty Hump was Shock G's alter ego, after all. But what makes "The Humpty Dance" feel real happens midway through the song when Shock G raps that he likes to write. It's a tone shift that gives the words the earnestness of your tenth-grade class clown letting his guard down with just you after school. It compels you to move backward and forward in the music to ferret out other truths.

In the music video, shot on what looks like a nearly nonexistent budget, Shock G rocks the mic as Humpty Hump. He's dressed in a white faux-fur cap, tag still dangling, a plaid blazer, a white polka-dot tie around his neck, with a second black polka-dot tie slung across his shoulders, and fake glasses with a big plastic nose. When Humpty opened the song rapping about how funny he looks, my kindergarten self couldn't disagree.

In the '90s, we may have had Heavy D, the overweight lover in the house, but fat was still, much as it is today, synonymous with unsexy in most circles. Yet when Humpty Hump calls out to ask a fat girl if she's ticklish, it didn't sound to me like a cruel punch line made at the expense of a woman's body. It sounded playful. And once I'd gotten older, after experiencing how a man would hock up and spit out the words "Fat b————!" when he was rejected, Humpty's bars sounded joyful and hedonistic.

He was a man making his desires known and making it plain that bodies of all shapes and sizes can be lusted after publicly and are deserving of pleasure. In my white-wine-induced tribute to Shock G on Instagram story, I passionately made this same argument. A skinny friend slid into my direct messages to share that those bars didn't just resonate with fat girls who want to be flirted with. He'd used Humpty Hump's reference to having a thin frame as a pre-hookup self-affirmation for years.

I don't want to force a body-positive lens onto Shock G. The directives for "The Humpty Dance" have not aged well and are ableist, the girls in the music video are all skinny enough to be modern-day social media influencers, and who knows who Shock G was actually sexing down.

But I believe his egalitarian views on pleasure extended beyond this snippet. Later in the song, Humpty raps that he ain't ashamed of his nose. And on the same album, on "Doowutchyalike," Shock G invites folks of all classes and colors to strip down and jump into the pool. A year later, Digital Underground released "No Nose Job." While the song does tip into some body-shaming territory, its primary message is that Black women's noses, lips, and hips don't need to be corrected by plastic surgery. And Shock G even calls out celebrity greed for furthering the problem.

Shock G pointed out that little girls can have their view of themselves warped by the media they consume. So maybe it's not all that unusual that tiny Minda tucked a few words about lusting after a fat girl down into her core to return to over and over again as the years progressed and my body grew and blossomed. That when a culture invested in skinny supremacy tried to teach me that I wasn't allowed to enjoy my body past a certain weight nor was I worthy of being desired, I had a directive, no matter how minor, to believe otherwise, to continue to seek pleasure and be pleased. How the masses think I should feel about my body never stopped me from getting busy. No Burger King bathroom required.

If you are mindful about who you follow on Instagram, you'll push past the influencers using their thigh gaps to compel you to buy whatever they're selling. Your feed can feature fewer backs arched just right in bikinis hitched up high on thighs and more Lizzo blessing you with her body in motion, gleefully being praised and lusted after. You might even tumble into #bookstagram and see books beautifully staged next to cups of tea such as Sabrina Strings's *Fearing the Black Body: The Racial Origins of Fat Phobia* that makes the link between fatphobia and racism. Or Sonya Renee Taylor's *The Body Is Not an Apology: The Power of Radical Self-Love* with Taylor's Black body luxuriously splayed on the cover, inviting you to revel in your own physical presence. Or a video of Adrienne Maree Brown, author of *Pleasure Activism: The Politics of Feeling Good*, talking that talk to fill you up, not bring you down. If Instagram insists on selling you something, why not buy what nourishes you?

These books and these Black femme messengers mean I no longer need to protect my desires and my need to be desired with lyrics from a thirty-year-old rap song. But it speaks to the power of Shock G's persona that in just a few words he created a life raft sturdy enough to help keep my self-esteem afloat through culturally engineered waves of self-hatred. Shock G and the Digital Underground will be remembered for their contributions to music, but may Shock G's memory also be honored for guiding us all toward more pleasure.

Originally published April 27, 2021

CAN A **BLACK HEROINE** FIX THE **RACIST STEREOTYPES** INFECTING *KING KONG*?

Actress Christiani Pitts
steps into the role first made
famous by Fay Wray.

BY SORAYA NADIA MCDONALD

WHEN *KING KONG* opened on Broadway in 2018, actress Christiani Pitts became the first Black woman in history to play Ann Darrow, the legendary damsel in distress who gets carted off by a gargantuan silverback gorilla on his way to the top of the Empire State Building.

Before Pitts's casting, Darrow had been portrayed in film by a parade of young, white blondes. Fay Wray famously originated the role in the 1933 film directed by Merian C. Cooper and Ernest B. Schoedsack. A 1976 remake starred Jessica Lange, and director

Peter Jackson (*The Lord of the Rings*) resurrected the story again in 2005 with Naomi Watts.

The Broadway musical, a $35-million production that stars a two-thousand-pound puppet, was a commercial success despite being almost universally derided by critics. But consideration of Pitts's role as Darrow has been scarce. Her casting raises plenty of questions about whether a character like King Kong can, or should, ever truly be divorced from the context of prejudice and panic that birthed him. Since Cooper and Schoedsack first brought him to the screen, Kong has been an enduring symbol for white Americans' imagined fears of Black male sexuality.

Still, this new production of *King Kong* comes amid a flowering of race-neutral casting that has led to Black actors playing some of the biggest roles available. A Black woman (Denée Benton) played Natasha in an adaptation of a segment of Tolstoy's *War and Peace*. Another (Alexia Khadime) portrayed Elphaba Thropp in *Wicked*. And still another (Noma Dumezweni) played Hermione Granger in *Harry Potter and the Cursed Child*. On Broadway, Aaron Burr and George Washington are supposed to be Black and Norm Lewis can be the half-masked phantom of the Palais Garnier.

What makes Ann Darrow so different? Well, for one, her whiteness has always been central to the role. Americans didn't historically worry about Black men attacking Black women, but they did worry about white women, hence the effort to dehumanize Black men by using an ape to symbolize them. Is it even possible to see King Kong as merely an ape? It's a question Pitts has given a great deal of thought to.

"I would love to see that happen, but unfortunately I don't think that we can," Pitts told me. "And I think that it's important to acknowledge it, especially because of when it came out. . . . Although it would be great to be able to watch that film and disregard the subliminal narrative, it's almost important that we do see it and do realize that for one of the first action movies with talking, there's a racial undertone. I think that has huge historical importance."

FEAR AND LOATHING ON SKULL ISLAND

Before we can understand what it means for Pitts to play Darrow, we must first understand what her costar symbolizes, and the troubling history behind him.

That's because the story of the giant gorilla kidnapped from his home on Skull Island is a nesting doll of racialized anxiety, mixed metaphors, and white hubris. It's also a thematic follow-up to D. W. Griffith's *The Birth of a Nation* (1915). Both films center on the fear of Black men sexually victimizing white women. It's just that *King Kong* uses an ape instead of white men in blackface to convey the threat.

When *Kong* was released in 1933, it reflected the misery of a country in the midst of the Great Depression. Bread and soup lines abound in Cooper and Schoedsack's depiction of New York. Poverty, along with a wish for celebrity, drive Ann to board a ship to an unknown destination with a strange director named Carl Denham only hours after she's met him.

They sail to a secret island enveloped in fog that's inhabited by people who've never experienced contact with the outside world. Denham, Darrow, and the ship's crew arrive as the natives are about to sacrifice one of their maidens to the giant gorilla that lives in the jungle beyond their village gates: King Kong.

In the film versions of *Kong*, the Black natives kidnap Darrow from the ship under the cover of darkness and offer her, terrified and screaming, to the ape king. Denham, the crew, and the love interest she's cultivated aboard the ship go back to the island to save her, with many of them dying along the way. They fall off cliffs, get eaten by nightmarish beasts, and evoke Kong's rage. Meanwhile,

Kong takes a liking to Darrow–or at least decides not to eat her the way he has all the Black virgins who've been offered to him in the past. Once Darrow is rescued, Denham insists on subduing Kong and bringing him back to New York. There, he sells tickets to a show where a giant ape in chains is beguiled by a blonde in a white evening gown.

Of course, Kong's handlers overestimate the power of American steel to subdue the wild animal, who goes nuts onstage amid the flashes from newspaper photographers. He takes off with Darrow, wreaks havoc on the city, climbs with her to the top of the Empire State Building, and finally gets shot down and killed by military planes.

Uncivilized, inferior brown people, the irresistible white woman, and the destruction of an oversized symbol of Black virility are the recurring tropes of *King Kong*. Kong's zombielike, loincloth-sporting worshippers kidnap Darrow and shove her through a gate with a locking mechanism that doubles as an unmistakable metaphor for penetrative sex. They're never, *never* depicted as sympathetic. Each subsequent film adaptation changes slightly to reflect the time in which it's made, but those key elements remain.

John Guillermin's 1976 version reflects a world defined by the energy crisis. Kong is taken back to New York in the hold of an oil vessel, supplanting the millions of gallons of inky black gold that had been its intended cargo. In Jackson's bloated 2005 take on the story, the human natives of Skull Island barely register as people but instead are presented as a feral, languageless horde with a predilection for decorating with human remains. They emerge from the environment, barely distinguishable as human and covered in mud, similar to the undead crew of the *Black Pearl* in *Pirates of the Caribbean*: "part of the crew, part of the ship."

Before writing the original *King Kong*, Cooper and Schoedsack had embarked on their own *Heart of Darkness*-style journey. They traveled by ship to Ethiopia, where they met the prince who would later become Haile Selassie I. But Cooper and Schoedsack's America was also in the midst of a lynching epidemic. *The Birth of a Nation*, a silent Civil War epic, had been released eighteen years before *King Kong*, yet the violent racism reflected and encouraged by the movie was ever present.

The Birth of a Nation's costume design inspired the white robes and hoods we've come to singularly associate with the Ku Klux Klan, and its release single-handedly resurrected the organization after years of dormancy. It was wish fulfillment for whites resentful of a changing society in which Jack Johnson fought his way to the world heavyweight championship title in 1908 and retained it for the next seven years. Not only was a large, dark-skinned Black man the best fighter in the world, he had a white wife, much to the consternation of many, many racists.

The Birth of a Nation told its audience they were right to consider Johnson and men who looked like him to be an affront to white Christian sensibilities. Its depiction of the white woman as the pinnacle of virtue, who would rather pitch herself off a cliff than face the clutches of a cartoonishly evil Black predator, helped justify a wave of extrajudicial torture and murder against thousands of Black men that lasted for decades. (Billie Holiday recorded "Strange Fruit," the protest dirge written by Abel Meeropol, in 1939.)

Griffith's ideas about Black male predation clearly informed *King Kong*, to the point that Cooper and Schoedsack had trouble being honest about its true villain. That would be Denham, whose love of money and fame dooms everyone who goes into business with him. Rather, they absolve Denham (and white men writ large) of his responsibility in Kong's tragic death. The film ends with Denham proclaiming, "Oh, no, it wasn't the airplanes. It was beauty that killed the beast."

This is the baggage that has followed the story of *Kong* all the way to the stage of New York's Broadway Theatre: an unwieldy albatross of fear, resentment, control, and racial hierarchy that is enforced with firearms and gas bombs.

CAN AN APE EVER JUST BE AN APE?

Kong may be a tragic hero, but he and his species remain inextricably conflated with stereotypes of untamed animal savagery, lasciviousness, and other ugliness that gets heaped onto Black people.

There has arguably never been a less racially neutral animal in the history of the country. *King Kong* opened on Broadway the same year Roseanne Barr was fired from the reboot of her eponymous hit show after calling Valerie Jarrett, former chief of staff to President Barack Obama, the progeny of the "muslim brotherhood & planet of the apes." The words "ape" and "gorilla" remain favored pejoratives for racists seeking to malign Serena Williams and Michelle Obama, and they also persist overseas, where soccer fans are known to pelt Black players with bananas. When LeBron James was pictured on the cover of *Vogue* with model Gisele Bündchen in 2008, evoking the memory of Kong and Darrow, then–ESPN columnist Jemele Hill admonished the basketball star to "be more careful with his image."

"It's make-believe on the surface, but when you dive in and look at it from a different lens, the truth becomes really harsh, and not only was saying a Black person was a monkey an insult, but you look back historically when Black people were three-fifths of a person and were put in the same category as livestock during slavery," Pitts said. "It's really, really, really disgusting when you dive into what it can mean to so many people."

All of that makes it exceptionally difficult to accept Kong as a positive figure, even when the new Broadway version transforms him into a fearsome but misunderstood softy instead of a god requiring human sacrifice. (This version, by writer Jack Thorne, has blessedly done away with the human inhabitants of Skull Island entirely.) Does the fact that Kong is now a sympathetic figure matter more than the racist conflation of Black people with apes? Can it? I'm not so sure.

If Kong were widely interpreted as good, Denzel Washington's indelible line from *Training Day* wouldn't have nearly the same effect. His character, the corrupt cop Alonzo, doesn't yell, "King Kong ain't got s--- on me!" because he's tragically misunderstood. It's a chest-beating declaration that Alonzo ain't nuthin' to f---wit, ya dig?

Nevertheless, we must also consider the atmosphere in which Darrow and Kong exist on Broadway, where a perceived racelessness of certain characters is more commonplace. Shouldn't we extend the same generosity of imagination to the character of Darrow?

Perhaps, if in Thorne's version, a gorilla is just a gorilla. Except he's not. When Kong is revealed in New York, he's constrained by massive shackles that look like a supersize version of ones a visitor might see in a slavery exhibition at the Blacksonian. Kong is trapped, stolen from his homeland, and brought to America to make a profit at the behest of Denham, the white man who owns the rights to his exploitation.

Furthermore, Darrow feels guilt for her complicity in Kong's capture and weirdly, in expressing her remorse to him, ends up as the Black woman who sold out the gorilla/Black man in service to her own ambitions. Darrow is both a guilty, opportunistic accomplice and the heroine who tries to set Kong free.

Is that . . . better?

Pitts struggled with how to approach this.

"It became a heavy load on me," she said of the history that surrounds *King Kong*. "These are all things that I have known, and that I've learned about, but it'd been a long time since I sat with this material.

"My character, being in her early twenties in the 1930s, didn't have the access to this kind of research. She was just living it. So what that means for her is that she doesn't exactly know the trauma until she's in it. So I had a lot of challenges in dealing with the comment on slavery in a very nuanced way, because [she doesn't realize] until it's happening right in front of her eyes, which is why there's a moment in the show where she sees Kong in chains, and that is the first time that she makes the connection.

"The first time I read the script, and the second the captain says that were going to rope Kong and take him to America, that was the first time that I as the actor noticed the connection. But I had to realize that this person [Darrow] is living it. Her connection to slavery, which is her grandmother, and her great-grandmother, knowing that it's something that happened in the past but that she wasn't still reliving. It wasn't until she actually sees the chains in front of her eyes that she has to sit with the connection."

Characters can be racialized, or they can be raceless, but they can't be both. Inside the Broadway Theatre, the audience is asked to see Darrow as simply a lady and Kong as a tortured circus spectacle of an animal. But taking in *King Kong* without some twinge of ethical compromise requires either Magritte-level mental acrobatics or complete ignorance of the role of race in American history. In each of those circumstances, it doesn't really matter what color Darrow is.

BROADWAY KONG'S ROOTLESS FEMPOWERMENT

Just as each version of *King Kong* says something about the era in which it's created, so too does each version of Ann Darrow.

Previous iterations of Darrow have been helpless (Wray), dumb to the point of absurdity (Lange), or nice ladies who just want a job in showbiz (Wray, Lange, and Watts). Their perceived virtue is always a key part of the character. Lange ends up surviving a yacht wreck because rather than sit with a bunch of men watching *Deep Throat*, she goes to the deck in protest. She winds up joining the journey to Skull Island when the crew of the oil vessel spots her drifting on a lifeboat and hauls her aboard.

She develops a friendship with Kong, and when she's rescued, her love interest (played by Jeff Bridges) cannot understand why she harbors an ounce of sympathy for the beast.

"He risked his life to save me," she explains.

Bridges gazes patronizingly into the eyes of his imbecilic beloved. "No, honey," he tells her. "He tried to rape you."

Every version of *King Kong* featuring a white woman as Darrow has relied upon the threat of rape as motivation for the ships crew to return to Skull Island and save her. They perpetuate Griffith's original white knight archetype, with Darrow as the recipient of their benevolent sexism. Griffith's idea that white female virginity must be preserved against all odds is one that Lange's character has internalized, even in a world where sexual attitudes have been transformed by Helen Gurley Brown and Hugh Hefner.

But transposing these characteristics onto the body of a Black woman is more intellectually cumbersome. While white female sexual purity is seen as a commodity to be preserved for the sole enjoyment of white men, Black women, especially in the 1930s, were seen as opportunities for sexual practice. Whatever harm they experienced was no one's concern but their own.

Pitts's Darrow, then, cannot be helpless and in need of constant protection. Instead, Pitts imbues her with a plucky bravery one might associate with the Dorothy of *The Wiz*. Pitts's Darrow has no interest in being victimized. When Kong roars at her and beats his chest, she does the same right back.

Like Dorothy, once plopped into unfamiliar environs, Pitts's Darrow sets about finding her way home and calling upon her own nerve and determination to do so. She comes to regard Kong as an animal like the ones on the farm where she lived before leaving to pursue her acting dreams in New York. Just as Dorothy sees past their shortcomings to befriend a tin man, a lion, and a scarecrow in an unfamiliar land, Darrow makes an unlikely connection with a wild gorilla.

Pitts's Darrow is adventurous, independent, and determined. But she's also a Black woman who, like Kong, is ensconced in a production that doesn't seem to have taken full account of what that means beyond a mealymouthed, post-racial conclusion that anyone can play anything! And it's totally fine! Progressive, even! Perhaps, more than anything else, that's what ties Kong and his Black Darrow together on Broadway, even more so than their victimization at the hands of the arrogant Denham. Both remain suspended in a parable that, however well-intentioned, remains grafted onto a fundamentally racist foundation.

Originally published January 3, 2019

"GAME, **BLOUSES**"

The real story behind the famous Chappelle skit about Prince's late-night hoops challenge.

BY JERRY BEMBRY

WHEN MICKI Free checked into a Nashville, Tennessee, hotel not too long ago, the clerk, glancing at the name on the reservation, did a double take. "Are you *the* Micki Free?" the clerk asked. "The guy who played basketball with Prince?"

Free laughed as he recalled the encounter. "Happens all the time when I check in," he said.

It started on February 18, 2004, when comedian Dave Chappelle's Comedy Central series aired a skit called "Charlie Murphy's True Hollywood Stories." In the segment, Murphy–comedian Eddie Murphy's older brother–describes a late-night basketball outing that portrayed Prince as a shot-calling, trash-talking baller.

It was a made-up comedic masterpiece, right? A fictionalized account of a scrawny, five-foot-two musician as a dominant athlete, right?

"Everything in that skit is true," said Free, a Grammy Award-winning songwriter who was a member of Shalamar in the 1980s. "I played in that game. And Prince was Steph Curry all m---f-- night!"

Prince wasn't just some famous dude who was breaking the ankles of other nonathletic famous dudes in late-night runs. Prince could actually play, a guy who might have been an impact high school basketball player under different circumstances while growing up in Minneapolis.

He played two years at Central High School in Minneapolis, and his high school coach, Albert Nuness, says he was extremely talented.

"His game was quickness. He wasn't the best shooter, but he could split the seams and pass the ball and because of his size people loved to watch him," Nuness said. "The player he reminds me of–Spud Webb. He didn't have the leaping ability like Spud, but his quickness was very similar."

One of the reasons Prince quit basketball was because he was unhappy about his playing time.

"At the time, that team was considered the greatest ever assembled in Minnesota," Nuness said. "So it would have been hard for him to get time with us, and a lot had to do with his size. But had he gone to any other school in the city–West or South–he would have played. A lot. No question."

During 1975-76, Prince's senior year, Central finished 25-1 and had four players receive Division I scholarships, including Prince's half brother, Duane Nelson, who played for the University of Wisconsin–Milwaukee.

Although Prince's basketball skills weren't widely known at the time the *Chappelle's Show* skit aired, there were signs that he had talent: He had a basketball court on the stage during his

1988 LoveSexy Tour, for instance, and during the concert he would shoot baskets and spin a basketball on his finger.

In his video for the song "The Daisy Chain," which was recorded in 2000, Prince handles a basketball throughout. The closing seconds of the video, which was shot in his indoor court at the Paisley Park complex in Minneapolis and didn't surface until after his death, show perhaps the only known footage of Prince playing basketball.

Going back to the basketball game made famous on *Chappelle's Show*: Free said it happened sometime in the mid-eighties as he was hanging out with Prince, Eddie Murphy, and Charlie Murphy at a private club, Tramps!, at the Beverly Center in Beverly Hills, California. When the club closed, Prince invited the group to his Beverly Hills home.

While playing music for his guests, Prince asked the group, "Do you want to play basketball?" The invite was met with laughter, but once the Murphy brothers saw Prince was serious, they geared up and took to the court at his house.

The TV skit portrayed the game as five-on-five, half-court. In reality, it was the Murphy brothers and their uncle Ray against Prince, his brother Duane, and Free.

Murphy's crew changed into athletic gear. And Prince's crew?

"Yes, it's true, we had on blouses and frilly shirts," Free said. "The same clothes we had at the club. Prince played in six-inch heels!"

Free remembered that Murphy's crew didn't take the game seriously at first. "They checked the ball to me, I gave it to Prince and he went to work," Free said. "You know that one move where Curry dribbles up and they got him covered, but he steps back behind the three-point line and hits nothing but net? That was Prince."

In the TV skit, Murphy described Prince as a combination of basketball greats Allen Iverson and Charles Barkley, a scoring and rebounding machine. Prince dominated the game, according to Murphy's account, and capped off his game-winning shot with these oft-repeated words: "Game, Blouses."

And after the game?

"It was just like they showed on TV," Free said. "His chef served us blueberry pancakes, for real!"

Free first met Prince in the early '80s, and over time, the two became friends. Prince offered to buy Free out of his contract with Shalamar and place him in his Minneapolis-based group, Mazarati. But the owner of Shalamar's label declined and the two grew apart as Prince's star began to shine brighter following the success of *Purple Rain*.

"What happened between us? He became Prince," Free said. "He got huge and I was just one of many people he knew. I was just lucky to have my experiences with Prince, because anytime you got a chance to spend one-on-one with him, it was like a religious experience."

Memories of their time together returned on February 18, 2004, with an out-of-the-blue email from Charlie Murphy.

"I got you, m−−−−f−−−−," the email read.

Free was still trying to figure out what he meant when he got a hysterical call from his mother.

"'They're talking about you on TV, son,'" he recalled her saying. "'They're calling you a girl.'"

She was watching the portion of the skit where Charlie Murphy described her son: "And Micki Free was like the new cat in Shalamar, that when he joined the group I heard mad cats like, yo, Shalamar got a new girl, man, that b−−− is fine like a m−−−−f−−−."

Free's reaction was the total opposite of his mother's. "I was rolling," Free said. "It was hilarious. And it was true."

The skit captured the true competitiveness of Prince, which stretched beyond basketball.

David Z, a sound engineer, told the *Minneapolis Star Tribune* that Prince once challenged Michael Jackson to a game of Ping-Pong while the two were recording in the same studio. Apparently, Jackson wasn't a player. And it didn't end well for the gloved one.

Prince asked Jackson, "You want me to slam it?" As Jackson cowered, Prince did just that, and Jackson was humiliated. "Did you see that?" Z recalled Prince saying. "He played like Helen Keller."

After Prince's death, Jimmy Fallon, the host of *The Tonight Show*, described being destroyed by Prince during a late-night game of Ping-Pong. Prince delivered the beatdown while wearing a "double-breasted crushed blue velvet suit."

That's exactly how Free remembers Prince: a man who took everything seriously.

Originally published July 27, 2016

WAKE UP! IN THIS #BLACKLIVESMATTER ERA, **SPIKE LEE'S** *SCHOOL DAZE* IS STILL RELEVANT

BY KELLEY L. CARTER

IT WAS late summer of 1986. Jasmine Guy was standing on the streets of New York City, fresh out of a dance class at the Ailey School, when she heard a word unfamiliar to her: "wannabe."

She'd just run into director and eventual cultural purveyor Spike Lee. She first met him back in 1979, when she was a high school senior and he was a senior at Morehouse College who was directing the coronation at the school where she danced. Back then, he was telling folks that he planned to go to film school and had aspirations of being a director—although, at the time, Guy wasn't entirely sure what that meant.

Spike had some news for her. "I just finished my first movie, you've got to see it," she remembers Lee telling her. He was talking about 1986's *She's Gotta Have It*, which is now of course a lauded Netflix series of the same name. She saw the movie and was mesmerized by the very contemporary film that was in black and white and dealt with sex, relationships, and intimacy. She'd never seen anything like it before. With Black people. And she was impressed.

She ran into him again on those New York streets, and this was the time that he added a new word to her lexicon. "I'm doing another movie, and you're going to be in it, so send me your head shot. You're going to be a wannabe." She was confused. "You know how *you all* are," she remembers Lee saying. She had no idea what he was talking about. *Wannabe.*

But she soon learned. As did everyone else who would consume Lee's epic portrayal of a fictional historically Black college in *School Daze*, a movie that altered how we publicly talked about Blackness and HBCUs. For the uninitiated, the idea of a wannabe was a caricature of (for the most part) a high-yellow, lighter-skinned woman with long hair whose physical attributes look more European than African. "Wannabe" was also an attitude: *wannabe better than me.*

School Daze. It's been three decades since theaters were lit up with a historically Black campus waking up–this was when Nelson Mandela was still locked up and students called for divestment from South Africa. Three decades since Lee brought us a story of conflict, of a time when students pledging fictional Greek fraternities were pitted against those who desired global and local social change. The Gamma dogs. The Gamma Rays. The Fellas. The Wannabes. The Jiggaboos–oh yes, the Jiggaboos. *School Daze* was about the tensions between light-skinned Black folks and dark-skinned Black folks.

Everything was right there on a fifty-foot screen. No escaping it. We had to consume it. And address it. "It was like, Wow, this guy's really going to go there," said renowned director Kasi Lemmons, whose first film role was in *School Daze*. "He's really going to explore these issues. It occurred to me, when I saw it, how important it was because it explored so many things that you just hadn't seen."

In so many ways, *School Daze* was an extension of what was happening on campuses. It tapped into activations that were happening in the mid-1980s, and after it was released, it inspired and engaged other students, amplifying the work that was already taking place.

Darryl Bell—who was one of the "big brothers" in *School Daze*, his first role—was quite active as a real-life student at Syracuse University. He attended rallies where Black and Latino students were mobilizing, much in the same way that Laurence Fishburne's Dap did on Lee's fictional campus of Mission College. In real life, Bell pledged Alpha Phi Alpha.

"I wanted to know more about these Alpha fellas," said Bell. He remembers seeing them at rallies. "The idea that Alpha men were involved in, and on the forefront of talking about, issues that mattered—the divesting of South Africa—it encouraged me to be part of student government. All of these things . . . my experience at Syracuse, you saw in the film. . . . We were engaged in voter registration. We put on a fashion show to raise money to give scholarships to high school students. . . . That was the life I was living. That's why I was so desperate to be in the movie. . . . This is all about me and what I'm living every day. It was an extraordinary example of art imitating life."

The film was more than entertainment; even before *A Different World*, it really illuminated HBCU campus life. It shed a light on colorism, one of the most uncomfortable and unspoken issues among Black folks—something we'd been battling for generations and, in a lot of ways, still are.

"There was . . . division between the men and women," said Joie Lee, who portrayed Lizzie Life in the film, "in terms of what constitutes beauty. I wasn't fine. I wasn't considered that. I did not fit that standard of beauty, perhaps because I was brown-skinned. Perhaps because my hair was nappy, and natural. The women that are considered fine . . . were light-skinned or had good hair–I'm using that term loosely. Those were some of the issues that [we were] grappling with."

More than thirty years later, the film still holds up. Replace *School Daze*'s international concerns with the Black Lives Matter movement and the activism, especially in this current political climate, most certainly feels familiar. "It does have a relevance to what's going on today," said Kirk Taylor, who portrayed one of the Gammas. "In terms of the look, in terms of the content, in terms of the final message about waking up . . . we need to wake up as much now as we did then–and stay awake. It's easy to be lulled into a false sense of security, or false peace, and not be aware that things still need to be addressed. Things still need to be changed."

Stay woke, indeed.

Originally published February 12, 2018

DIDDY'S WHITE PARTY
KICKED IN THE DOOR, ANNOUNCING **"WE UP IN HERE"**

From 1998 until 2009,
his White Parties hopped from one
exclusive location to the next with a
strict all-white dress code.

BY ROGER REEVES

WAS P. Diddy's Labor Day party in 1998 in the mostly white, wealthy enclave of the Hamptons, New York, the end of the world as some of its neighbors feared? Was this raucous and luxurious display of hip-hop party culture, Black culture, and white celebrities eating and drinking at the Veuve Clicquot and Chandon founts of Black wealth a type of apocalypse?

This new Black money was not interested in sequestering itself in the previous vacation and summer homes of the Black elite of generations past. Highland Beach, Maryland; Oak Bluffs, Massachusetts; even Sag Harbor, New York, lacked the luxury and hallmarks of elitism that this burgeoning class of Black wealth desired. This burgeoning class of Black wealth that Diddy helmed felt at home in both the boardroom and the Bed-Stuy reggae club in Brooklyn, New York, and desired to mingle with businesswoman Martha Stewart and actor Ashton Kutcher in their enclaves. They had the George Jefferson ethos—they wanted to move on up and into the old White Anglo-Saxon Protestant communities of white wealth.

However, they were not going to change their manners or replicate those of their white neighbors. This new Black money in the form of Sean "P. Diddy" Combs (aka Puff Daddy) dripped in swagger and braggadocio, and wanted you to know it. Diddy's White Party signaled to the neighbors in the Hamptons that "we up in here," acting like we want to act.

Five years after starting his record label Bad Boy Entertainment, Diddy had signed and worked with an illustrious list of artists such as Biggie Smalls, Mary J. Blige, Mariah Carey, and Aretha Franklin. Bad Boy Entertainment allowed him to straddle the streets and high society, moving in a black car from Harlem, New York, to the Hamptons and back again. The streets were never more vocal and vociferous than in the East Coast–West Coast beef that led to the assassination of Smalls in 1997 with Diddy himself in the truck on Wilshire Boulevard in Los Angeles. Before the launching of his beverage empire of DeLéon Tequila and Ciroc Vodka, and one year after the release of his multiplatinum debut album, *No Way Out*, with "I'll Be Missing You," a tribute to the slain Smalls, 1998 found Diddy astride the entertainment and fashion industry with the start of his couture house, Sean Jean.

Diddy was Cecil B. Rhodes-ing the competition, straddling the map of commerce in America. Bad and boujee before the then-grammar-school-age Migos could remix "bourgeoisie" into "boujee." Funky and fastidious about it. On September 7, 1998, in East Hampton, New York, on Hedges Banks Drive, Diddy's White Party "kicked in the door, waving the four-four," announcing this new era, this new mogul, this bridegroom cometh. This apocalypse.

And Diddy wanted his apocalypse, his takeover all in white. White clothing, known as summer whites, became a popular manifestation of elitism, virtue, and leisure beginning in the Victorian era, and gathered a tremendous amount of traction in the twentieth century, where white clothes became a signal of wealth, exclusivity, and even fantasy. Think Wimbledon. Think fashion spreads in *Vanity Fair* of models next to long-haired, white-haired dogs while sitting next to a fire on a beach. Think white plantation owners and scions of the industry from the Northeast yachting on the Chesapeake in late July. Think Truman Capote, writer of *In Cold Blood* and *Breakfast at Tiffany's*, sitting by a pool with a notebook scribbling out names of Hollywood's who's who to invite to his Black and White Ball in 1966. Think Capote's Black and White Ball in the Grand Ballroom at the Plaza Hotel, 450 bottles of Taittinger champagne sweating beneath the tinkle of a chandelier.

Diddy's co-opting of this tradition melds this notion of fantasy, wealth, and leisure with Blackness, which is both subversive and not subversive at all. The subversion is in the tethering of Blackness and Black people to concepts such as leisure and exclusivity, which normally are not the domain of Blackness. For instance, if I asked what you think of when you hear the words "wealth" or "leisure," you are more likely to think of former president Donald Trump on a golf outing, ambling over an overly green piece of earth, rather than of Diddy descending out of a helicopter with the Declaration of Independence tucked beneath his arm, which he did in 2004 when he entered that year's White Party in the Hamptons from the heavens.

From 1998 until 2009, Diddy's White Parties hopped from one exclusive location to the next. East Hampton; Beverly Hills, California; and Saint-Tropez, France, were a few of the locations Diddy descended upon with his exclusive guest list, all-white dress code, and white carpet runway that led into the lavishness of his nouveau riche remix of Jay Gatsby's imagination.

Let's stay here for a while, with this surreal and almost impossible image: a Black man descending out of a helicopter with a copy of one of America's founding documents beneath his arm. It's a moment that I imagine in an unpublished novel by Ralph Ellison. I would be a poor poet and critic if I slipped this moment into the file folder marked "absurd" and left it there for the dust mites. It is a powerful image that anticipates and, in some ways, predicts Barack Obama's presidency four years later, as well as calls back to Jack Johnson, the American boxer and heavyweight champion who was convicted of trafficking white women across state lines in 1912 for "immoral pleasures." Though the white woman was his wife, a woman named Lucille Cameron. Johnson, like Diddy, was clutching one of America's sacred and sacrosanct treasures.

In the brandishing of this iconic piece of paper, Diddy aligns himself with that cultural lineage and heritage of the founding fathers, the *Mayflower*, and the mystique of the country's creation myth, which means also aligning himself with the genocide of Native Americans, slavery, Jim Crow, and countless other atrocities. Diddy's White Party becomes a type of "constitutional convention," wherein what is being legislated is not so much the laws of the land, but who constitutes an American. But not just any American: a founder, an aristocrat. Diddy's White Party is him putting in his application.

Which might also be called a cult of the American dream. It is a misinterpretation and flattening of Martin Luther King Jr.'s "I Have a Dream" speech, where we focus on the multicultural kumbaya moment where all the white and Black children of the world hold hands in postracial harmony and elide or forget the call for reparations at the beginning of King's speech, a call that has yet to be answered.

Because the guest lists at these White Parties reach across the aisle, office, and couture house, bringing together the burbs, bank presidents, the bourgeoisie, and the boujee, some would interpret this as a victory over the old evils of a segregated America. Reverend Al Sharpton appearing in a white tunic and baggy pants, Aretha Franklin in a white, wide-brimmed hat, rhinestone-studded, floor-length duster-style white coat, white chiffon top, white pants complete with a large rhinestone-studded Chanel purse—even the tips of Franklin's toes painted white; all of this occurring while supermodels sit on white swings wearing white bikinis over a blue pool might appear as a type of paradise in 2004. The breezy, easy life of excellence. And hard work. But actually, it is a celebration of cultural elitism, a place and space that none of us could afford to get to nor would be welcome.

This type of paradise is the American dream. It is what we all secretly desire–to be among the rich folk without the funk of our credit card debt, car payments, payday loans, student loans, gas and electric bills. This is America without our elders, firmly tucked away and out of sight, without our sick, our shut-in. And we're all wearing white as if we've just entered heaven.

Diddy's White Party becomes the escape we cannot afford but put away on layaway. The year 1998 was the end of a furious century–a century that began in a horse and buggy and ended in a rocket ship.

And the end of the century was not going down with a whimper: Y2K was less than two years away, and everyone expected computers to crash and bring down the world's banking system. School shootings began to mar the Middle American landscape, and parents began grappling with the notion that schools were no longer havens of safety. We were six years out from the last urban rebellions via the Los Angeles riots, which were not limited to just L.A., but made their way to Philadelphia, Baltimore, and Newark, New Jersey. And with the O. J. Simpson trial having reached its clown-car-strapped-with-dynamite-crazy conclusion nearly two years before, the racial tension in America was no longer sequestered in its hills. It seemed to come out of its mountains, down out of the forest, and rage all over the place.

And out of this turmoil, a flicker of white, a white flag of sorts in the guise of Diddy in an all-white outfit inviting a thousand or so guests to his house in the Hamptons for a party on the last possible date that one can wear white, Labor Day.

Maybe, it was the end of something and simultaneously the beginning of something else. An apocalypse that was simultaneously a creation myth. An America drunk on vodka and stumbling toward the edge of a pool.

Originally published May 14, 2020

TONI MORRISON
MADE ME STOP WANTING
TO BE WHITE

Slavery took our bodies. Cultural
hegemony tries to take our minds–
and destroy our hair. Morrison gave
it all back to us.

BY RAINA KELLEY

I'M HERE to give thanks. Toni Morrison freed me. She freed me
from the burden of wanting to be white. She taught me how to put
down blue eyes and use my own brown ones.

I had promised myself that when the day came that Morrison
passed, I would not be afraid. But it is a promise I cannot keep.

Even now, I feel the keyboard rise unevenly against my fingers
and my heart feels like a possum trapped in a box. *What will*

people think? They'll judge me. They'll pity me. My race card will be snatched. I'll get canceled. The whole world knows her résumé: Nobel Prize, Pulitzer Prize, Princeton professor, speaker of truth. No adjective is too big, and no verb can contain the glory of her oeuvre, the ripple of her effect.

I would no more appreciate Toni Morrison than Harriet Tubman could eulogize the North Star. She, as she says in *Song of Solomon*, is a woman who could fly. With her words, I can see the mountaintop. She taught me real freedom, freedom of the mind.

Slavery took our bodies. Cultural hegemony tries to take our minds—and destroy our hair. Morrison gave it all back to us—if we have the strength to take it. What did she say in *Beloved*? They do not love your body. So you have to love it and love it hard.

This is not about being *seen*—a watered-down approximation of affirmation if ever there was one. We are seen every day and seen wanting, thanks to the economic demands of a scientifically ignorant people who built a sweet land of "liberty" on the backs of other, darker humans. It's not right to own people. But it seems almost worse to convince yourself and those you enslaved and their descendants that it has something to do with their own inferiority. That's twisted. Morrison put it back straight.

It can be hard to remember to be free—to remember whose best thing I am.

My world sometimes looks like a series of planks I hammer together in front of me, stepping on the last to hammer the next. But it's mine, free and clear. There can be long breaks between finishing one board and picking up the next, but Morrison understood that. Her books are full of magic, but there are no magical Negroes.

Examining her loss, I feel as if Morrison has always been with me. *The Black Book* haunted me with nightmares of what they would do to my brown body if they caught me, *Song of Solomon* strengthened my mind when I thought being brown was wrong, *Beloved* soothed my soul when being a brown girl felt worthless and then again when it felt like too much.

Her stories are mine, although the names and details were changed. Here is the spot under my chin where I burned my neck trying to look like Laura Ingalls. This is the elderly Italian woman who works at my local grocery–always eager to tell the white woman ahead of me how to braise her beef but anxious and silent when bagging my groceries. Here's how I wear Hall & Oates T-shirts to short-circuit racial profiling.

Lately, I'd been dwelling on omens. Sullen, murderous days slinking one into another, casting shadows of old terrors. Nine in Charleston, eleven in Pittsburgh, twenty-two in El Paso, so many more in ones and twos. Earthquakes in pairs. Countless aftershocks.

But Morrison taught me to pity those empty bags of death who think automatic rifles can stop us. She showed me that first at Pilate's stove and then in the clearing behind Sethe's house.

My wings hold the shape of her words, and so they cannot fail. I know now that as the shadows gather shape in the wagon to take me back to Sweet Home that I will hold my chin high, pick up the hammer, laugh, and say:

"Me? Me?"

Originally published August 8, 2019

WHITLEY'S WORLD:
A BRIEF HISTORY OF **BAD** AND **BOUJEE** BLACK GIRL **STYLE**

Jasmine Guy's Gilbert is the blueprint for *Insecure's* Molly, *Dear White People's* Coco, and *Living Single's* Regine.

BY DANIELLE CADET

NO OTHER show explored the life of coeds at a historically Black college as thoroughly as NBC's *A Different World*. The show's colorful characters gave us everything we didn't know we needed, from a young Black man who made solving for x extremely sexy to a free-spirited redhead who would certainly be on the front lines of any and every Black Lives Matter protest today.

But if "bad and boujee" was trademarked by Migos, it originated on the fictional Hillman College campus and was created by the grande dame of the dorm known as Gilbert Hall: Whitley Marion

Gilbert. The Louis Vuitton luggage–toting, siditty Southern belle, as portrayed by Jasmine Guy, had a legacy at the prestigious university that went back generations. At five-foot-two, her frame was petite, but her style was colossal. The Whitley character not only reflected the most fashionable trends of the '80s and '90s, but she also influenced contemporary style and served as an inspiration for many young Black women and Black creatives today.

As one of the first examples of young, Black affluence on television, Whitley paved the way for a long list of pivotal TV personalities. *The Fresh Prince of Bel-Air*'s Hilary Banks, *Saved by the Bell*'s Lisa Turtle, *Living Single*'s Regine Hunter, *Clueless*'s Dionne Davenport, *Girlfriends*'s Toni Childs, *Dear White People*'s Colandrea "Coco" Conners, and even *Insecure*'s Molly Carter all seem to draw inspiration from the Richmond, Virginia–born beauty queen who, now via streaming apps, continues to personify the style and essence of bad and boujee Black girls everywhere.

Her impact also went beyond the small screen. In 2015, when the show started streaming on Netflix, Pinterest boards, Instagram handles, and Halloween costumes (including one from yours truly) dedicated to mimicking Whitley's style became a dime a dozen. But imitation certainly is the highest form of flattery, and nobody knows that better than Whitley Gilbert.

THE DEVIL IS IN THE DETAILS

Three decades ago, we got a first-class ticket to a historically Black college in Virginia. A group of students evolved from inexperienced adolescents to dynamic adults. From 1987 to 1992, we came to know and love Dwayne Wayne's nerdy swag, Whitley Gilbert's style, Freddie Brooks's free-spirited eccentricity, Kimberly Reese's steadfast level-headedness, and Ron Johnson's zany antics. And although the show initially aimed to follow the coed life of Cosby kid Denise Huxtable (Lisa Bonet), it shifted its focus in its second season to the whole crew's college experience and to Whitley and Dwayne's love story.

A *Different World* touched on relevant social themes such as workplace sexual harassment and racial injustice, and it celebrated Black heritage. It also featured iconic dayplayers such as Patti LaBelle, Diahann Carroll, Whoopi Goldberg, Jada Pinkett, and even Tupac Shakur, ushering in a wave of classic Black television shows. "It deepened the tone of Black sitcoms," said Guy, who at the time was filming season two of BET's *The Quad*, which is set at a historically Black college not named Hillman.

To authentically portray the character, Guy says, she created a backstory for Whitley that helped bring her to life. She decided Whitley had attended a primarily white, private school–so for her, Hillman's campus truly was a different world. "She thought she was Black, and she is. But there are all different kinds of ways to be Black," Guy said. "And . . . the Hillman College experience gave her a new sense of who she was and the community she belonged to. I noticed in the writing how she grew. Over the arc of a season you could see that that character had a lot to learn."

The show was mostly written by Susan Fales-Hill and Yvette Lee Bowser. The creation of a character with as much style development as Whitley, and the whole A *Different World* crew, started with the script, says Ceci, who worked as costume designer on the show for five seasons (1989–92).

"The inspiration comes first from the writing," Guy said. "[It] shaped who these characters are, absolutely and situationally. . . . Whitley is waking up in the morning, but what is she waking up to do? You should be able to turn your TV on mute . . . and kinda know what's going on when you see the character. I'm supporting the dialogue and the intentions that the writer and director are trying to convey. I'm doing that visually, through the wardrobe."

Ceci's résumé includes work on iconic shows such as *Living Single* and *Sister, Sister* and she was the costume designer on Netflix's *Dear White People*. Each of these shows features personalities communicated via style, a characteristic she says was used extensively on *A Different World*. "You'd never see Freddie Brooks wearing anything the Whitley character would wear," she said. "Jaleesa wouldn't wear anything Whitley would wear. Each of those characters are . . . being true to who they are."

Whitley Gilbert is certainly in a world of her own. There aren't many episodes in which the girl with the sass and twang isn't draped in Chanel suits and/or silk scarves. Unlike so many college students who roll out of bed in sweats, Whitley spends her days in heels, fur coats, and pearls. "She's a society girl," says Mel Grayson, a designer who worked on the shows early seasons before Ceci took over as costume designer. "She was highfalutin."

Grayson, a Dallas native, drew his inspiration for Whitley from his own upbringing—and shows that featured affluent characters like the women of CBS's *Dallas* (1978–91). "I kept it sexy and hip, taking elements of French couture . . . elements of Southern church ladies who sat in the front row," he said. "I'd take a bit of that kind of styling and move it down a few levels. Cut off the shoulder pads, kill the big heels and the big ruffles, but still make her regal, and still make her stand out as somebody that had class."

Whitley's wardrobe wasn't cheap. Both Ceci and Grayson say they shopped at high-end stores such as the Dallas-based Neiman Marcus but also had to get creative to stretch what was a meager budget. They augmented new purchases with consignment shop pieces. Tailoring was important: It was hard to come by clothes that fit Guy's petite frame. "There were clothes that you'd know [were] quality just by the way they fit the body," Grayson said.

"Everything had to be altered to fit her perfectly," said Ceci. "Thought was given to each decision–is this fitting too close, or too tight? No, she'd wear silk, she wouldn't wear cotton. She'd wear probably pink, not black. Black is too harsh. Every time you look at Whitley, she's not out of place. Everything about her is supporting this one style aesthetic."

Ceci would often swap basic original buttons for gold ones, or choose a classic pump over a slouched boot. The key was to capture an authentically upscale young Black woman who consistently remained true to herself. Would Whitley wear an unbuttoned blazer? Would she ever have a pimple? If so, how many? That pimple question alone sparked a production meeting debate that lasted at least thirty minutes.

"Those are the details," said Ceci, "that help subconsciously round out a character."

BOUJEE–AND BLACK

The first season of A Different World received scathing reviews and is often ranked last on lists of fan's favorite seasons. Season four–it begins with Whitley's epic shade toward Dwayne's new girlfriend, Kinu, and ends with Dwayne asking Whitley to marry him–is the best season by far. And while season two was a good-bye to Bonet's Denise Huxtable story line and a largely white production staff, it was a hello for legendary director and producer Debbie Allen, who ensured the show was both authentic and unapologetic about it.

During Allen's tenure, the show created endless opportunities for Black Hollywood professionals and designers. The Howard alum even took the writing staff on annual "field trips" to the Clark Atlanta, Spelman, and Morehouse campuses for inspiration.

What emerged was a show that was very Black. "When Debbie Allen came on the show in the second season, she made it more specific, and more clear, who all these people were–including Whitley," Guy said. "Because she did know people like that. She brought little things like 'How can y'all have a cafeteria with no hot sauce on the table?'"

Despite Whitley's often insufferable sense of entitlement and occasional disregard for peers outside of her tax bracket–in one episode she defends Kimberly's scholarship from a company that hasn't divested from South Africa and separates herself from the anti-apartheid struggle with a flippant "I don't know those people"–Whitley maintains a shatterproof pride in her Blackness.

"Yes, she's a socialite, she's got her nose in the air, she's got great hair–and it's straight," said Grayson. "She's got a light complexion; she could pass the paper bag test. But she's a girl that wants to be a Black girl. She's not about trying to be white, or anything else. She's being very Black, and this is a very Black situation."

"There's a distinction," Guy said. "And I guess that's why they call it bad and boujee, because there are bougie Black people that are not trying to be white. I think that is a misnomer that Whitley was WHITEly. I was determined not to go into that direction because this kind of character does exist in the Black community and has the same issues as her friends."

For Ceci, communicating that Black self-confidence through Whitley's clothing meant altering the styles that luxury brands were creating, particularly as those styles weren't often intended for Black girls.

"A lot of times when you go to high-end stores, that classic look is a color palette that is better for blond hair and blue eyes," said Ceci. "We can wear those colors [and] we can be more bold. I tried to let Whitley . . . *not* try to emulate what an affluent white person would look like but what an affluent African American young woman in college would look like. But that really didn't exist [on television]. It was up to me to imagine what that looked like. The trick with her was trying to make her look affluent but still approachable."

Throughout the show, Whitley comes to life draped in jeweled tones rather than monochromatic ones. She'll wear cream pants with an emerald blouse, or pair a black pencil skirt with a golden peplum blazer. A delicately placed brooch here. A chain-linked belt there. Classic, polished styles mixed with elements of youth. "The trick with her was color," said Ceci. "If I couldn't find something colorful, I would often dye things. If she wore all taupes and beiges it would be like, 'Okay, who are you?'"

Maintaining that authenticity was particularly important when it came to portraying Whitley's wedding day. This was long before wildly popular Black wedding sites and Instagram handles like Munaluchi Bride existed. Seeing a Black woman in a bridal gown was rare. "*Brides* magazine would never, ever have anybody of color in their magazine," said Bethann Hardison, a pioneering African American runway model and advocate for runway diversity whose son, Kadeem, portrayed Dwayne Wayne. "If they thought to do it, it was maybe a bridesmaid–but that came a lot later. We never saw anyone in a bridal gown that was of color."

A *Different World*'s pivotal 1992 wedding episode gave viewers something they couldn't get anywhere else. It not only featured iconic guests–including Joe Morton, Diahann Carroll, and Orlando Jones, among others–but it also served up the proverbial peak of Dwayne and Whitley's relationship. Whitley had been dating future senator Byron Douglas III (portrayed by Morton) and was at the altar when Dwayne interrupted, asking her to reconsider.

According to Guy, the whole scene was done in one take, and Dwayne's epic "Baby, please!" followed by Carroll's "Die, just die!"

weren't actually written into the script. The episode–in which Guy wore a delicately embroidered fit-and-flare gown with puffed, capped sleeves reminiscent of Princess Diana's and a dramatic train with bow detail–put "Black" and "bridal" in the same sentence long before anyone else would. And if anyone knows how to dress for a momentous occasion, it's Whitley Gilbert. So the pressure was on.

"We were trying to go with something that was sophisticated but still Southern," said Ceci. "Something that had some sweetness . . . not over-the-top but still a little sexy. It had to have a little bit of everything . . . this one dress, striking the balance of demure but still sophisticated–and not too mature or revealing." Unlike other episodes where she had the chance to communicate who Whitley was in multiple outfits, Ceci had to sum up all the character's elements in one ensemble. "Wedding dresses are a challenge," she said. "I've got one shot."

The pressure was also on for Guy, who knew seeing a Black bride on television was particularly significant for young Black women. "Little girls dream of those things, and they don't necessarily know it's possible for them," she said. "All the little girls are looking at Whitley being bougie, getting knocked down, getting up, and then realizing, 'Look at what she had to learn before she got married.' That's what I'm hoping young people will see: Look what it took to get to this point, and look how it's worth it."

The gown, which was made in-house rather than purchased, not only matched Whitley's boujee bridal needs but also echoed Bethann Hardison's words to magazine editors: "Black people get married too."

WHITLEY'S "WORLD"

The impact of *A Different World* goes far beyond the small screen. Its story lines tackled topics such as HIV/AIDS, interracial dating, and apartheid–and enrollment at HBCUs drastically increased while the show was on during prime time. "The show was so contemporary at that moment," said Bethann Hardison. "*A Different World* was the first show that ever tackled all the issues, from date rape to race relations. It's a show that stands the test of time."

Networks also started making room for more Black TV shows. "We were a part of a wave," said Guy. "I didn't realize that we were the end of the wave. I thought the business had changed. And then it went back to very few Black people. It wasn't until cable, and the birth of all these other outlets, that the networks couldn't afford to be so cocky about what they put on and don't put on."

As for Whitley, her style and boldness showed up in other shows. In the 1990s, the presence of affluent young Black women became less rare with the creation of characters such as Lark Voorhies's Lisa Turtle, Karyn Parsons's Hilary Banks, or even Stacy Dash's Dionne Davenport. There was also another strain of young female TV personalities who weren't born with money but via hard work became accustomed to the finer things in life, such as Kim Fields's Regine Hunter, Jill Marie Jones's Toni Childs, and Antoinette Robertson's Coco Conners. That sensibility is also evident in *Insecure*'s Molly on HBO, as portrayed by Yvonne Orji, whose power suits and fashion sense are a contemporary remix of Whitley's wardrobe. There's also, of course, Olivia Pope of *Scandal*, who stakes a claim to bad and boujee herself.

"I saw a lot of Whitley-esque influence in a lot of characters," said Grayson. "In *Living Single* and *Girlfriends*. They were a bit more risqué, but they had that same sensibility."

Ceci said she wasn't as aware of the influence in real time. But looking back, she sees correlations. However, she said the clothes she chose for characters such as Regine and Coco signify more aspirational efforts than did Hillman's own pride and joy. "The

Regine character . . . she wasn't born with money. She has . . . humble beginnings and is a little more sassy and expressive," said Ceci. "Coco didn't have the affluence that the Whitley character has. So while there might be some parallels in terms of trying to be pulled together . . . those two characters are never gonna be able to hit the mark in terms of the polish and the etiquette of the Whitley character."

Guy said she was more aware of women who paved the way for her as Carroll did in *Dynasty* (1981–89). While she agrees that both Hilary Banks and Regine Hunter fall into the same category as Whitley, she said they each had unique characteristics. "We were all a part of that theme, we were just different in our bougieness," she said.

Both Grayson and Ceci acknowledge that although Whitley can be antagonistic, even when you hate her, you still want to dress like her. "Now, when kids look at Whitley," said Ceci, "they feel like she's like a baby baller. They're like, 'I wanna look like her when I grow up.'"

"It just made young girls realize that you don't have to be that . . . dowdy girl and just wear . . . jeans and your old flannel shirt," said Grayson. "You can pull yourself together and go to school . . . and look a little more elegant, and not care what other people have to say about that–because you wanna be dressed."

And Ceci is proud and humble at the same time. "You can't unsee *A Different World*," she said. "You've seen it. It's kind of engraved in your psyche. And perhaps subliminally that's a reference point, or even consciously. . . . I don't know if I defined what African American female affluence was at that time, but . . . I'm just coming to embrace the impact the show had, and my part in it . . . I feel proud and privileged and honored to have . . . been a part of that."

As a fan of fashionable jewels and a collector of fine art, Whitley knows that reprints are acceptable. But there's nothing like the original. Although her character set a part of #BlackGirlMagic in motion, no one has matched her level of polished sophistication, and perhaps no one ever will. Ms. Gilbert would have it no other way.

Originally published September 21, 2017

AN ODE TO *JET* MAGAZINE'S "BEAUTY OF THE WEEK"

BY MARTENZIE JOHNSON

THIS WAS the point, my dad once told me, when I knew you were interested in women.

I was six years old, waiting for a haircut from our regular barber, Clarence. (To this day, I don't know Clarence's last name. He is my Cher.) My older brother and I took out about twenty of the pocket-sized weekly magazines, lined them up in a row, and flipped each to page 43–it was almost *always* page 43. We probably didn't even need the table of contents; we knew exactly what we were looking for.

We found out on our own that we liked girls right there in the pages of *Jet* magazine, in "Beauty of the Week."

In 2019, Johnson Publishing Co., which published *Jet* magazine and its sister publication, *Ebony* magazine, from the 1940s until 2016, filed for Chapter 7 bankruptcy in U.S. Bankruptcy Court for the Northern District of Illinois, effectively ending the Black-centric publisher's seventy-seven-year run. It had already sold *Jet* and *Ebony* to private equity firm Clear View Group in 2016, so the filing didn't affect those publications. Nevertheless, the fate of Johnson Publishing brought back thoughts of "Beauty of the Week," which placed just ahead of professional wrestling and *Power Rangers* on the *Family Feud*-like board of my pastimes.

Your level of fondness for "Beauty of the Week," the magazine's famous section dedicated to Black women decked out in swimsuits, depends on your perspective.

For some Black men, it was somewhere between adoration of the Black female body . . . and Lawd Have Mercy. Whether on the bus, in the barbershop, on the end table at your grandmother's house, or even in prison cells, from teenagers to middle-aged men, some among us went straight to the centerfold of *Jet* as soon as we set our eyes on the pint-sized glossy cover. Black boys and men (and women too) ogled the pretty brown-skinned women with the voluptuous curves and breathtaking smiles. And while it wasn't *Penthouse* or *Maxim*'s Hot 100, Johnson Publishing exploited Black bodies and sexuality, sometimes printing photos that straddled the line between tasteful and lustful.

At the same time, "Beauty of the Week" brought Black female bodies into the mainstream, said Cornell University professor Noliwe M. Rooks, whose research focuses on beauty, race, and fashion. As a pushback against pinup girls in other magazines of the early twentieth century, Johnson Publishing founder John H. Johnson created a domain for Black women and their sexuality. These images were a sharp contrast to the all-white bodies presented in other publications. And though *Jet* was never known for featuring plus-size women, its models came in different colors, sizes, and shapes–the antithesis of the blond bombshell.

"They're not stick figures," Rooks said.

Stick figures they were not. At the time I was way too young to understand the meaning of sex or even what it was, but I could somehow recognize Black beauty (among *other* things) and how it differed from other suggestive images I saw on television. Sure, there were the hidden dirty magazines around the shop of my dad's trucking company, or the always-weak-signaled Channels 32 and 33 on the "black box," but I just *knew* there was something different about the women on the 5-$\frac{1}{8}$-by-7-$\frac{3}{8}$-inch pieces of paper.

Former *Jet* editor-in-chief Mira Lowe came to the publication during its twilight in 2007 but grew up reading the magazine, admiring the risks Johnson Publishing was willing to take with Black women featured so prominently on its covers and throughout its pages. Before *Jet* and *Ebony*, Black women simply didn't appear on magazine covers. *Vogue* (in 1974), *Glamour* (1968), *Life* (1969), and *Playboy* (1971) didn't put Black women on their covers until almost twenty years after *Jet*'s first issue in 1951.

"*Jet* helped with the penetration in the Black community," Lowe said. "[It] laid the groundwork and was the pioneer to what we see today in mainstream magazines."

Dudley Brooks, who was *Jet* and *Ebony*'s photo director from 2007 to 2014, said *Jet* was forward-thinking at the time in choosing to showcase Black women in a way they hadn't been before.

The early incarnation of "Beauty of the Week" debuted in 1952 in the centerfold. One of the first models was Florida-born Ruth King, who was working a clerical job in a New York City courthouse when she appeared in the August 14 issue. As would come to be *Jet*'s trademark, King's full-page portrait was accompanied by a short bio and body size measurements that Sir Mix-a-Lot would rap about some forty years later.

Outside of King, it wasn't just aspiring models looking to be the next "It" girl appearing in "Beauty of the Week." There were women majoring in speech at historically Black colleges and universities, beauty consultants from California, and aspiring politicians and musicians. There was Beverly the waitress, Denise the inhalation therapist, and Noni, who liked to deep-sea fish and Jet Ski. These women were everyday girls who were given the opportunity to show the world what "normal" looks like.

But there were also those who used "Beauty of the Week" as a launching pad. Former television personality and author Janet Langhart Cohen graced the section in 1966. She told *Jet* in 1986 that it was "where I got my start." Janet Dubois, who played wisecracking neighbor Willona Woods on *Good Times*, appeared in 1977. The most famous of the bunch was blaxploitation film actress Pam Grier, who was set to star in 1971's *The Big Doll House* when she posed for the magazine in a two-piece bathing suit in Chicago.

"I think it was just after I finished *Black Mama White Mama*, and things were starting to blow up, and they said, 'You've got to do *Jet* and *Ebony*,'" Grier told *The Undefeated* in 2016. "You can see I am so rough. I just seemed not like the beauties of today: toned and tanned and shiny. I was ashy, no makeup, my hair was all over the place."

While "Beauty of the Week" was an opportunity to uplift and portray Black women in a non-disrespectful manner, at the end of the day it was what it was.

"It was eye candy," said Brooks. "Things that used to be considered normal or accepted widely years ago move on."

The women, for the most part, were photographed solely in swimsuits and, from 1959–93, were accompanied by their body measurements.

The photos have been called a "quick dose of random, incongruous cheesecake" meant to offset the more serious news stories in the magazine, no more obvious than in 1955 when *Jet* published the gruesome images from Emmett Till's funeral just twenty-six pages ahead of fifteen-year-old Judith Stewart in a two-piece bathing suit.

The merits of presenting Black women in next to no clothing can be argued every day of the week, but, at the same time, the editors and art directors appeared ahead of their time in the mid-twentieth century, showcasing women of various skin tones, waist sizes, and hair lengths. A 2011 research study found that *Jet* presents "a larger female body size ideal . . . contrary to mainstream Caucasian media's practices," which may reflect a "broader definition of female attractiveness." From Saartjie Baartman to former first lady Michelle Obama to Serena Williams, Black women's bodies have been ridiculed, mocked, and simultaneously ignored for centuries, but *Jet* (and older publications such as *Tan*) had the audacity to put Black women front and center for the world to see.

There's not much I remember about my childhood. I vaguely recall learning to ride my bike or almost getting lost at a Six Flags theme park or dressing up for Halloween. But "Beauty of the Week" is one of those things that sits in the back of your memory. I haven't picked up a physical copy of the magazine since the early 2000s, but I can envision being in my grandparents' living room as everyone else watched television, wading through the first forty-two pages of the latest *Jet*, anticipating which pretty woman I'd get to see that week, like an adult LOL. Surprise! doll box. (*Jet* switched to a digital-only operation in 2014.)

When I was commissioned to write this story, I was told by my editor to keep it classy and tasteful. But crossing that line never crossed my mind. "Beauty of the Week" didn't make me the man I am today, in that clichéd kind of way, but I can say without a doubt that it helped me learn to appreciate and respect Black women and their bodies.

And now the dissolution of Johnson Publishing means a part of *Jet*'s soul is gone forever.

And with it, a part of my adolescence.

Originally published April 19, 2019

UNCLE PHIL FROM *THE FRESH PRINCE OF BEL-AIR* MAY BE THE **BEST TV DAD** IN HISTORY

BY JUSTIN TINSLEY

TATYANA ALI is fighting back tears.

"James Avery taught me that acting is actually a noble profession, and that there's great purpose in it," says Ali. "If we took it seriously enough, we could help our people. We could lift them up . . . make people see who we really are." Ali, of course, played Ashley Banks, the youngest daughter of Vivian and Philip Banks and the first cousin of the title character on the landmark '90s sitcom *The Fresh Prince of Bel-Air.*

Ali remembers Avery as a man who understood the importance of representation and felt it was a kind of spiritual obligation. "Uncle Phil" was a former hippie-activist in the sixties turned Princeton-educated Los Angeles judge who was down to quote

Malcolm X and call the criminal justice system out on its flaws at a moment's notice. *The Fresh Prince of Bel-Air* was hip-hop in spirit, from the title on down.

The country was coming off nine years of Cliff Huxtable, who rose to power in hip-hop's infant stages (1984-92) but was never hip-hop's father figure. That title goes to James Avery as Uncle Phil, even if it wasn't about fandom. "We didn't really speak a lot about hip-hop," says DJ Jazzy Jeff, Will Smith's real-life musical partner who played the role of Will's friend Jazz, who would frequently, and literally, be thrown out of the Bel-Air mansion by Uncle Phil. "But he loved Will and I. He loved what we were doing. He loved the fact 'Summertime' encompassed Summer Madness by Kool & the Gang."

Fresh Prince, a collaboration of Quincy Jones and the then-married team of Andy and Susan Borowitz, was based loosely on the life of Will Smith's then-manager Benny Medina (and on the lifestyle of Jones's own family) and ran on NBC from 1990-96. NBC was wary of a project starring a rapper, and the show was derided at first by some for a lack of grit. Ultimately, critiques proved ignorant, as the sitcom became part of the cultural DNA of the '90s.

There are many classic episodes of *The Fresh Prince*—like "72 Hours," in which Carlton goes to Compton. In "My Brother's Keeper," it's Will vs. Allen Payne with a Georgetown basketball scholarship on the line. And "Banks Shot" includes the classic "Geoffrey, break out Lucille" line. But there's no singular installment that holds the significance of the "Papa's Got a Brand New Excuse" episode. It aired on May 9, 1994, in the middle of the fourth season, and in it, Will's father, Lou (played by Ben Vereen), reenters his life after fourteen years—only to abandon him again.

"I shed a tear or two every time this episode comes on!" LeBron James tweeted in April. "Can't help it. I've had that same feeling my whole life." Dwyane Wade responded to his friend James, but it wasn't the first time James would refer to the episode, mentioning the emotions that swelled inside him upon seeing Will collapse into his uncle's arms.

The last scene is the most brutally honest in the series' most emotionally jarring episode. And in the streaming and social media era in which we live, it never goes away. LeBron James grew up without his father, while Wade's was active in his life. Their upbringings were very different, but their emotional attachments to the scene are almost identical. It's because the scene dramatizes a deep, complex, and universal pain. And James Avery is, at center, a rock. The dad everyone wishes they had.

James Avery passed away on New Year's Eve 2013 after complications from open-heart surgery. He was sixty-eight. A Suffolk, Virginia, native who served in the U.S. Navy, Avery was a classically trained actor with more than 175 credits–*L.A. Law* (in which he also played a judge), *The Closer, Star Trek: Enterprise, 8 Million Ways to Die*–to his name. Prior to *Fresh Prince*, Avery's most recognizable role was as the voice of the villain Shredder in *Teenage Mutant Ninja Turtles* for 106 episodes between 1987 and 1993.

He was Judge Philip Banks/Uncle Phil for six seasons, though, and Avery embraced the younger cast members as extensions of his own family. Even when not in scene, he referred to both Ali and Karyn Parsons (Hilary Banks) as "Daughter."

The scene between Avery and Smith helped establish Smith as the kind of dramatic actor who would go way beyond being a funny comedian and good rapper. He'd already done *Six Degrees of Separation* (1993) to great reviews and portrayed himself on shows like *Blossom*. Ahead of him was 1996's *Independence Day*, 1998's *Enemy of the State*, and the *Bad Boys* and *Men in Black* franchises. Smith was nominated for an Oscar for his performance in 2002's *Ali* and 2007's *The Pursuit of Happyness*. But his performance alongside Avery in "Papa's Got a Brand New Excuse" was an undeniable turning point in his career. Everyone on set knew it the moment it happened.

Ali remembers Avery's boundless support of Smith. "James [was] telling him, 'Don't try to cry. Try not to cry.'. . . His performance just completely took on a whole new light." The episode, and the final scene in particular, have become a cultural phenomenon. A *moment.* Will's titanic final words, "How come he don't want me, man?" stick to the ribs of an entire generation.

Will and Uncle Phil regularly had scenes where their personalities and egos clashed. The results were usually hilarious. But it's in this scene that Uncle Phil becomes *Uncle Phil.* His character lived in all of our households. Regardless of race, ethnicity, religion, or whatever difference that makes the human experience unique. The love, respect, and adoration Uncle Phil exhibited and commanded universally appealed to the most innate human desire: to be loved and protected. And in this scene, an older Black man was comforting a younger Black man during a time of unbearable grief and heartbreak. Rare for television, for mainstream media.

"It brings tears to your eyes," says Shelley Jensen (*Friends, Hannah Montana, The Jamie Foxx Show*), who directed eighty-seven episodes of *The Fresh Prince*, including "Papa." "To get there for an actor, on Will's part, who is a comedian—and at that time in his career wasn't known as a dramatic actor—James helped him so much from an acting standpoint."

Joseph Marcell portrayed Geoffrey the butler on *Fresh Prince.* "[James Avery] and I actually met when I came to America," says Marcell. The two, both smoking cigarettes when their paths first crossed, quickly bonded. "One classical actor from one side of the world, and another one from the other side. And both Black. It was magical."

Years after *Prince*'s final episode, Avery is referred to by castmates with reverence. *Larger than life. Loving. Gentle as a lamb. Jazz connoisseur. Cultured. Endless wisdom.* "James Avery was the one who gave me my appreciation for travel," says DJ Jazzy Jeff of the man he saw as a kindred spirit and big homie. And one with whom he shared a deep, almost spiritual appreciation for jazz music. "He would talk about how every summer he and a bunch of his friends would get in a car and drive cross-country. I thought that was the coolest thing in the world. He gave me an appreciation for leaving . . . your comfort zone. . . . He was a real, actual father figure on [the set of] that show."

"James and I hit it off when I auditioned," says Daphne Maxwell Reid, who played Avery's wife, Vivian ("Aunt Viv" Banks), from 1993–96. "Then I fell in love with the man. He was just such a dear. We'd dance down the halls together because he was a great dancer. His talent . . . his sincerity, he was a nice person . . . a smart person." It was her character who said to Vereen's, "Lou, if you walk out of Will's life now, don't you ever come back." And then Avery picked up the ball with that offhand but strict "Sit down."

Avery knew, Ali says, that for a Black actor, portraying a Black father on a television show came with responsibility. Every scene, every relationship Uncle Phil had with his kids, his nephew, his butler, his wife, or his mother–all of it would be reflective of actual Black families in the world. "He knew that kids would be watching," says Ali. "Those meaningful moments, the heart of the show. *He was the heart of the show.*"

Fresh Prince had dealt with heavy topics before–"Just Say Yo" (season three, episode nineteen) and "Blood Is Thicker Than Mud" (season four, episode eight). Donald Trump even appeared in a

1994 episode–which is, if nothing else, ironic ("I like to keep a low profile," said Trump) and prophetic ("Thank you for ruining my life!" says Ali). But for the entirety of the series up to that point, Will's single-parent household had been represented by the close relationship he had with his mother, "Vy," portrayed by Vernee Watson. Taking on the issue of Black single-parent households before a massive American audience was complex. Everyone had to play their part.

"Marcell and, of course, Alfonso [Ribeiro] were very funny in that episode. So was Karyn Parsons," Jensen remembers. "They had strong jokes. . . . You needed them because you were about to get hit in the face with this hard story. That's what makes good TV."

Legend has it that the scene was largely freestyled, and that Smith drew from personal experience. Smith was involved in the creation of the episode, as he was with all the others. But this one held a special significance for him. Cast members recall a collaborative process in the making of the first six seasons that was fruitful and commonplace. The actors mostly appreciated the perspective of the writers, while the writers mostly embraced the feedback from the Black cast. Both Smith and Avery were very much involved in the creation of "Papa." Smith's relationship with his real-life father (who died in November 2016) was a far cry from the one he had with his on-screen father, Vereen–whom Smith requested personally for the role in 1994. It's the close relationship Smith had with his father, and the respect he had for him, that Smith tapped into. And it was more than powerful.

"A big reason Will was able to pull that scene off was the relationship he had with his dad. He could not necessarily draw on personal [experience], but the exact opposite," says Jazzy Jeff. "When you have that relationship, and then you realize what it would be like if you didn't, then that's enough to bring you to tears also."

During the taping, Avery was in constant communication with Will about how he might react. How he might respond. How he might block his own emotions and let the character's emotions overtake him. There was a process involved. "We didn't get that [scene where Will breaks down] until the night we shot it," says Jensen. "It was very difficult for Will to get to that place."

What happened in the moment was pure emotion. It wasn't scripted for Will to say, "To hell with him!" in reaction to his father leaving him once again–this time for good. No one expected what they saw.

"I remember being on the set when the scene went down," says Parsons. "It was devastating. I wasn't expecting it. It hadn't gone like that in rehearsal."

"That line [asking Avery], 'How come he don't want me?' I get chills because that's the saddest childlike expression. It's not intellectualizing. Why does he do this all the time? Why is he this way? He's not saying any of the cliché statements. It was such a raw expression. He was taking the blame–like 'It's me. How come he don't want *me*?' I think that's what rings true for a lot of people, is that child inside of them that feels somebody is rejecting them because they're not enough. . . . It's so painfully sad because it had nothing to do with him. That's what I think a lot of people carry in their life . . . that kind of trauma from having somebody leave you, and [you] feel like it's because of you. Even as they grow into adulthood, they still have that little person in them that feels so vulnerable."

Reid says, "It was just so painful to watch. When Will finally collapsed into James's arms, it was just–everybody was crying."

"Every one of us was teary-eyed because it was real. It was raw emotion," says Jensen. "At that point it wasn't acting, and that's the best acting you can do." The episode, specifically its final scene, is a jewel of *Fresh Prince*'s crown. A classic moment that, for some, still comes with present-day consequences. "I can't tell you," says Vereen, "how many women have come at me and yelled at me for leaving Will."

Avery's "daughter," Ali, always remembers his advice that artists should be educated so that when they do speak, they "heal" and "push things forward." For Parsons, his other daughter, the importance of individuality and becoming comfortable in one's own skin is a foundational pillar of her life–thanks to Avery. For Marcell, Avery gave him friendship.

Whenever he visited America, Marcell stayed with Avery and his wife, Barbara. "He wouldn't let me get a hotel or apartment," says Marcell with a laugh. It was Marcell and Barbara who took Avery to an emergency room near Glendale, California, in November of 2013. He visited his friend every day for a month. Sometimes with Barbara. Sometimes alone. Avery's last words to him still make him laugh because they remind him of the friend who he worked with to make America laugh for six years. And also the vibrant friend who "absolutely savored life."

"The last thing he actually said to me was 'Hey, man, can you make them bring my dogs to me?'" Marcell recalls. "'And could you get me [some] McDonald's?'"

Avery is unique in the lineage of powerful Black television fathers like John Amos (*Good Times*), Sherman Helmsley (*The Jeffersons*), and even the disgraced Bill Cosby (*The Cosby Show*). Philip Banks was vulnerable because of his weight, the target of constant jokes from his butler and his nephew, yet he could dish it out as well. There was never a dull moment with Uncle Phil, not because of the way he spoke but because of the way he carried himself. His confidence was soothing. His love, unlike Cliff Huxtable's, felt available to all, and all-encompassing.

"Philip Banks was Philip Banks," Marcell says with a profound sense of pride. "That is his legacy. . . . He just was."

Originally published June 15, 2018

WHAT
MICHAEL K. WILLIAMS
TAUGHT ME ABOUT BEING
A MAN

He was an icon for queer Black men, but he was also a beacon for what's possible to ask of straight Black men.

BY DAVID DENNIS JR.

ABOUT FIFTEEN minutes into the third episode of *The Wire*, Omar Little is sitting on a stoop with two of his crew members. One of the men, Brandon, is under Omar's arm, his head leaning on Omar's chest. The second member, John, looks on uncomfortably. As the scene progresses, Omar and Brandon tenderly play with each other's fingers, leading to Omar delivering a light forehead kiss and a tender caress of his chin.

By this point in the series, we've already watched Omar, trademark shotgun in tow, and his posse rob a drug house. He'd been established as a snarling Rambo who struck fear in the hearts of everyone who heard his name in Baltimore. And now the audience learned that he was gay, not as the crux of a plot twist played up for shock, but in a quiet moment of affection.

I was twenty-two when I saw Omar kissing Brandon in that scene, and it floored me. I had been catching up on the series after it had just ended a few months earlier, in March 2008–using a now-prehistoric version of Netflix to get the DVDs delivered to my door every three days or so. I'd grown up in Mississippi and gone to college in North Carolina, and could probably count the number of openly gay men I'd met on my fingers and toes; a smaller number I'd call friends. The idea of someone like Omar, who, just an hour earlier I'd considered one of the most intimidating characters I'd seen on TV, as also being gay, was an epiphany.

A lot has and will be said about what Michael K. Williams contributed to the world of acting, art, and representation for the LGBTQ+ community. But he also helped me, a young Black man who is cisgender and heterosexual, understand masculinity and what it means for me and those around me. I'd considered myself an ally and supporter of my LGBTQ+ friends, but Williams showed me how much further I had to go and what was possible with full-hearted and fearless love.

It would be sensationalistic to say that that one moment when Omar romantically loves another man undid two-plus decades of toxic masculinity, stereotypes about gay men, and ideas of what it means to be a man. But Williams's portrayal of Omar and his subsequent career changed me, reshaping what I believed about manhood.

Mainstream society had presented queerness and masculinity

as polar opposites. Strong or muscle-bound men often portrayed gay characters for laughs or irony–I think about Terry Crews in *Friday After Next*, whose whole comedic presence was built on the idea that men who looked like him couldn't lust after other men. Omar, though, stood in his truth and did so in a way that shed a light on many queer Black men. He broke stereotypes I'd allowed to coalesce into my consciousness without even realizing it.

Omar was a superhero on-screen, having spaghetti western standoffs, taking on drug lords, and gunning down Stringer Bell. But when it was time to show Omar in love, Williams displayed a deep affection, revealing that even the most ruthless can be emotionally vulnerable. Williams would kiss, hold, caress, and care for men on-screen with his whole being.

It's important to mention the way Black men playing queer characters has been weaponized to amplify antigay bias. When Williams went on then–MTV personality Sway's show on Hot 97 in 2003, the host called Williams kissing another man on-screen repulsive and morally reprehensible (the two later made peace, with Williams appearing on Sway's show multiple times). Williams's portrayal of Omar landed in one of the more complicated and enduring battlefields among Black men: the idea of America's obsession with "emasculating" the Black man.

In 2006, for instance, in the middle of *The Wire*'s popularity, comedian Dave Chappelle went on *The Oprah Winfrey Show* and delivered a speech about what he saw as Hollywood's fascination with seeing Black men in dresses for comedy as a way to emasculate the men. It was a stance that I, at the time, saw as pro-Black without understanding how one can't be pro-Black and anti-LGBTQ+. The same outrage is present in the way bad-father actors such as Lil Boosie have attacked Lil Nas X for spreading the mythical "gay agenda." These acts of faux concern about things like "family values" and how Black men are positioning queerness as a detriment, especially in light of the way we equated queerness with emasculation, lack of manliness, and weakness.

But neither Williams nor Omar was weak. Omar's love of men didn't emasculate him, just like Williams's portrayal of a gay man didn't make him less of a man. Omar loved men in the face of antigay bias that made him a target for the same hate crimes that killed his lover. Williams loved Omar in the face of a community that saw his portrayal as betrayal. Seeing those examples of strength helped me reckon with the ways I had allowed antigay bias to infect the ways I saw the LGBTQ+ community and folks I had proclaimed to love and embrace in my life.

Williams's entire career post-*Wire* has been a testament to his fearless pursuit of showing the parts of us we're scared to face, let alone reveal to millions on camera. As Chalky White in *Boardwalk Empire*, he was rage and survival in the face of a world that wanted him dead. As Bobby McCray in *When They See Us*, he was scared, insecure, and trying to love his son the best he could. As Montrose Freeman in *Lovecraft Country*, he was confused, conflicted, and tormented by his internal antigay bias.

But Williams was at his most beautiful when he was himself. He got his start as a dancer and choreographer, touring with George Michael and Madonna. He loved to use his body to express himself with freeness and happiness. Watching him dance, especially in the viral videos that have circulated online in recent years, was like watching someone who had broken the chains that hold so many men back from loving our bodies and the way we make them move. To smile with nothing left to hold us back. It's these videos, as much as Williams's iconic roles, that are the lasting images of his legacy.

How does Williams become a Black queer icon? He loves those

who are so often cast aside. He sees the fullness of people so often relegated to being the punch lines, violence, and the worst of our cruelties. He holds men near on camera and off. And through all of this, he takes the hands of men like me, shattering what we thought we knew about the world and rebuilding a brighter, better, more loving reality in its place.

Originally published September 10, 2021

THE UNBEARABLE **WHITENESS** OF *OKLAHOMA!*

In a Broadway revival, the blinding sunshine of the Territory exposes the violence beneath the romantic myth.

BY SORAYA NADIA MCDONALD

THOUGH IT hasn't always been acknowledged, Rodgers and Hammerstein's *Oklahoma!* has always been a musical about whiteness.

Oklahoma! has often been summarized through a lens of racial neutrality as a romantic musical about a woman named Laurey Williams who is trying to make a choice between two suitors: Jud Fry, a hardworking farmhand who lives in the smokehouse of a farm owned by Laurey and her aunt Eller. And guitar-strumming Curly McLain, who is more socially adept, but doesn't offer much beyond a pretty face. Set in the Claremore Indian Territory of Oklahoma in 1906, *Oklahoma!* delivers a rose-tinted view of history that centers on happy white people whose greatest concern is a town dance that will raise money to build a new school. It's a classic example of willful erasure and ahistorical mythmaking.

In 1838 and 1839, President Andrew Jackson forced thousands of Native Americans to abandon their homes east of the Mississippi. Even though Oklahoma was the end point of the genocidal forced migration known as the Trail of Tears, *Oklahoma!* doesn't feature a single Native American character. In fact, its only explicitly nonwhite character is Ali Hakim, a Persian peddler who seeks romantic encounters that don't come with marital strings.

Director Daniel Fish's new, stripped-down Broadway revival of *Oklahoma!* doesn't play by those rules, though. In this version, Laurey is played by a Black woman, Rebecca Naomi Jones. Laurey's best friend, Ado Annie, is played by Ali Stroker, who uses a wheelchair, the first actress to do so on a Broadway stage. When Stroker won the Tony for best actress in a featured role in a musical, she was the first performer who uses a wheelchair to be nominated, much less win.

Suffice it to say, this ain't your granny's *Oklahoma!* The musical, which won the 2019 Tony for best revival, has been popularly characterized as the "Sexy *Oklahoma!*" That's largely because of the horny howling of its handsome leading man, Damon Daunno, who plays Curly, and its shamelessly libidinous Ado Annie. But I did not find *Oklahoma!* to be sexy so much as darkly terrifying– and I mean that in a good way.

That's because this version, which faithfully maintains the original script and lyrics of the 1943 musical while updating the orchestrations with modern arrangements, subjects toxic whiteness and masculinity to the glaring bleach of the noonday sun.

The revival is unique because of its deft interrogation of the whiteness and toxic masculinity that have long been romanticized in the American western, and in the many treacly iterations of *Oklahoma!* that have been mounted since 1943. This version asks its audience to consider a familiar world in an unfamiliar way: through the eyes of a Black woman with little to no physical security or power of her own.

The first thing one notices upon entering Manhattan's Circle in the Square theater is the aggressive brightness of the room's lighting (more than a few members of the audience wore sunglasses throughout the performance). The second is that the walls are lined with racks upon racks upon racks of shotguns.

The lighting turns out to be subversive. Much like a black light held over the surfaces of a sketchy motel room, it illuminates all the ickiness lurking on surfaces that appear otherwise innocuous. It welcomes you to the Oklahoma Territory, where flowers fill the prairie and the june bugs zoom, and then it ensures that you cannot turn away from the ugliness that lurks there. "Everything's going my way" certainly applies to the men of the Territory. But its female residents? Not so much.

It's strange to see *Oklahoma!* when the horrors of mass shootings are still in the shallow recesses of one's consciousness. But mostly, I was reminded of violence specifically linked to virulent misogyny, and so Alek Minassian, Elliot Rodger, and George Sodini entered my mind within minutes of the introduction of Jud (Patrick Vaill). Minassian, Rodgers, and Sodini are white men who committed mass murder because they were angry, lonely, and felt entitled to attention from women when they weren't getting it. Minassian identifies as an "incel," or involuntary celibate.

There is a rhythm to the news of mass shootings, and one beat in particular is frustratingly metronomic: the killers, more often than not, have a history of abuse or antipathy toward women. In *Oklahoma!*, Jud is armed with an unshakable crush, a shifty attitude, and a revolver. Vaill imbues Jud with a patina of gentle shyness, underneath which beats a familiar pulse of resentment, entitlement, and a violent temper precariously held in check. Jud might be an excellent farmhand, but he is not a good man. It makes for a terribly dangerous combination for Laurey.

To survive in the modern world, women develop a spidey sense about men who would potentially harm us, and we mold our lives around the avoidance of male aggression. We move to a different subway car if someone stares a little too long or brushes up a little too close. We slow our gait to let someone pass rather than take the chance that he may be following when we must walk late at night. And we get very good at managing–managing expectations, managing tempers, and managing egos.

The same reality of ever-present male danger is true for the women of the Territory. For them, the most effective way to guard against it is to get married. (Nothing sucks the romance out of courtship quite like knowing you're seeking a man in hopes that his presence will prevent your rape or murder.) Laurey has a decision to make about who she will choose for the dance and her life afterward: Curly or Jud? By Laurey's second interaction with the seemingly mild-mannered Jud, I felt my stomach grow queasy with worry. Oda Mae Brown from *Ghost* made an entrance in my notebook: "Laurey," I wrote furiously, "you in danger, girl!"

Before Fish reimagined her, Laurey was usually portrayed as a lucky woman blessed with a surfeit of romantic possibilities. Nowhere is that more clear than in Fred Zinneman's 1955 film adaptation. In Zinneman's *Oklahoma!*, Laurey is played by Shirley

Jones, a sunny, self-assured blonde whose good looks, tiny waist, and homespun charm are enough to tame any man.

When Shirley Jones sings "Many a New Day," she's surrounded by white women pirouetting in bloomers and petticoats, and she's laying out a philosophy that Ellen Fein and Sherrie Schneider would come to monetize some four decades later in *The Rules*, possibly the worst self-help book about dating ever published. Essentially, it is a doctrine that tells women that all their power and moral authority lie in their sexual availability or lack thereof, also known as playing hard to get.

But this display of performative reluctance isn't an indication of power, so much as the lack of it, especially when you consider the presence of armed threats like Jud. From the beginning of the musical, Aunt Eller is telling Curly how much her niece likes him, no matter how much Laurey's behavior indicates the opposite. It's strategic: Aunt Eller's trying to provide some security for Laurey, in the limited way that she can, by playing matchmaker. Sexual violation is a constant threat for women, even for Ado Annie, who is generally portrayed as a ditsy, well-meaning slut with her rendition of the song "I Cain't Say No."

Stroker's Ado Annie, on the other hand, delivers a rollicking, proudly sex-positive rendition of the song, a recognition of the character's agency.

Still, in both scenarios, Ado Annie's choices are protected by her father's ever-present shotgun–to a point. She may get around, and she may like it, but she's still got to marry *somebody*, and furthermore, someone with money. Ado Annie's father insists that a man vying for her affections have at least fifty dollars to his name before he'll let him marry her. (Remember, it's 1906.)

Laurey doesn't really have two viable options so much as she's faced with making a choice between a man who will almost certainly kill her if he doesn't get what he wants and a well-meaning dunce who thinks the height of being gentlemanly means getting down to the dirty business of dispatching the Territory's resident incel.

Jones is not the only member of the *Oklahoma!* company who is Black, but her Blackness serves to reinforce just how vulnerable and disenfranchised Laurey is in a place where men hold an overwhelming amount of sociopolitical power and women have nearly none. That social order is enforced and maintained with guns:

- When Ali Hakim won't commit to Ado Annie, her father threatens him with a shotgun.

- When Jud and Curly want to intimidate each other, they shoot holes into the roof and wall of the smokehouse.

- When Laurey finds herself in need of protection from one bad man, it comes from another wielding–you guessed it–a gun.

Jones plays Laurey as a woman moving through the world with tense, uneasy reluctance. At times, she exhibits an attraction to Curly, but it never seems to permeate too deeply, perhaps with the exception of the dream ballet (danced with magnetic athleticism by Gabrielle Hamilton) that explores Laurey's subconscious. It concludes with Laurey's id scooching crotch-first offstage toward Curly–she's made her "choice."

But even when Laurey agrees to marry Curly and enters the stage in her wedding dress, she's bereft of the glowing, floaty ebullience typically associated with brides. Instead, the subtle hesitations in Jones's movements and the drawn expression of her face leave the viewer wishing poor Laurey had a trusted maid of honor to ask, "You okay, sis?" It's a beautifully crafted performance, full of simmering internal contradictions that Laurey dare not raise aloud. She seems more resigned than anything to spend her life with Curly, if only because he provides protection from the Juds of the world and she knows that she needs it.

I could not help but see parallels between Laurey and the protagonist of *Test Pattern*, a film from director Shatara Michelle Ford. *Test Pattern* explores the aftermath of sexual assault for a Black woman living in Austin, Texas, named Renesha. Renesha (Brittany S. Hall) is in a loving inter-racial relationship when she is sexually assaulted during a celebratory night out with a friend. (Coincidentally, the two works share an actor; Will Brill plays Hakim in *Oklahoma!* and Renesha's boyfriend, Evan, in *Test Pattern*.) Like Laurey, Renesha ends up spending a great deal of time managing the emotions of two white men, one of whom is ostensibly "good" and the other who is "bad." It turns out the two men are not so different. Like Jud and Curly, they both prioritize their own wants over the needs of the Black woman who is the object of their desire or devotion. This is not accidental. In both the Territory of 1906 and modern-day Austin, the world is constructed to serve these men, and that's what they've come to expect. This is their version of neutral.

Oklahoma! becomes a jaunty horror show when Laurey is splattered with Jud's blood on her wedding day after Curly guns him down and the entire company belts out a lively rendition of "Oklahoma!" The residents of the Territory ignore the cancer destroying their community in favor of singing, dancing, and the avoidance of discomfort, in much the same way that no amount of tragic deaths seems to spur meaningful action on gun control.

Ultimately, *Oklahoma!* provides a nuanced opportunity for audiences to reexamine systems of power from the view of those least protected by them. The artists will even serve you chili and corn bread during the show's intermission. The timing is key–better to eat a bowl before "pore Jud is daid," when its contents can't remind you of his bullet-blasted innards.

Originally published September 16, 2019

A LESSON
IN EMPATHY
DO CRY ##

PR

VER 'AUTHENTIC' BLACKNESS

TS

UNDER THE **CORONAVIRUS LOCKDOWN,** A FATHER AND SON **REDISCOVER** THEIR LOVE FOR **BASEBALL**

Basketball rims and tennis nets were gone, but the diamond was still open for a game of catch.

BY DWAYNE BRAY

I COULD see his frustration growing. My son Nick's high school basketball season had ended in late February. Nothing had been normal in his life since then. He came home from boarding school in early March, expecting to return to campus later in the month. Of course he never went back, as the country shut down due to the coronavirus pandemic. I could see the absence of his routine was eating at him.

COVID-19 wreaked havoc on our nation, causing widespread illness and death, and shutting down the economy. There's nothing good associated with this horrible disease. That said, during this forced time-out, Nick and I rediscovered one pleasure that we'd lost over the years–the power of a father and son spending an hour or two on a baseball field, sharing a laugh and growing closer in these most uncertain of times.

Nick and I have always loved baseball. We used to practice it together three to four times a week until he turned twelve. That's when Nick, like a lot of other boys around that age, began specializing in a single sport, which in his case was hoops.

Like many sports-minded young Black men raised in the 1970s and early 1980s, I grew up idolizing baseball stars such as Jim Rice, Gaylord Perry, and Reggie Jackson as much as I idolized Dr. J and Magic Johnson. Over the years, while my wife and I raised Nick and his two older siblings, we transformed ourselves into a basketball family. But during the pandemic, Nick and I learned that if we wanted to play sports together, baseball was the best option. While cities were removing basketball rims and tennis nets from parks, no one closed off the local baseball fields. Like running trails, they were still available.

Nick was born in Arlington, Texas, and when he was a baby, I started rolling balls of all kinds his way. Baseballs. Tennis balls. Basketballs. Footballs. Golf balls. Before he was four, I took our games outside into the Texas heat. In our driveway and on the side of our home, I'd show him the art of dribbling with his off-hand, fielding ground balls, catching and throwing a spiral, running sprints and distances, as well as hitting a forehand and putting a golf ball. By age five, I was no longer pushing him. He was pulling me, demanding to go outside and "do sports."

Nick has two older siblings, but they were teenagers when he was born. A whole 'nother generation. I felt I needed to be even closer to him since he wasn't growing up with a brother or sister close to his age. His siblings were off to college by the time Nick began joining sports teams at age six, plus we'd moved to Connecticut and left the siblings in Texas to finish school. In our family, my wife dealt with all the serious stuff such as taking Nick to the doctor, feeding him nutritious meals, and making sure he was good at school. I'll admit it: I was lucky enough to be the "sports parent." My contribution was coaching my son's sports teams and making sure he had the skills to be able to play for as long as he chose.

Once we got to Connecticut, we signed Nick up for T-ball and for a basketball league. He loved both sports and also dabbled in cross-country, soccer, and tennis.

Things changed when Nick got to the eighth grade. That's when the high school coach at Kingswood Oxford School in West Hartford, Connecticut, put him on the varsity basketball team. He was about five-foot-seven, 135 pounds. I remember one game against Canterbury School, in which middle-school Nick got caught up in a switch and was matched up against Canterbury's top varsity player, Donovan Mitchell, the future NBA star (and onetime college baseball player). Nick gave up at least eight inches and seventy-five pounds to Mitchell. Needless to say, Mitchell got the best of Nick and his teammates, but we were proud that Nick was playing against such high-level talent. It was at that point that Nick decided he had to give up baseball if he wanted to compete against the best players in New England. Nick, now five-foot-eleven and 170 pounds, ended up with four hundred 3s in high school and was a first-team All New England player.

Before basketball took over Nick's life, he and I used to enjoy going to the park and hitting and throwing a baseball around the yard. Our sessions would always end with me on the mound and

Nick getting one final at-bat. He'd hit the ball as hard as he could and run the bases. Wherever the ball went, I'd have to run after it and then try to tag him out before he rounded home. It always seemed as if that last play ended at the plate. Most of the time he would score, but occasionally I'd run him down.

Through the years, I noticed that fewer Black fathers were taking the time to teach their children the fundamentals and intricacies of baseball. In our Connecticut community, only a handful of Black kids would come out for Little League baseball tryouts. But a couple of dozen Black kids would show up for travel basketball tryouts.

Baseball has been losing Black players for decades. The numbers are down in Little League, high school, and college. In 1981, nearly 19 percent of MLB was Black. Today, that number hovers around 7 percent. Only one Black kid who grew up with Nick is playing college baseball today, while dozens are playing some level of college hoops.

Shortly after the NBA suspended its season, our local recreation center shut its doors. No sweat, we thought. Nick and I would go to the park so he could stay sharp and put up hundreds of 3s a day. But officials advised people not to play ball in the park and removed the rims from all hoops throughout our community.

Nick suggested going to the golf range and driving some balls. But the golf ranges, like the golf courses, were closed. Next thing you know, the city was removing the nets from tennis courts. We were in full shutdown mode.

I was getting tired of watching Nick play video games and stream movies.

Then it dawned on me. Nick and I should restart the father-son baseball sessions we had abandoned once he became a varsity basketball player. They're part workout and part bonding. Nick liked my baseball idea. In fact, his face lit up when I mentioned it.

Our first trip back to the diamond happened the Saturday before Easter. The last time Nick and I had played baseball together, I was forty-eight. I'm now fifty-five. He was twelve. He's now nineteen. Years ago, skin-and-bones, wide-eyed Nick would jump into the passenger side of my car with his baseball glove and buckle up. Now a more buff Nick has facial hair. I thought we were riding to the baseball field together, but he jumped into his own car and said he'd meet me at the park. They grow up so fast.

We arrived at Elizabeth Park, which is across the road from the home of Connecticut governor Ned Lamont, who had issued strict orders about social distancing and staying home. The governor could look out his window and see Nick and me pulling up to the diamond. Nick joked that he'd gotten a robocall from the governor hours earlier, updating citizens on the virus. What if the governor saw us and sent state troopers to get us? Our crime: playing baseball in public during a pandemic.

They'd also have to arrest a few others who were in the park: a few joggers and a family flying a kite.

The field wasn't in good shape. The grass hadn't been cut, so the infield was overgrown with crabgrass and dandelions. The sun bathed us, and we smiled and stretched. It all seemed surreal, the times we were living in and the fact that dad and son were back on a baseball field for the first time in about eight years.

I began by tossing Nick some balls that he could hit into the fence above the backstop. That was always how we started things, back in the day. Next, he walked through the crabgrass and out to the mound. I crouched behind the plate and caught about twenty-five fastballs—some high, some wide, and some down the middle. Years earlier, I'd let him send fifty pitches my way, but bending down to catch fifty pitches isn't in the cards for me anymore.

We moved to short toss, and once our arms were loose, we tossed the ball long. I hit Nick some infield grounders, and he fielded most of the balls cleanly, given that he was working with uneven turf and tricky hops. Then we got to our main activity, which was dad hitting long fly balls to son, who would roam center field and shag them. We only had two baseballs and that was plenty.

"Hit it farther," Nick yelled after my first few flies were more shallow than he wanted. "Make me run."

As best I could, I tried to jack the ball but soon remembered the best way to hit it far was to relax and just make contact. It was all coming back to me. When I tried to hit the ball hard and far, I hit dribblers or missed altogether. When I relaxed and swung, I was more apt to send it soaring over Nick's head. He couldn't get to a few, but chased others down as if he were a Mookie Betts starter kit. After one good catch, Nick hollered, "Call the Mets!"

After about ten minutes in the outfield, Nick sprinted in and said, "Let's switch up. You go to the outfield and I'll do the hitting." After about another ten minutes we switched back.

After about an hour, I was spent. I knew we had one more thing to do. I pitched Nick a fastball and he jacked a screamer into deep left center. I ran as fast as I could after it. By the time I reached the ball, Nick had already crossed the plate. He didn't slow down to give me a chance. He just wanted to crush the old man. We laughed.

If it weren't for the isolated world of coronavirus that we live in, I doubt that Nick and I would have ever revived our baseball ritual. This was about dad and son and a game that we both love.

"I had forgot how much fun baseball is," Nick said to me as we packed up our equipment. "When I have kids, I'm going to make sure I play baseball with them.

"And when MLB comes back, I'm going to watch more of it," he said.

As I headed off to my car and he to his, he had one more thing to say.

"Dad, as long as things are shut down, let's keep doing baseball, okay?"

Three days later, we were out there again.

Originally published April 21, 2020

A **PGA VETERAN'S** CALLOUS JOKE ABOUT **BLACKFACE** AND **TIGER WOODS** TURNED INTO A LESSON ON **EMPATHY**

BY MICHAEL WILLIAMS

THERE ARE many pro golfers whose careers wax and wane, and there are a few players who endure. For two decades, Charles Howell III has been one of the most consistent players on the PGA Tour. Since turning professional in 2000, "Chucky Three Sticks" has amassed ninety top ten tournament finishes, including three wins and nineteen second-place finishes. He has accumulated $40 million in winnings while barely making a ripple on the general sports conscience because, at five-foot-ten and 160 pounds, Howell has been playing in the shadows of Tiger Woods, Dustin Johnson, and other bigger, stronger athletes.

As befits a player with such a strong record, Howell has made multiple appearances in the game's major tournaments: the PGA, the Open, the Masters, and the US Open. In 2019, he qualified for the US Open, which was being held at Pebble Beach Golf Links in Pebble Beach, California.

The competition on the course that year was amazing, with a resurgent Woods, fresh off a win at the Masters, in contention on the course where he had played perhaps the greatest golf ever in winning the championship in 2000. The combination of an iconic course and a stalking Woods made for a US Open that captured the interest of even the most casual of golf fans.

I had been invited to the tournament by one of the corporate sponsors of the USGA, the organization that owns and operates the US Open. One of the perks was the opportunity to attend private post-round interviews with players, including Howell, in the sponsor's hospitality tent beside the 18th fairway. As a golf journalist, I was familiar with Howell as a player, but I didn't know much about him personally. While he wasn't a contender to win (Howell finished tied for 52nd, 17 strokes behind winner Gary Woodland), I decided to attend to get some insight into how a physically unremarkable guy had willed himself to a remarkable career.

Todd Lewis of the Golf Channel was slated to ask Howell and fellow pro Patrick Cantlay about how the players thought they did, what their chances were, the difficulty of the course, etc. Typically, the players' answers would match the banality of the questions.

But after a couple of softballs, Lewis started recounting a story that Howell had shared with him when asked for an amusing anecdote. "You all remember the night Tiger Woods hit the fire hydrant with his car, right?" The seventy-five or so people in the tent laughed nervously and nodded, unsure why the 2009 accident outside Orlando, Florida, that contributed to Woods's tragic fall was being discussed at the national championship.

Lewis continued: "Now, just to set the scene, there were reporters' crews, camera crews, outside the gates of Isleworth from all over the world. I mean, it must've been a hundred fifty to two hundred people there. There were helicopters flying above, trying to get pictures of Tiger's house, the hydrant, Tiger, [whoever]. And looking for [his then-wife] Elin. Well, Charles decided he'd have some fun with all of that. Charles, pick up the story from there."

Howell then told a story about how he thought it would be funny to punk the media looking for Woods. "So, a friend of mine in the community drives a black Escalade, very similar to Tiger's. Now, this idea should have ended there because [Woods] had wrapped *his* Escalade around a fire hydrant and wasn't driving it. But we took the black Escalade and a friend of ours, who happened to be a blond female. So, we put her in the front seat, okay?

"And then I took a lot of shoe polish and Magic Marker and whatnot. And I made myself look like Tiger. . . . I put on a black Nike hat with a black Nike swoosh and we drove out the front gate really slow and they thought they found [Tiger and Elin]. And we saw how far around Orlando we could drive these people. . . . We drove to Disney. And, basically, they were following us, right. . . . Literally, we drove through Disney, we drove to Universal Studios, and we just kept driving. As far as we could do that. They thought they had found Tiger."

I was sitting about fifteen feet from Howell. I couldn't tell what was making me angrier: the ignorant, callous story or the laughter that was coming from the crowd. I moved to the back of the room and tried to compose myself. Did Howell really just publicly admit to wearing blackface as a joke? I knew that I would respond, but I didn't yet know exactly what that response would be and the impact it would have on me, on Howell, and on the game of golf.

My parents moved from the segregated South to Washington in the 1950s to make a life of opportunity for themselves and their children.

They succeeded, and their reward was a resting place in Arlington National Cemetery. Along with my sister and two brothers, I grew up never feeling limited because of my race. I attended the prestigious Sidwell Friends School, enrolling shortly after the school was integrated. When I graduated in 1980, I was the first African American male to attend the school from kindergarten through twelfth grade. Sidwell was overwhelmingly white, but I recall ethnic and economic differences making no difference there. But living in America, I was familiar with racism and bigotry.

We lived in a mostly Black neighborhood, and my school friends and my neighborhood friends were of very different hues and castes. My father was a human resources specialist for the State Department and one of the people responsible for establishing the Equal Employment Opportunity Commission, so we were always aware of systemic racial injustice and the toll it took on the country. My father also spent two decades in the Army Reserve and would brook no disrespect from those closest to him, much less from anyone attempting to discriminate against him. If he sensed racism in an interaction, he would react with the fury of a man who grew up in South Carolina, a state where sitting in the wrong seat or smiling at the wrong woman could cost you your life.

Golf was not a part of my upbringing. I had been to a driving range or golf course only a handful of times as an adult when, at the age of forty-one, I took a job as the marketing and communications director for the operator of the three National Park Service golf courses in Washington. I quickly became infatuated with the game. Part of the fascination was trying to improve as a player, but the far more engaging aspect was the extraordinary places that host golf's finest courses and the wonderful people you meet who frequent and operate them.

After seven memorable years managing courses, I became a

member of the golf media, one of only a few minorities to host a golf radio show in a major market for a network affiliate (CBS Radio). In 2014, I was named Media Person of the Year for the Middle Atlantic PGA Section, making me the first and only person of color to win an award in any category in the ninety-year history of the section.

Over the years, I have found those who love golf to be among the most fair-minded people I have ever met. But I also experienced the fact that people of color are at times a rare and unwanted presence. I have become accustomed to being the only African American in any clubhouse, media gathering, or industry meeting. And there is often the assumption that if a Black man is present at an elite golf course or resort, he must be a part of the staff. If I had a round of golf at Augusta National for every time someone handed me the keys to park their car or asked me to put their bag on a cart, well, I'd have more experience at Augusta than most of the players on the tour.

As I stood in the room at Pebble Beach, though, my roots in the game were in the distant past and the events of summer 2020 were still in the future. The only thing on my mind was finding the proper way to respond to what Howell had said.

Earlier that year, there had been calls for the resignation of Virginia governor Ralph Northam because of the discovery of blackface pictures of him that were thirty-five years old. The fact that a public figure such as Howell could tell that story seemed to me either the height of arrogance, colossally self-destructive, or a combination of the two.

I decided to wait until the question-and-answer portion of the talk to address the issue with Howell. Several people asked questions, but none had to do with the blackface comment. I could feel the eyes on me in the room, wondering if I was going to do it. I wasn't sure myself. I was there as a guest and I didn't want to blow the event up. But as a journalist and as a man, I had to address this.

When I felt that the last question had been asked and answered, I raised my hand. I said that I had a question and a comment. First, I asked a question about how he had managed to be so persistent in his career, mostly to make sure that my voice would not be shaking with anger. He answered, but I barely heard him because my mind was searching for the right words to raise the blackface story.

And then I decided to just say it like I felt it. "Charles, I want you to do yourself a favor and never, ever tell that story in public again, because it's embarrassing and it's ignorant. And in one moment you could blow up everything you've worked twenty years to achieve. You just don't know what you've said, and it's so dangerous and so offensive and you need to never ever do it again." The room was silent. Howell seemed puzzled. He looked at me and said, "Well, I don't know . . . they asked me for a funny story. And I gave him this one. Sorry. . . ."

The awkward exchange brought an end to the event. Afterward, about twenty people came up to me and said that they were glad I had said something. The PGA Tour representative there had Howell come over and apologize to me, which was basically, "I'm sorry if you were offended." (Later that day, I met with Lewis, who said Howell hadn't previously told him the part about donning blackface.)

After Howell's lukewarm apology, I was livid all over again, but also conflicted. This was my favorite tournament. I didn't want to blow up the entire week because of something that one guy said.

What I wanted to do was to take this incident and do some good with it. Rather than make a "gotcha" out of it and destroy this guy's life, I wanted to see if that's the way he really felt and, if it really was, to help him see things differently. I wanted to tell the story of the aftermath of that day at Pebble Beach. If it was a positive story, great. If it was the story of somebody who had no remorse, then so be it. But I was determined that I would, in my own time, tell the story.

Charles Gordon Howell III seemed destined to be a professional golfer. He was born June 20, 1979, the son of a pediatric surgeon, in Augusta, Georgia. Howell noted, "In a lot of towns, a lot of cities, you know, the cool thing is to play basketball or football. But in Augusta, we have this little tournament called the Masters that rolls around every April. Myself, and a lot of other kids in the area, we were introduced to golf via the Masters."

Howell excelled in junior golf tournaments, earning a reputation as one of the best young players in the country. But the combination of a privileged upbringing and playing a privileged sport in a city segregated by race and class—as well as his tendency to be an introvert—put Howell in a social bubble that is common among professional golfers. Ironically, golf also provided young Howell an opportunity to play at the local public course with the Black men who made their living caddying at Augusta National. "The caddies taught me how to play the game," Howell said. "They taught me the importance of short game. And they taught me a little bit about the art of gambling and trash-talking."

He earned a scholarship to Oklahoma State University, one of the most storied programs in college golf, which has produced no fewer than fifty PGA Tour professionals. Howell was a three-time All-American and winner of the NCAA men's individual championship his junior year. He seemed to have a lock on stardom on the PGA Tour. But by the time Howell joined the pro ranks, Woods was already changing the game with a combination of skill and power.

Howell had been aware of Woods since they both were junior

golfers, but coming from opposite sides of the country, they did not play against each other. Once on the pro tour, though, Howell saw the majesty of Woods's game. Like every golfer who has competed against him, Howell speaks of Woods in reverent tones. "It was Tiger and it was everybody else. He changed the whole world. He changed the whole golfing world to where he made golf cool."

In 2003, Howell moved to Isleworth, Florida, an exclusive gated community near Orlando that many of the world's top professionals call home. They are attracted by the sunshine, the luxurious amenities, and the absence of a state income tax. On any given day, you might see top-ten golfers playing practice rounds together while laying side bets that would be a month's rent for most people.

Once there, he established a cordial, if not close relationship with Woods, whose superstardom put him at arm's length for all except his family and a select group in his circle. "Tiger liked me because I minded my own business, I practice hard, and I never got in his way. He'd let me tag along sometimes and that turned into working out together in the morning. We'd play and practice all day, then maybe a quick dinner at night. I turned into sort of a . . . a practice buddy, if you will."

Three years after Howell joined the tour, he and Woods were both selected for the 2003 Presidents Cup, an international team competition. Howell and his wife joined Woods and his wife on a private jet ride to the event, which was held that year near Cape Town, South Africa. Woods also provided a boost of confidence and mentorship. "Hey, listen, you're going to see how good you are this week, number one," Howell recalls Woods saying. "And number two is I got you. You just stay under my wing all week. I'll show you everything." Howell partnered with Woods in every pairs match in the competition, and he got his first look at what life was like for Woods on the golf course. "I never appreciated it until then. My goodness, like this guy is a walking bull's-eye. Like, everywhere you go, there's thirty-five photographers, there's twenty-five cameras. I'm like, 'How do you do it?' And he would just look at me and just laugh."

Over time, the connection between the two men faded. "I haven't had a long conversation with him in a long while," said Howell. "He became very private and to himself as the years have gone on."

In some ways, Howell was fortunate that day at Pebble Beach. I was the only journalist in the room and the only one recording the event. The crowd in the room was forgiving. I decided not to go public with the story immediately; the scandal of a tape of a tour player joking about wearing blackface would have been difficult to weather, for the tour and for Howell. But Howell's sponsor required that he undergo racial sensitivity training. It was during those sessions that Howell realized the gravity of what had happened, and how much worse it could have gone for him.

"I spent six hours with this gentleman who works in diversity, inclusivity. And I said, 'I want to know it all,'" recounted Howell. "I said, 'I've lived my whole life not wanting to upset a soul–I mean, to a fault. And I've been a Christian in my faith, something I'm extremely proud of. I don't want to hurt anybody.' What did I learn? The concept of intent versus impact."

Howell described how the counselor explained it. "Let's just be honest. There are some people who intend to hurt other people. But, Charles, there's a lot of people, like you on that day, where there's zero intent whatsoever. But you did hurt someone. And that's when it hit me, like, 'Holy cow, thank you. I've got to understand and learn better.'"

Howell said he fell into a period of depression that prompted more counseling. Afterward, he sought advice and insight from the Black people in his life. "I set off on a whole lot of conversations, a whole lot of group messages, a whole lot of group chats, everything. And I reached out to a lot of different people. . . . What can I learn? What can I do?"

Bruce Berryman is a forty-three-year-old sports performance specialist who works with a number of elite athletes in the Orlando area, including Howell. The two struck up an acquaintance in the gym that evolved into a professional and personal relationship. Howell says that Berryman is "one of my best friends . . . I love him."

Berryman has nothing but good things to say about Howell. "[Charles] has this amazing ability to adapt very well as an athlete. And one of the first things that drew me to Charles was his character. . . . He's always been an upstanding guy and always been straightforward with me and . . . and very respectful."

Berryman is a faithful friend to Howell, but he is also an African American, familiar with racism and its cancerous effect on society. When asked about the conversations he had with Howell about the blackface incident, Berryman processes it through both of those filters.

"Knowing Charles, I know where it came from. It came from a place of really trying to tell something funny," he said. "I definitely can see how it could be taken differently, for sure. But like I said, knowing him and knowing his character, it wasn't being told in a way to demean anyone."

Berryman said he explained to Howell about schisms in society that his life and career had shielded him from, the kinds of experiences that were fueling the unrest in the country.

"Growing up, I experienced racial discrimination and police profiling. And we talked about, you know, the conversation that is very common in the Black community, the conversations I had with my father telling me how to say 'Yes, ma'am' and 'Yes, sir.' Cops pull you over, have your registration already out, keep your hands on the steering wheel, you know, look them in the eye. So we have that conversation because, you know, he never had that conversation or had to experience dealing with that."

"So in that regard, his eyes opened up, like, 'Wow, this is a whole new world,'" Berryman said.

After the protests began over George Floyd's death while in police custody, Howell reached out to PGA Tour commissioner Jay Monahan and fellow tour professional Harold Varner III, one of the few African Americans currently on the tour, to listen to ideas and offer suggestions for how golf could make a meaningful impact. He later announced on Instagram that he was partnering with the Advocates Pro Golf Association (APGA), a small professional golf circuit that serves as a gateway for minority golfers to sharpen their game in hopes of ascending to the PGA Tour. "I believe in a better America, and I want to be a part of the solution," Howell wrote.

Because of the COVID-19 pandemic, this year's US Open was moved from its traditional mid-June slot. I had wanted to meet with Howell around the anniversary of last year's competition, but the restrictions around travel and access made scheduling difficult. We finally managed to get together in Greensboro, North Carolina, in August before the Wyndham Championship, one of the events that had been rescheduled due to the temporary shutdown of the tour. (Howell finished thirteen-under in a five-way for fourth place.)

As I prepared for the five-hour drive from my home in Washington, any feelings of trepidation that I had about the trip were connected to traveling. I had been sheltering against COVID-19 for months. I normally log twenty thousand miles a year in air travel, but in 2020 I had barely seen the other side of my own city. When I arrived, the hotel lobby was almost deserted, the complete opposite of the typical hustle and bustle of the host hotel at a PGA Tour event.

I suspected that some self-preservation instincts would kick in for Howell before our interview, prompted by Howell's manager floating the idea–contradicted by my tape from the event–that he had not actually done the blackface prank but was repeating a story he had heard about two teens who had done it. I worried that the announcement of the donation to the Advocates Tour was an attempt to put "foam on the runway" before my story about Pebble Beach became public. But whenever I talked or texted with Howell before our meeting, he assured me that he trusted me to tell the story fairly, so I persisted with my efforts to meet in person, confident that once in the room with him, I would be able to assess his sincerity.

We met in a conference room at the hotel. As I waited for Howell to arrive, I took the measure of my own emotions. This was a meeting that had been a full year in the making, and I wanted to be sure my motivations were in the right place. The Black Lives Matter movement against racial injustice had impacted me. I resolved to make the interview not be about any perceived grievance or reckoning for things outside of the events that had occurred at Pebble Beach.

I had a mask on when Howell arrived. But he immediately took off his mask, so I took a deep breath and did the same. In a nod to his faith and mine, I asked him if he minded if I said a prayer before we began. He smiled and said, "Yes, please." I said a short prayer, thanking God for bringing us together and asking that he use our meeting and our relationship to make a positive change in the world.

As our conversation evolved, I found a man who had gone through more than just counseling. Howell had been through a transformation and was unafraid to talk about it. He told me that what happened that day and the counseling that followed affected his relationships, his playing ability, and his mental and spiritual well-being.

He told me he wanted to see if he could make what he called "the worst day of my life" into something positive. I found someone who had gone a long way from the person who gave a cursory apology for a very hurtful story. Howell told me, "Michael, I'm sorry about what happened, but I went through a lot just because I knew how much I had hurt you."

It became clear that our interaction at Pebble Beach was far more impactful for him than it was for me. Golfers are unique because they are required to know the rules and call penalties on themselves. Howell had come to understand that he had made two mistakes, the clumsy blackface prank and the use of it as an amusing anecdote, and he was calling the penalty on himself.

He said that he felt he had hurt and embarrassed me. The truth was I was angry, but I was embarrassed for *him*, not myself. I also found it incredible that he would be so concerned about the response of one individual that he would be prompted to go through all that he had been through, but he insisted that was the case. He said the interaction with me had triggered a chain reaction, and when he shared what had happened at Pebble Beach with the Black people in his life and understood how hurtful it had been to them, it added to the pain and to his sense of debt and burden. He also told me that from the time in mid-June when he agreed to speak with me for this story, he felt he had begun to play better. "It just feels like a weight has lifted," said Howell.

I applaud the work he's doing now with the minority golf tour, but it's important that the real reasons that spurred this be told. Otherwise, it is just another person saying, "I have some extra money, let me throw it at a couple of people who have a little bit less." Howell has redoubled his efforts with the Advocates Tour, providing not only cash but his time by mentoring young players, providing tee times and instruction to players who have talent but lack the connections and intangibles that make the difference between tour dreams and tour titles. He is also rallying his fellow PGA pros and the tour itself to invest in the APGA tour or other efforts to promote diversity, equality, and social justice. If he sustains his efforts, it is quite possible that Howell's impact off the course will outstrip his playing accomplishments.

"Some amazing things are happening around the Advocates Tour and some other things we are doing. I hope the momentum continues," he said. "We are really affecting lives in a positive way and I love it."

It's tempting to think that Howell is just trying to buy a good reputation. But the truth is more complex than that. The hole that he's seeking to fill is not only in society and in the community—he's seeking to fill a hole within himself.

At the end of this story, two people who were strangers become friends. I know that because he said so. During one of our conversations to arrange the Greensboro meeting, Howell said to me, "Michael, I'm sorry that this all happened. But in a way, I'm glad because I'm a better person because it happened. And I got to meet you because it happened. And I can tell you that you're going to have a friend for life because of what this is."

I accept Charles's friendship and he has mine. And I tell this story in the spirit of friendship and spirit of service to the wider community, because we can all use a story of redemption right now. I sat down with Charles for a face-to-face conversation. We talked about what had happened during the past year. We talked as colleagues in the golf world. And we talked as people who have a unique relationship because of what happened in a different conversation a year ago. It is my hope and his that our experience can serve as a template for others, an example of the curative powers of patience and understanding.

Originally published September 17, 2020

THE **THANKSGIVING** AN IMPRISONED **JACK JOHNSON** FOUGHT TWO MEN AT **LEAVENWORTH**

BY ROBERTO JOSÉ ANDRADE FRANCO

THE WARDEN at Leavenworth Federal Prison had scheduled the fights to start at three in the afternoon. But guests started arriving at noon and officials struggled to find enough seats to accommodate the crowd of two thousand, including three hundred reporters, state officials, and other notables.

The rest of the crowd was made up of prisoners dressed in their usual striped outfits, who, after eating Thanksgiving dinner, were led out to the yard by guards and armed soldiers. A band made up of inmates played while snipers and cameras looked down on the specially constructed outdoor boxing ring. The former kept watch while the latter filmed the momentous event. It was the first time in years that Jack Johnson–Inmate #15461–would box on U.S. soil.

Most Americans hadn't seen Johnson since he fled the country seven years earlier. When he fought on that Thanksgiving afternoon in 1920, Johnson was forty-three and at least a decade past his athletic prime. But he was always more than a boxer. The first African American heavyweight champion and a man unafraid to cross racial lines in his romantic life, Johnson embodied the country's anxieties over race. His success prompted a backlash from people as high as former president Theodore Roosevelt, who advocated for boxing's banishment, to those who invited Johnson to Mississippi to show him their brand of hospitality.

In 1913, Johnson was convicted under the Mann Act of allegedly transporting a white woman across state lines for immoral purposes. During the trial in Chicago, protesters hanged Johnson in effigy. A dummy with its face blackened with paint swung from a tree and included a placard reading "This is what we will do for Jack Johnson." Three weeks later, a group in Midland, Texas, sent a letter to the prosecuting attorney, informing him that if he killed Johnson, they'd contribute $100,000 for his defense. When rumors spread of Johnson's assassination–either by a white woman or her relatives, depending on the version– several newspapers published regrets that the boxer remained alive. When a reporter informed Johnson of the rumor, he replied, "Do I look dead?"

Eight years later, he was in Leavenworth, still alive. Johnson entered the ring that day wearing a skullcap and bathrobe while the prison band played and inmates cheered. It was likely the first time most people at a Johnson fight had rooted for him. But despite all the people there, his wife, Lucille, the one person who'd always cheered for Johnson, was missing. "Sorry you can't come to see me," Johnson wrote her in a telegram, "but you will understand– no ladies admitted."

Johnson planned to fight twice that day. In the weeks beforehand, he relied on his wife to send along supplies: boxing shoes size ten-E, or "ten half D," and five-ounce boxing gloves. For his training, he asked her to send arm bracelets to "pull against horses." They communicated through long letters and telegrams, and Johnson ended his correspondence each time with a loving phrase: "Love and kisses to you," "Best love for you," "Love with kisses." Their love was strong, although they had a complicated relationship–to say the least.

Lucille, who was white, was at the center of what landed Johnson in prison. When they first met, she was eighteen and, some sources suggest, may have been a sex worker. He was thirty-five and widowed. Soon after they met, her mother demanded that police rescue Lucille from Johnson, who she claimed had abducted her daughter. It didn't matter that Lucille repeatedly mentioned that she loved Johnson and planned to marry him. Authorities and her mother dismissed those claims as lunacy. Lucille's mother would later claim that she'd rather see her daughter "spend the rest of her life in an insane asylum than see her the plaything of a n––––."

Police arrested and charged Johnson with violating the Mann Act and raided his Chicago nightclub in search of white slaves. They also arrested Lucille, hoping to use her as a witness against Johnson, but also out of worry that she'd run away and marry him. Authorities released her only after her mother promised to take her from Chicago. Lucille quickly ran back to the city and married Johnson in a ceremony at his house filled with what one newspaper described as "color-blind kisses." The case against Johnson collapsed until authorities found another woman to testify against him. During the second trial, an all-white, all-male jury convicted

Johnson after deliberating for ninety minutes. The judge sentenced him to a year and a day in prison.

"This defendant is one of the best-known men of his race," the judge explained during sentencing, "and his example has been far-reaching, and the court is bound to consider the position he occupied among his people. In view of these facts, this is a case that calls for more than a fine." Johnson and his wife fled the country.

In his first fight that Thanksgiving Day, Johnson toyed with his African American opponent, Frank Owens, a modestly talented pro from Chicago and a friend of Johnson's who had come down for the exhibition. Johnson knocked Owens down twelve times before ending the fight in the sixth round with a left hook to his jaw. Afterward, Johnson stood in the ring and rested a few minutes before facing his second opponent.

It was no more than forty degrees outside–average for that time of year in northeastern Kansas. As Johnson told his wife in one of their many prison telegrams, "Weather doesn't bother me." By that point, compared with everything that had occurred, whether it was cold or hot must have felt trivial.

When Johnson chose self-exile, he and his wife traveled across Europe and Latin America for seven years. In the nine months before arriving at Leavenworth, Johnson was a guest of Mexican president Venustiano Carranza. This was the same Carranza who in 1914, when the Mexican Revolution had devolved into civil war, threatened to capture and turn Johnson over to the United States if he set foot in the country. The threat came after Carranza's foe, Pancho Villa, attempted to increase his war chest by hosting a fight between Johnson and Jess Willard in Ciudad Juárez. But with Johnson unable to arrive safely, promoters moved the fight to Cuba, where Willard defeated Johnson on April 5, 1915.

The symbolism of Willard, the latest Great White Hope, standing over a beaten Johnson wasn't lost on anyone. That picture became a common decoration in speakeasies across the United States. Johnson would later claim to have intentionally lost to Willard, saying representatives of the Justice Department had promised that if he lost, they'd be lenient on his prison sentence. Whether anyone made that promise is unknown, but no leniency was granted and Johnson remained in exile, eventually landing in Mexico.

For much of their history, Mexico and the United States have had a contentious relationship. So it wasn't surprising that the Mexican government saw Johnson as a victim of the American justice system and embraced him as a brother fighting against oppression.

With the government's blessing, Johnson taught self-defense to high-ranking military officials and put on boxing exhibitions. There were even plans to make him into a movie star, playing an adventurer named Pedro Cronolio–the polar opposite of how films in the United States portrayed African Americans. (In the end, Johnson never made any movies in Mexico. But after his imprisonment, he starred in two films in the United States: *For His Mother's Sake* and *The Black Thunderbolt*.) Johnson also headed a land company that advertised in African American newspapers, essentially recruiting others to join him south of the border.

One advertisement read: "You, who are lynched, tortured, mobbed, persecuted and discriminated against in the boasted land of liberty, the United States. Own a home in Mexico. Here, one man is as good as another, and it is not your nationality that counts but simply you." The advertisement ended by stating, "Best of all, there is no race prejudice in Mexico, and severe punishment is meted out to those who discriminate against a man because of his color or race."

Despite Johnson's advertisement, Mexico was not a paradise of racial equality. And soon the Mexican Revolution's violence claimed the life of Carranza. Fearing for his own safety after the assassination of the president who had welcomed and protected him, Johnson decided to leave Mexico to serve his time in the United States.

On July 20, 1920, Johnson, accompanied by his wife, walked from Tijuana across the United States–Mexico border and presented his passport to a San Diego County deputy sheriff. Authorities then took Johnson to Los Angeles before returning him to Chicago. Johnson asked only that they not travel through Texas, his home state, because he feared residents would attack him. Authorities changed their travel plans and drove around the state.

In Chicago, thousands of African Americans welcomed Johnson's return—even though he was in custody. Police fought back the crowd to make way for Johnson and his wife. Johnson spent months in Joliet Prison and Geneva Jail before a judge ordered him to Leavenworth, where he entered on September 19, 1920, to a crowd of cheering inmates. Five days later, he sent a telegram to his wife in Chicago informing her he'd arranged for her to receive fifty dollars every two weeks.

Johnson's second fight that Thanksgiving came against another African American pro boxer, thirty-seven-year-old "Topeka" Johnson. The fight went four full rounds, with the former heavy-weight champ dominating the other man.

Observers who had received the warden's special invites noted Johnson's conditioning—he had entered the prison two months earlier at six-foot-one, 225 pounds—and that, despite his age, he "still retain[ed] much of his cleverness and punching power."

After the two fights, Johnson telegraphed his wife. "Everything went lovely yesterday," he wrote. "Was sorry that you weren't there." A few days later, he wrote her again, informing her that during the event, he—the great symbol of racial anxiety, whom detractors often portrayed as subhuman–had caught a cold, had a toothache, and had hurt his hand.

Johnson asked his wife to send along a recipe for "nerve medicine" and write him a long letter to help him pass the time. Inmate #15461 ended the telegram by writing, "Love and kisses," before signing it "Jack."

Originally published November 22, 2017

KAEPERNICK AND THE DEBATE OVER "AUTHENTIC" BLACKNESS

Some supporters of the controversial quarterback criticize others as traitors or sellouts, a tactic that goes back to Du Bois and Malcolm X.

BY MICHAEL A. FLETCHER

HOW DID Colin Kaepernick become a litmus test for authentic Blackness?

Some of Kaepernick's supporters have denounced people who disagree with aspects of his protest as racial traitors. The repeated attacks formed a disturbing subplot to the Kaepernick saga not long after he began kneeling during the playing of the national anthem to call urgent attention to police brutality and racial inequality. The discord has arisen repeatedly as Kaepernick's exile from the NFL looked like it would become permanent.

The quarterback's closest backers have suggested that they feel betrayed by anyone who partners with the league they accuse of blackballing him—even if those partners share his goals. Ironically, even as Kaepernick remains sidelined, legions of Black NFL fans have been tuning in to watch a new generation of Black quarterbacks lead a resurgence of interest in the NFL. But that has not stopped Kaepernick's backers from firing rhetorical salvos at African Americans they see as lending comfort to the NFL.

The tension burst into view when Kaepernick supporters called out hip-hop mogul Jay-Z after his company, Roc Nation, signed a deal to advise the NFL on social justice and entertainment projects, including the Super Bowl halftime show. Jay-Z's past support of Kaepernick and his long history of using his money and cultural cachet to promote social justice hardly seemed to matter to his critics. Not long after the deal was announced, for instance, the hashtag #JayZSellout was trending on Black Twitter.

Carolina Panthers safety Eric Reid, one of Kaepernick's closest friends, was no kinder in 2018 when he denounced Philadelphia Eagles safety Malcolm Jenkins, a leader of the Players Coalition, as a "neo-colonialist" after the NFL announced an $89 million pledge to the coalition to promote social justice advocacy and programs.

Similar views were echoed in a torrent of social media posts directed at ESPN's Stephen A. Smith and Jason Whitlock of Fox Sports. Both had criticized Kaepernick for turning his back on an NFL-arranged workout that was billed as an opportunity for him to get back into the league. Many of the critics pointedly questioned the racial loyalty of the two prominent Black commentators.

Racial authenticity is often invoked to simultaneously raise the stakes in a dispute and shut it down. "To use race is also a form of coercion," essayist and cultural critic Darryl Pinckney said. "It says, 'My argument is unanswerable because it comes from the moral high ground of my inherited history.'"

That can be true even when the parties on either side of a disagreement share the same history–and the same goals. All of that is intensified by the hothouse of social media, where many of these arguments play out. People are "canceled" all the time, mainly for being willing to compromise or otherwise demonstrating their impurity. Nuance or context is often taken for weakness on those platforms.

"I think it is very unfortunate that people choose to engage like that around Kaepernick, because everyone is trying to pursue their own path of activism," said Samuel T. Livingston, director of the African American Studies Program at Morehouse College. "There is no one way to engage in that activism. There is no one way to be Black or to be Black and an activist."

The most visible opposition to Kaepernick's protest has come from prominent white people, including former president Donald Trump and Fox News commentators Sean Hannity and Tucker Carlson. Polls have shown that while most Black NFL fans hold a favorable view of Kaepernick, the reverse is true for white fans. All of that has added to the racial cast of the debate surrounding Kaepernick, leading some of his supporters to contend that if you in any way oppose him, or his tactics, you are lending credence to the views of his (mostly white) detractors.

After Dallas Cowboys owner Jerry Jones said he would not tolerate players on his team protesting during the playing of the national anthem, Black quarterback Dak Prescott said he was unbothered. "We know about social injustice," he told reporters. "I'm up for taking the next step, whatever that step might be, for action."

For that, Prescott was pilloried–often in racial terms. "When

Jerry Jones, who owns 'America's team,'" drew a line in the sand, "Dak Prescott is out here basically saying he's happy being a lemonade serving house negro," tweeted Shadow League columnist Carron J. Phillips.

The desire for ideological purity and the way people line up behind a perceived leader are not unique to African Americans, nor do they come into play only around racial issues. Some fervent supporters of Senator Bernie Sanders said "Bernie or bust," meaning they weren't sure they would back the 2020 Democratic nominee if Sanders wasn't on the ballot. On the flip side, for many years, some conservative Republicans derided moderates in their party as RINOs–Republican In Name Only.

In some ways, the on-and-off friction over Kaepernick among Black people is as old as Black activism itself. In his 1903 classic, *The Souls of Black Folk*, W. E. B. Du Bois said Black Americans have tended toward three basic responses to their circumstances in America: revolt and revenge, an attempt to adjust to the will of the majority, and a focused effort at self-development.

Over the decades, many have viewed "revolt and revenge" as the most authentically Black, even if elements of all three responses might be necessary to achieve lasting progress. That may be why the poet Amiri Baraka once disparaged writer and playwright James Baldwin for being popular among white liberals. Or why Malcolm X called the likes of Martin Luther King Jr., Thurgood Marshall, Adam Clayton Powell Jr., and Jackie Robinson "Uncle Toms" for, one way or another, compromising with white people.

Sometimes, the insults become circular. Du Bois himself was called an Uncle Tom by Marcus Garvey, who did not like interracial coalitions and integration. Then Garvey was deemed a sellout–and much worse–for his many statements supporting the racist rhetoric of white supremacists, and for collaborating with the murderous

Ku Klux Klan. Garvey, who thought returning to Africa was the best hope for African Americans, reasoned that he and the Klan shared a goal: racial separation.

Marshall, who had been criticized by Malcolm X, used a similar tactic in criticizing Nat King Cole. After the celebrated singer performed in front of a segregated audience in Alabama, Marshall, then a crusading civil rights lawyer, called him a racial traitor. "[All] Cole needs to complete his role as an Uncle Tom is a banjo," Marshall said.

Until recently, no one would have guessed that Kaepernick would be seen as the test of Black authenticity. He is the child of a white mother and a Black father, who grew up with adoptive white parents in the small city of Turlock in central California. His political awakening began when he joined the Kappa Alpha Psi fraternity while he was a star quarterback at the University of Nevada. But that did not result in any overt activism for years. An outstanding and curious student, he read Black history and sought out mentors, but he did not emerge as an activist until a rash of highly publicized police shootings of Black men led him to begin his protest in 2016.

"I am not going to stand up to show pride in a flag for a country that oppresses Black people and people of color," Kaepernick said then. "To me, this is bigger than football, and it would be selfish on my part to look the other way. There are bodies in the street and people getting paid leave and getting away with murder."

He has rarely spoken publicly during his exile from football. While he has millions of social media followers, he uses those platforms mainly to echo posts from his tight circle of supporters, to promote Nike products he is paid to endorse, and to update people on how long he has been kept off NFL gridirons.

Much of his activism is achieved through symbols, and many of them are of what Du Bois would call the "revolt and revenge" ilk that contribute to the idea that Kaepernick somehow represents authentic Blackness. There are shots of his billowing Afro, photo shoots evocative of 1960s Black activists, and provocative T-shirts, such as the one bearing the name of the defiant (and fictional) slave Kunta Kinte that he wore to his abortive NFL tryout.

There can be little argument that Kaepernick's stance has transformed him into a cultural force. If Kaepernick were still playing football, who would care when he was spotted in the stands at the US Open? Would it make news if he objected to the use of the original American flag on a pair of sneakers designed by Nike, the sporting goods behemoth he endorses? Or would his $110 Nike "True to 7" sneakers sell out in just hours? Certainly, there would not have been a dozen children's books written about him if he were still playing.

Yet, as uncomfortable as Kaepernick's growing status as an icon of protest may be for the NFL, it is also true that the league has enjoyed a period of renewed prosperity since he has been sidelined. Led by the play of several top Black quarterbacks, the NFL is enjoying a surge in popularity, even as one of its best-known Black quarterbacks, Kaepernick, remains unsigned. Television ratings are up, and interest in the game–including from African Americans, the league's most ardent fans–is high.

"It remains true that the NFL is a great unifier for American sports fans, and the story lines just keep on coming," said Jay Rosenstein, a former vice president of programming at CBS Sports. "It is hard to measure the effect of the debate over Kaepernick. For every person who says his actions were virtuous or unpatriotic, there seems to be many more people who are just going to watch their teams."

Many African Americans are no doubt angry about what they see as the blackballing of a figure who risked his career to speak out for racial justice. But while Black fans may be with Kaep, apparently few have gone as far as abandoning the NFL to show their support. And no one is questioning anyone's racial authenticity because they are interested in seeing Patrick Mahomes or Lamar Jackson perform on the field.

"The Kaepernick dilemma is the Black American dilemma in a nutshell: Black folk are outraged by the manifest mistreatment of a man who as a result of his principled stance has become an icon mentioned in league with some of our most noteworthy figures of the past," said Michael Eric Dyson, a social critic and Georgetown University professor. "Black folk wisely protest the administration of the Kaepernick case but affirm the value of the NFL–which has been horrible to a Black man like Kaep, but has provided opportunity to Black men by the thousands."

None of that has diminished Kaepernick's impact. His activism has undoubtedly raised awareness of issues civil rights leaders work on daily, even if it at times has caused dissension.

"I have a lot of respect for how he has used the platform that he has to model what change looks like," said Rashad Robinson, president of Color of Change, a civil rights group. "His cultural advocacy has forced people to reckon with something they didn't want to reckon with. What he has done has been a tremendous help to those of us who are working to kick out district attorneys who don't value Black lives. To change laws around money bail. To expose issues of policing and mass incarceration in deep ways. He has provided an on-ramp for people to have these conversations, to debate, to feel uncomfortable."

Originally published January 22, 2020

THE **MORAL ARGUMENT** FOR KEEPING **BARRY BONDS** OUT OF **COOPERSTOWN** DOESN'T HOLD UP

The Hall of Fame has enshrined mediocre talents and stone-cold racists. It can open its doors for the home run king.

BY JUSTIN TINSLEY

WHEN THE 2019 Baseball Hall of Fame class, led by New York Yankees closer Mariano Rivera, was formally enshrined in Cooperstown, New York, it was the seventh consecutive year that Barry Bonds failed to get enough votes from the Baseball Writers' Association of America to be included. For years, people have passionately argued for excluding Bonds, Roger Clemens, and other benighted characters of baseball's "steroid era." Yet it may be time to revisit both the wisdom and the morality of that position.

John Thorn, Major League Baseball's official historian since 2011, makes an obvious point about Bonds's performance on the field.

"I would say that if I were asked, apart from pitchers, who were the greatest baseball players of all time, and your answer were to be someone other than Willie Mays, Babe Ruth, Ted Williams, or Barry Bonds, that you're crazy."

He pauses momentarily before picking back up. "[Bonds] is at that level."

Bonds, a left fielder, began his twenty-two-year career with the Pittsburgh Pirates in 1986 before signing with the San Francisco Giants in 1992. His Hall of Fame–caliber career, solidified well before the allegations of performance-enhancing drugs, is quite literally one-of-one: seven-time MVP (including four consecutive from 2001 to 2004), fourteen-time All-Star, eight-time Gold Glove winner, twelve-time Silver Slugger winner, two-time batting champion, three-time TSN Major League Player of the Year, the all-time leader in home runs (762), walks (2,558), and intentional walks (688), and still the only man to hit at least four hundred home runs and steal at least four hundred bases (500/500 too).

Other organizations have seen fit to honor Bonds. He was inducted into the Bay Area Sports Hall of Fame in 2015 with former Giants manager Dusty Baker. The Giants retired his number 25 jersey in 2018. And in 2019, Bonds was inducted into the California Sports Hall of Fame.

But Bonds was passed over for the starting lineup in MLB's All-Century Team in 1999 in favor of the more popular Ken Griffey Jr. And his deliberately confrontational approach to the media–David Halberstam once called it an "abuse of power" in which Bonds engaged in "unprovoked, deliberate, gratuitous acts of rudeness towards all kinds of people"–may be hurting him now.

Of course, the behavior that poses his biggest obstacle to Cooperstown is his alleged connection to performance-enhancing drugs. Bonds was the highest-profile player linked to a federal investigation of illegal doping at the BALCO lab in the Bay Area. According to a 2007 federal indictment, anabolic steroids were found in Bonds's system in November 2000–three years before baseball implemented a drug testing system. A mistrial was declared over three charges that he made false statements to a grand jury that he never knowingly received steroids or human growth hormone. But a jury did find him guilty of obstruction of justice for evasive testimony about his drug use. Bonds appealed, and in 2015 a federal appeals court overturned the verdict. He never admitted to nor was he convicted of using performance-enhancing substances, although in many pockets of the court of public opinion, especially the one holding court over his spot in Cooperstown, Bonds remains a stain on the game's legacy.

For Claire Smith, Major League Baseball's first female beat reporter and a longtime voter in favor of Bonds, there's always a sense of what-if.

"If there wasn't that constant cloud following him, I think that period would have been really without compare in terms of the brilliance of an artist at work at the plate. But it always was under a cloud," said Smith, who has been honored by the Hall of Fame for her work. "It was always accompanied by Barry being closed off and scowling and not being the easiest person to be around.

"I just regret that we didn't get to see him in a vacuum. That it always had the baggage, it always had the era. Other people had been allowed to shed the era and go on with their lives and rehabilitate their image. [Barry] never had that opportunity."

In 2017, Joe Morgan, Cooperstown's vice chairman and a 1990 Hall of Fame inductee, sent a letter to Hall of Fame voters urging them not to consider steroid users for future inclusion. "Players who failed drug tests, admitted using steroids, or were identified as users in [MLB's] investigation into steroid use, known as the Mitchell Report should not get in," he wrote. "Please keep in mind I don't speak for every single member of the Hall of Fame. . . . I do know how many of the Hall of Famers feel."

More than a decade removed from the Mitchell Report, which identified more than eighty-five players and rocked baseball to its core, the debate about whether players connected to PEDs should have a place in the Hall of Fame is still hot. Protecting the integrity of the game is most important, some argue. Bonds's inclusion would be an insult to Hank Aaron, others claim. A few, such as Reggie Jackson, Chipper Jones, and Andruw Jones, stand on the other side of the aisle. Pete Rose, baseball's most infamous exile, said that without Bonds the Hall of Fame didn't deserve its name.

Cooperstown is already full of questionable inductees based on their on-field performance alone. When you add questions of morality, there are Hall of Famers who now don't look so great. Consider the story of Adrian Constantine "Cap" Anson.

Cooperstown officially opened its museum doors on June 12, 1939. Anson, considered the greatest player and manager of the nineteenth century, was among the class of '39 after being voted in posthumously by the Veterans Committee. He had the stats: the first member of baseball's three-thousand-hit club, he led the league in RBIs eight times and was a four-time batting champion who averaged .415 in 1872 and .399 in 1881, albeit in far fewer games than today's standards (and even those numbers are apocryphal).

Anson, as many baseball purists are well aware, was a racist. Famously, on July 14, 1887, Anson, of the Chicago White Stockings, refused to play against the Newark Little Giants because of its Black pitcher, George Stovey. It wasn't the first time Anson had objected to competing against Black players. But on this particular day, the directors of the International League met and decided that contracts would no longer be offered to Black men except for those already employed in the league. In a separate gentlemen's agreement, Blacks were excluded from the major leagues beginning in 1885, and baseball's color barrier would last another sixty years, until the name Jackie Robinson entered the American consciousness and changed the course of history.

How can Major League Baseball, which proudly celebrates Robinson's legacy every season, continue to keep Anson, whose name has become synonymous with the history of segregation in baseball, in its most hallowed halls while Bonds remains a pariah? Segregation was far more destructive than performance-enhancing drugs in regard to evaluating talent in baseball. This much is irrefutable. Baseball history would be completely different if players such as Josh Gibson and Satchel Paige had been given the opportunity to suit up against Babe Ruth and Lou Gehrig.

"If you're going to have an asterisk in baseball at all—and the commissioners have already ruled you should not," Thorn said, regarding the assertion that Bonds's records should be recognized as tainted, "then that asterisk might more easily apply to every white player prior to 1947 because those players did not face the best possible competition. From my standpoint, moralism ought not to enter into it. You've got some very dubious characters already with bronze plaques. It's a little late to close the barn door, because those cows have already left. If you've got Cap Anson in there, then I think your moral barometer is very difficult to keep high."

Another inconvenient truth in this debate over morality is that drugs didn't enter baseball for the first time in the '90s. Players introducing chemicals into their bodies was anything but new by the time the Nike-endorsed catchphrase "Chicks dig the long ball" made its way into the public lexicon.

"There was a lot of performance enhancement in the pre-steroid era," noted Jon Light, author of *The Cultural Encyclopedia of Baseball.* "I would say most likely it began after the war, in the late '40s and early '50s. Then it became a taboo subject as word leaked out in the '60s and '70s."

It can even be argued that the steroid era helped save baseball. By the mid-'90s, the game was in a dark place. The 1994 work stoppage 112 games into the season had exponential effects: the Montreal Expos were the prohibitive World Series favorites. Had the team won it all, there is an alternate universe where the franchise never leaves Canada for Washington, D.C., a decade later. Halted too was Tony Gwynn's quest to be the first player since Ted Williams in 1941 to bat .400–he was batting .394 when the strike began. Fans quickly soured on the game and turned almost exclusively to the NFL and, soon thereafter, Michael Jordan's return to the NBA.

Two things helped erase the bad taste of 1994. The first was Cal Ripken breaking Gehrig's fifty-six-year-old record for consecutive games played. The second was the 1998 home run race between Mark McGwire and Sammy Sosa.

If not for the steroid era, "you wouldn't have had these guys who did the so-called wrongs doing what they did and keeping baseball in the spotlight. Period. It would be like boxing now," said St. Louis–based *Yardbarker* columnist Matt Whitener. The McGwire/Sosa home run race "was the most timely, lifesaving occurrence in the history of baseball. It is one of the biggest pivot points in the popularity and the financial success of this league now. Bryce Harper, Manny Machado, Nolan Arenado, Giancarlo Stanton. All these guys who are cashing checks now are doing so because baseball survived that winter on the backs of Mark McGwire, Sammy Sosa doing what they did. And Barry Bonds is just as big a part of that picture as them."

Baseball has positional stars now. The Aaron Judges, Stantons, Machados, Harpers, Mike Trouts of the world. But there are no superhero or supervillain figures in the game today in the way the NBA has LeBron James or the NFL has Tom Brady, the towering strongmen who captivated the die-hard baseball enthusiast and made the casual fan cop tickets for a mere sighting. Bonds was, it seems now, among the last of a dying breed.

"I think the major difference between the steroid era and now is that people allowed themselves to believe in Paul Bunyan and follow players as larger than life," Smith said. "I think today people just say, 'Oh, okay, he's the best player in baseball, but there's no *it* factor.' The energy of that era has not been duplicated."

In his seventh year on the Hall of Fame ballot, Bonds finished with 59.1 percent of the votes. A player needs 75 percent to get into Cooperstown. This represented a small uptick from the previous year's finish of 56.1 percent. Now the all-time home run leader would need an alternative path into the Hall of Fame, most likely through the Veterans Committee. Players from Bonds's era are voted on twice every five years.

Bonds has never made a public spectacle about the honor. But for a giant, no pun intended, whose professional story is so intrinsically tied to America's pastime, it's hard to believe it's not important to him.

"I think every player who reaches a certain stature in the game, [Cooperstown is] the last exclamation point you want to put on a great career. In Barry's case, he probably would love to take that stage while his godfather, [eighty-eight-year-old] Willie Mays, could be there to applaud him," said Smith. "I'm pretty sure that [eighty-five-year-old] Hank Aaron would be there to applaud him because Hank has always been very generous in his approach to Barry and what took place. I'm sure that Barry would love to be on the stage with those two guys. Can he live without it? Sure, because he might not have an option."

For the time being, the all-time home run king appears destined to be an outcast.

"When Babe Ruth exceeded the average level of play in his era by two and three times, we imagined that no one would ever exceed the average to that extent ever again," said Thorn. "Yet the one person who has ever exceeded Babe Ruth on a season-to-season basis, exceeded the norm to his extent, is Barry Bonds. He did the impossible."

Baseball's gatekeepers aren't in a charitable mood now. A final home run trot for Barry Lamar Bonds may look unlikely. But don't count him out.

Originally published July 18, 2019

WHAT **REPORTERS** CAN LEARN FROM **KYRIE IRVING** CALLING THEM **"PAWNS"**

If the media wants athletes
to be better, then we have to
be better too.

BY MARTENZIE JOHNSON

ONE COULDN'T be blamed for reacting to the Kyrie Irving news cycle with a heavily sighed "Boy, if he don't get . . ."

The mercurial Brooklyn Nets point guard and his employer were each fined $25,000 by the NBA at the end of 2020 for Irving's refusal to speak to the media since the beginning of training camp. Three days later, Irving released a statement that read, in part, "Instead of speaking to the media today, I am issuing this statement to ensure that my message is properly conveyed. . . . I am committed to show up to work every day, ready to have fun, compete, perform, and win championships alongside my teammates and colleagues in the Nets organization.

"My goal this season is to let my work on and off the court speak for itself."

Irving, not letting his play do the talking, posted on social media an apparent reaction to the fine:

"I pray we utilize the fine money for the marginalized communities in need, especially seeing where our world is presently. [I am] here for Peace, Love, and Greatness. So stop distracting me and my team, and appreciate the Art. We move different over here.

"I do not talk to pawns. My attention is worth more."

Oh, brother. Here we go again.

The easy way out for everyone—the media, NBA fans—would be to chalk this up to Kyrie being Kyrie, ignoring the substance of what he said in order to further criticize—or laugh at—his bloated ego and even more bloated hotepery. (Irving also quoted Malcolm X in his statement.) Irving has repeatedly taken an ax to his reputation over the years, from his reported tumultuous relationship with his teammates on the Cleveland Cavaliers and Boston Celtics to boneheaded public comments, the most controversial being his thoughts on the flatness of Earth.

But, as is the case with most things, this Irving situation is complex. On one hand, Irving has an obligation to talk to the media. Not to get all slave-mastery, but the league has a $24 billion partnership with ESPN and Turner to broadcast games, and also has guidelines that require that players speak to reporters after games and practices. Irving knows this, as he is a vice president in the National Basketball Players Association. Irving may be annoyed by reporters and their questions, but the least he can do—the absolute least—is answer some questions for five minutes. (For the uninitiated, media scrums last only about that long.)

Irving makes the jobs of beat reporters harder by not answering their questions. Imagine if Irving didn't speak to the media after his season-opening fifty-point game last season on the one-year anniversary of the death of his grandfather. That career-defining moment loses a bit of its luster without Irving's cooperation. Not to mention, there's a risk other players would decide that they too don't want to talk to the media. Cooperation with the media means you get Damian Lillard's "Paul George got sent home by me last year in the playoffs" or LeBron James asking for some "damn respect." Less media access is not ideal for anyone.

At the same time members of the media, myself included, need to take a long look at ourselves as well. Irving didn't decide to call us "pawns" out of thin air.

Before the advent of social media and player-backed media outlets, journalists owned a monopoly on coverage of athletes. When you wanted to learn about your favorite athletes and teams, or conversely, when athletes wanted to set the record straight on something, they needed the local sports reporter. Newspaper columnists were once considered among the most influential people in sports, because they helped determine public opinion on this player or that coach.

But over the last decade–notably when James went on national television to say he was taking his talents to South Beach–things changed. Where there was once the local and national reporter, and maybe a blogger here and there, now there's James's UNINTERRUPTED media platform, Kevin Durant's Thirty Five Ventures, and the Derek Jeter-backed *Players' Tribune*, which broke the news of Durant's decision to join the Golden State Warriors in 2016, among other scoops. Plus there are the athletes' own social media accounts.

Players realized they didn't need the media anymore. And could you blame them? Many of us abused the relative power we had as purveyors of news. We called Durant "Mr. Unreliable." We turned James into a villain because he didn't want to play for Cavaliers owner Dan Gilbert anymore. We called Irving every four-letter word under the sun for questioning the circumference of Earth. Trolls on the internet and fans in arenas did the same thing, but we in the media are supposed to be better than that. The line between criticism and pure meanness was long crossed. These are the consequences.

It's easy to dismiss what Irving said because he's the wrong messenger. We–society, not just the media–did the same thing when Irving rightfully questioned the league returning to play in the middle of the COVID-19 pandemic and the protests following the police killing of George Floyd. Because Irving, like millions of others in this country, hadn't spoken up in the past about race and inequality, suddenly his opinion that the NBA would be a distraction from the social unrest was met with ridicule. For a Black man playing in a predominantly Black sport that's covered by an overwhelmingly white press corps that downplays his dedication to social justice, it should come as no surprise to that same press corps that this Black man no longer desires to speak with them.

If the media (reporters, journalists, writers, bloggers, podcasters, analysts, commentators, etc.) wants athletes like Irving to be better, then we too have to be better.

If not, it won't be a matter of whether or not we are pawns on a chessboard. We'll find we're the only ones playing the game.

Originally published December 11, 2020

HOW **BLACK UTAH JAZZ** PLAYERS EMBRACED **SALT LAKE CITY**

From barbershops to churches to soul food restaurants, here's how players past and present made themselves at home.

BY MARC J. SPEARS

AFTER CATCHING a rare sight of a Black man pumping gas in Salt Lake City in 1980, Utah Jazz guard Darrell Griffith felt the need to approach his fellow "brotha."

The only Black people whom the then–rookie guard regularly saw after coming to the city were his own Jazz teammates. At the time, Salt Lake City had a Black population of 1.5 percent. While Griffith hoped that the man had the blueprint for Black male survival in Utah, those visions of grandeur ended like a missed layup.

"I went to this gas station-store over by my motel to get a soft drink and I see this Black guy pull up in a black Cadillac Seville," Griffith said. "I went up to him to ask him where the Black population was. I told him, 'Hey, I'm just getting in town and I'm playing ball for the Jazz. I just want to know where the brothas are at?' He said, 'Man, I was just getting off the expressway to get some gas. I'm from California. Good luck with that one.'"

Of the thirty NBA teams, there isn't a market that seems less conducive to an African American player than Salt Lake City, the home of the Jazz.

Salt Lake City's population has always been predominantly white. In 2016, the city was 75 percent white and 2 percent Black. Utah itself was a mere 1.6 percent Black in 2010, according to the U.S. Census Bureau. While the lack of Black residents is a real issue for the Black players on the Jazz past and present, once they figured out their surroundings and met people, they loved playing there.

"I never had any problems. The people always treated me nice," said former Jazz forward-center Thurl Bailey, an African American who converted to Mormonism.

"There are a lot of great people out there. They try to help you as much as they can," said Jazz forward-center Derrick Favors. "Everybody speaks to you. Everybody smiles. Everybody says hello. I've never witnessed any kind of [racism] out there. It's a great place."

I spent time in Salt Lake City to investigate what it is like to be Black playing for the Jazz and got the rundown on one of the NBA's most unique cities.

WELCOME TO SALT LAKE, BROTHA . . .

The Jazz have not had a reputation for landing major free agents since arriving in Salt Lake City from New Orleans in 1980. Hall of Famers John Stockton and Karl Malone, 2017 NBA All-Star

Gordon Hayward, and defensive standout center Rudy Gobert were draft picks, as were other notable former players like Bailey, Paul Millsap, Deron Williams, Bryon Russell, and Mark Eaton. Favors, starting point guard George Hill and reserve forward Boris Diaw came from trades.

For most of the team's Black newcomers, there was some worry upon arrival.

"I come from a community that was predominantly African American," said Griffith, a Louisville, Kentucky, native who starred at the University of Louisville. "I was used to Black women. It was totally different for me. It was different.

"The scenic part of Salt Lake City is absolutely beautiful. It snows a lot, but it was a beautiful city."

For Favors and Millsap, their nervousness stemmed from a lack of knowledge about Utah.

"It was a big culture change. I was in the New York [area] first," said Favors, an Atlanta native who was traded by the New Jersey Nets to the Jazz in 2011. "To get traded to Utah, that was a big culture change. A lot of people in Atlanta heard of Utah, but they don't know nothing about Utah. . . .

"I was like, Utah? I didn't know anything about Utah. What was out there or what to do out there. I didn't know about the culture or the people."

"Before I went, I knew nothing about Salt Lake City," said Millsap, a second-round pick of the Jazz in 2006 who's now with the Atlanta Hawks. "I didn't even know where it was on a map. I remember getting out there and people greeting me. It was an amazing time."

Russell and former Jazz center Jarron Collins didn't complain about being drafted by the Jazz. Without guaranteed contracts, they were more worried about making it in the NBA than about the city.

"When I first got there is when my school [Long Beach State] went out there to play Utah State," Russell, the forty-fifth overall pick in the second round of the 1993 NBA draft, said. "I was like, 'Man, I hope I never come out there again. There was nothing to do out here.' The next thing I knew, 'The Jazz Draft Bryon Russell with the 43rd Pick.' I was jumping for joy. I forget every word I said. I was like, 'I'm happy as hell to be out here.'"

Collins, the Jazz's fifty-second overall pick in the 2001 NBA draft out of Stanford, said: "I didn't see things as race. I was excited for the opportunity to be in the NBA and live out my dream. I had an opportunity to play with Karl Malone, play with John Stockton, play for Coach Jerry Sloan. I was ready to go and excited through the roof.

"My experience was a little different because I was a second-round pick. I had to go make the team. It was all about opportunity."

Dominique Wilkins was drafted by the then-cash-strapped Jazz as the second overall pick in 1982 but didn't want to come to Salt Lake City. The Hall of Famer was traded to the Atlanta Hawks for John Drew, Freeman Williams, and $1 million and became the franchise's all-time leading scorer and biggest star. Twenty years ago, Dallas Maverick's guard Derek Harper also turned down a chance to be traded to the Jazz team that went to the 1997 NBA finals.

"There was a Utah deal, but you go live in Utah," he told ESPN. "Nothing against Utah or their team, but I don't want to live there."

Utah has had some respected free agent signees in Rickey Green, Raja Bell, Jeff Wilkins, John Starks, Antoine Carr, and Howard Eisley, but no grand slams. LeBron James, Carmelo Anthony, Kevin Durant, Dwyane Wade, and Chris Paul never considered the Jazz in free agency. The Jazz's most notable free agent signee is arguably Carlos Boozer, an African American who signed in July 2004 and was a 2007 NBA All-Star. Utah also got a surprising free agent signee in seven-time NBA All-Star Joe Johnson.

"It didn't bother me that there wasn't a lot to do. I'm from Little Rock," Johnson said. "There is not much for me to do there. I'm slow-paced. I was fine with that. I don't have a problem with that. I've lived in some great places around the country.

"I didn't really know about Park City. I didn't know it snowed that much. I was in New York with some tough snow winters. For me, it has been fun. I tell them, 'You have to come out here and see it for yourself, honestly.' For my close friends, family, because it's different from anywhere else I've been or played."

No one is more familiar with being a Black pro player or living in Utah than Ron Boone.

Boone was traded from the ABA Dallas Chaparrals to the Utah Stars in January 1971. The four-time ABA All-Star was a member of the Stars 1971 ABA championship team and was on the team when it folded in 1975. Boone also played for the Jazz from 1979–81 and serves as their television color analyst. The Omaha, Nebraska, native said that he was prepared for Utah after playing college ball in Iowa and Idaho, and he still lives there in the off-season.

"We don't have the ghetto. If you're a player and you have a problem with living here, look at the NBA schedule," Boone, seventy, said. "Out of the season, how many days are you in town? If you're a professional basketball player, you want to be a professional basketball player. You can dedicate yourself to being that player in a city like this for the short period of time you're going to be here."

But Boone certainly is very sensitive to any Black player who finds it difficult to live and work in lily-white Salt Lake City.

"What I don't like from people here, especially white people, is when they say they don't understand why Blacks don't want to come here to play. They don't have any right to speak on that," Boone said.

WHERE'S THE SOUL FOOD?

While there might not be many options, if Jazz players in Salt Lake City looked hard for soul food, they could find it.

The most legendary of all the soul food restaurants in the city was Mama's Southern Plantation. Jazz team members and visiting NBA teams were regulars. The restaurant, which once had several locations, is now closed.

"I used to go to Southern Plantation. That was the spot," Bailey said. "When other NBA teams would come in, they would go to Southern Plantation. It was like home. It was like how Mama made it. It was the closest thing."

Griffith said he ate at Mama's Southern Plantation regularly while playing with the Jazz from 1980–91 and was so serious about his meal choices that he often brought his own ingredients to the restaurant.

"It was really good," Griffith said. "It was so good that when they ran out of sweet potato I would go back in the kitchen and ask, 'What are y'all missing? Y'all missing some greens and sweet potatoes?' I would go to the [grocery store] and get some greens and sweet potatoes for them to cook. . . .

"We all went there after practice for breakfast. It kind of reminded me of my mom's cooking."

Like Mama's Southern Plantation, numerous soul food restaurants have opened and closed in Salt Lake City due to lack of patrons and financial backing. The co-owner of SoCo Restaurant, in downtown Salt Lake City, had to explain the fare to predominantly white patrons who had never heard of many of the items on the menu. One patron called Salt Lake City's health department after eating catfish for the first time because they thought it didn't taste right, restaurant co-owner Andrew Dasenbrock said.

"We have to explain everything," he said. "People are asking, 'What's hush puppies?' 'What's hopping john?' 'What are grits?' These are actual questions I get from about 50 percent of the tables. . . .

"When people order catfish, we have to ask them if they've had catfish. They were sending it back after one bite saying that the fish went bad. The fish isn't bad. It's catfish. It has a very distinct flavor. I don't know if they were expecting halibut or trout or what. They've never had catfish in their life and then one bite later they are telling us our food is bad."

Dasenbrock said one Mormon family came to eat at SoCo in honor of the Martin Luther King Jr. holiday, although their food selection was rather questionable.

"A white family of four came in after they searched on the internet for the best fried chicken in Salt Lake City. They ordered four fried chicken dinners in honor of Dr. King," Dasenbrock, who is Finnish, said.

SoCo, which was a drive of less than five minutes from the arena where the Jazz play, opened in July 2016 and closed the following year due to "complicated business reasons," Dasenbrock said.

"This town is lacking culture. It really is. This coming from the whitest of white people. My family is from Finland," Dasenbrock said. "You can [throw] a rock in this town and hit nothing but white people. Not that it is a bad thing, but a difference of opinions will make this society a better place."

Johnson hails from a town where Southern food and barbecue are a big deal. For the sixteen-year NBA veteran, getting oxtails, yams, and hot-water corn bread isn't a necessity in Salt Lake City.

"When you get my age, you stay away from that Southern cooking because you have to stay light on your feet," he said. "I haven't had none of that other than when my mom comes to town."

Hill has enjoyed having a private chef during his career but had a hard time finding the right one in his first season in Utah. "I've had probably four chefs already," Hill said. "What you're so used to, you don't find that. I like my food seasoned a lot. They don't do that there. They are stingy with the salt and seasoning. The cultures are totally different than where I came from."

THE BLACK CHURCH

Believe it or not, Salt Lake City has had a Black Baptist church since the late 1890s.

In June 1898, a building located in the back of a white church called First Baptist Church was used as a place of worship for Black Baptists and had its own full-time reverend. According to the *Salt Lake Herald*, the Calvary Baptist Church moved into an old frame building downtown that was described as the "little colored house of worship in the alley." In 1921, the Calvary Baptist Church was incorporated under the leadership of Reverend George Hart. France A. Davis became the pastor of Calvary Baptist Church in 1974. The church celebrated its 109th anniversary by dedicating a new house of worship in 2011.

Davis said the church is the best place for Black Jazz players or any African American looking to connect with others like them.

"They have to introduce themselves to people who are African American. There is no physical location where African Americans are. The church is the gathering place. Once they find it, then I think they will have a good sense that this is a good place to be," Davis said.

Davis served as a chaplain for the old ABA Dallas Stars and the Jazz. He said several Jazz players and their family members have been members of Calvary Baptist Church.

"I go to Calvary Baptist Church. It's very much like the one I grew up with in Nebraska," Boone said. "We have a few white members, but it is majority Black."

Millsap, who played for the Jazz from 2006–13, said that Calvary Baptist Church meant a lot to his family.

"It was a place we could go every Sunday, Wednesdays, to get away," Millsap said. "It was like an extended family. They treated us like family and welcomed us in. They've been great. They still keep in touch to this day."

THE BLACK MORMON

Bailey spent a lot of time in the Baptist church while growing up in Bladensburg, Maryland. The former North Carolina State star arrived in Salt Lake City in 1983 after being drafted seventh overall that year by the Jazz. While it was a "culture shock" living in Salt Lake City, Bailey quickly made friends who were white and Mormon in Salt Lake City.

"I would drive to practice and every now and then I'd see a Black person," Bailey said. "I'd pull up to a light and see a Black person. I'd wave at them. And then the next day I'd see the same Black people on the same route. I didn't really get to know them, but the point was there were very few.

"I never had any problems. The people always treated me nice. There was no outward prejudice. Maybe some of it was that sometimes when people see a high-profile person or celebrity, they don't see color. But I don't think that was the case here. Maybe it was the Mormon culture."

Bailey started learning about the Mormon faith.

"It wasn't like it was shoved in my face. It wasn't like I met missionaries. I would ask them to tell me about their church," Bailey said. "I would tell them how I was raised. So what's the difference? We still use the Bible, but there is another book, the Book of Mormon. I had a lot of questions; there is this thing called the priesthood. At a certain point, African Americans couldn't hold that priesthood. I was very curious about it. I was introduced by being in the culture."

Milwaukee Bucks forward Jabari Parker is a Latter-day Saint and said he grew up in a diverse Mormon church.

"I had a good church growing up," Parker said. "They were very liberal. There were Black people all around. If you have a good church, multicultural . . . it made it a lot easier to identify with certain people."

Bailey had two sons and a daughter with his first wife, whom he divorced. In 1989, he began dating Sindi Southwick, a white Mormon woman in Salt Lake City. They attended both Mormon and Baptist churches. But since Bailey wasn't a Latter-day Saint, they couldn't get married in a Mormon church. They got married in 1994 in Las Vegas.

Southwick's family disowned her for marrying a Black man, he said.

"There were things that happened from a personal standpoint where I wasn't totally accepted by her family," Bailey, who has three children with his wife, said. "Now I had kind of crossed that line. She was disowned. It was a tough period. A really tough period. She had to make a choice and she chose me. That told me something about her right there.

"I knew she was raised in a great home. I also knew having an ultimatum thrown at you by your family, that's a tough thing to do, especially when you're Mormon. It was the thing that brought us a lot closer."

Bailey decided to become a Mormon while playing basketball in Italy during the 1995–96 season while his wife was back in Utah.

He said his decision to become a Mormon was completely his own.

"I was in kind of at a crossroads of my life," Bailey said. "I knew my basketball career was coming to an end. I had a failed marriage that produced kids. I was always a God-fearing man. I prayed a lot. A lot was personal reasons. I was doing some soul-searching. I was trying to figure out what God had in store for me.

"My mom wasn't totally thrilled about it. My dad said to me, 'Son, are you happy?' I said, 'Yes, I am.' He said, 'I'm happy for you.' Then he said, 'When you come home I want to know a little bit more about it.'"

BLACK BARBERSHOPS

Longtime Jazz scout David Fredman was working for the franchise when it moved to Salt Lake City from New Orleans in 1980. There is one question he has heard from Black players more than any other when they arrive.

"The worst thing I heard was them trying to find a haircut. Once they got that squared away they were okay," Fredman said.

If you ask any current or ex–Jazz player who their barber was in Salt Lake City, the answer usually is followed by a smile and a name.

"I have a barber named Joseph. I ran across him on my Instagram page. He sent me a bunch of pictures on how he cut. He told me to give him a try and the first cut is on him," Hill said.

"They had Black barbers out there," said Russell. "I had a guy named John Lopez."

"We had one Black barber and his name was Billy. He cut everybody's hair," said Griffith.

There are a handful of Black barbershops in the Salt Lake City area today. Perhaps the most popular is Brickyard Barbers in the suburb of Murray. The shop's past Jazz clientele included Malone, Bailey, Raja Bell, and Ronnie Price. Jazz players Gobert, Johnson, and Dante Exum, Assistant Coach Johnnie Bryant, and

Salt Lake Tribune Jazz beat writer Tony Jones have gone there. Brickyard Barbers co-owner Romone Vaughn said that he often trims up visiting NBA players, including former Los Angeles Lakers star Kobe Bryant in his hotel room.

"When they come in here for the first time, they are surprised to see this many Black people," Vaughn said. "And then they are surprised we could give them a good haircut. They get skeptical that there is a Black barber in Utah, but we're pretty established now. When the new players come to town, they give them a heads-up and the coaches too.

"Karl would come and spend hours sitting here talking. He would end up paying for everybody's haircut because he'd be in the chair talking so much that we couldn't cut his hair. The barbershop is like a social club for them."

ENTERTAINMENT OFF THE COURT

Griffith recalls coming to Salt Lake City in 1980 and finding very little to do for entertainment. There were no radio stations playing Black music. He took his cassettes when he went on road trips. The cable on the television didn't have BET. He recalls calling his mom in excitement when *The Arsenio Hall Show* started being shown in Salt Lake City.

"You just adapted. I went to a lot of movies," Griffith said. "There was nothing on TV. Nothing on cable. Sometimes I would go to the movies saying, 'This movie comes on at two and goes off at 4:20,' then go to the next one. I'd go to two movies in a row. That's why I'm a movie buff until this day. My family gives me movie coupons for Christmas."

Dating was also hard for Griffith. While playing for the Jazz during the 1979-80 season, Hall of Famer Bernard King had five felony forcible sexual-assault charges in Salt Lake City. According to writer Peter Richmond, King pleaded guilty to one count.

Griffith arrived in the aftermath of this affair, which made dating challenging for a Black man in a predominantly white city.

"Single life there was tough, man. Really tough, man," Griffith said. "You had to suck it up. It was different. Especially with the situation that happened with Bernard King when he was out there. You were really just real cautious of doing anything, dating or anything."

Russell was quickly bored by the social scene in Salt Lake City but wasn't comfortable doing anything about it until he became established as a starter with the team. Around 1997, the nine-year Jazz forward began bringing comedy shows, concerts, and parties to Salt Lake City.

He said his first concert was a sold-out one for R&B artist Jaheim. He also had a comedy show that included Jamie Foxx as the headliner.

"I brought chocolate to White City. I put on concerts," Russell said. "I put on events. I had people saying, 'Well, damn, Utah is not bad at all.' It was about having fun while you were playing there and having a great atmosphere. We had a ball.

"Karl came out to the concerts and the comedy shows. All of the players used to come to my shows. Even John Stockton came to my shows. No, I'm lying. He didn't come. But all the brothas were there."

Today, there is much more hip-hop entertainment to choose from. The hip-hop radio station U-92 hosted concerts with the soul singer Kehlani and rapper T.I., and a rap concert called Mount Kushmore with Snoop Dogg, Wiz Khalifa, Cypress Hill, and Flatbush Zombies. Ariana Grande, Chance the Rapper, Young Jeezy, DJ Quik, E-40, Boyz II Men, and Mariah Carey had concerts in the Salt Lake City area too. There are a couple of bars and restaurants where you can hear hip-hop now, such as the popular Moose Lounge downtown.

"There are places to go out to on the weekends. There are a few that play hip-hop. You see more Black people there. It just depends on what you like. As long as I like the music and the girls, I'm okay," Gobert said.

HOME SWEET HOME

Salt Lake City will never be like Atlanta or Washington, D.C. It will never have a club scene like New York City or Los Angeles. It will never have a restaurant scene like New Orleans or Chicago or San Francisco. And with its snow and cold winters, Salt Lake City will never have the warmth of Miami or Houston. But the city has its strengths.

"You have to come out here and see it for yourself, honestly. For my close friends, family, because it's different from anywhere else I've been or played. To see this experience is great since the Jazz is the only professional team around here," Johnson said.

"The fans are phenomenal," said Hill. "They've embraced me with open arms and act like I've been here for ten years when I've only been here for a couple of months. That has been a great blessing for me."

"It was a good fit for me as far as basketball and the city," said Diaw. "I like the mountains. It's a nice state overall. Park City is right there and the nice parks. It was exciting."

"Friends were skeptical about coming," said Favors, who lives with his girlfriend and two children. "They were like, 'I don't want to come to no Utah.' Once they come out and visit Utah, they ask me if they can come out two to three times a summer.

"I told my mom when I bought my house that I was trying to stay out here year-round. She said, 'Go for it and see if you like it.' I tried it and fell in love with it."

Originally published March 13, 2017

BLACK MEN DO CRY—
IN THE NCAA
TOURNAMENT

Why is this the rare venue where we see public tears?

BY JESSE WASHINGTON

COLLEGE BASKETBALL is one of the rare public places where Black men are allowed to cry.

Central Florida senior Dayon Griffin wept in the handshake line after Duke stole a second-round victory in 2019, and the locker-room sobs of his teammates went viral. Kansas State players "cried like babies," their coach lovingly said, after they were upset in the first round by UC-Irvine. NBA-bound Murray State guard Ja Morant hid his tears under a towel as he exited a March Madness game.

And that was only one week. In 2017, DeAaron Fox and Bam

Adebayo cried in each other's arms after North Carolina sent the Kentucky Wildcats home from the Elite Eight on a last-second shot. In 2018, Fairfield coach Sydney Johnson wrapped his all-time leading scorer in a moist hug as he checked out of his final game. When Johnson was coaching at Princeton, he shed tears on the interview podium after his Tigers lost to Kentucky, 59–57, in the 2011 NCAA tournament.

Why do we grant permission to cry so freely in this particular venue? When Black men are killed, we see more tattoo tears than real ones. It's unheard of for Black men to cry in public if they don't get into college or can't get jobs. A brother would be ridiculed for crying on the job if he didn't get a promotion. When they learn that mass incarceration disproportionately sends Black men to prison, most Americans remain dry-eyed, while the convicted and their families weep. We use the term "soul-crushing" more often to describe the loss of a basketball game than a Black life.

Perhaps America thinks basketball is the most meaningful thing these young Black men will ever do. So we send the message: Feel free to show your pain—on the court.

Griffin, the UCF senior guard, said it's easier for him to show his emotions within the game than outside of it. "I've always loved the game. It has given me so many experiences and opportunities, which is why I let my emotions show," he told me. "March Madness was the opportunity of a lifetime. Emotions run high when you go to war with your brothers. The ball just didn't bounce our way."

Duke coach Mike Krzyzewski hugged Griffin in the postgame handshake line. "Coach K told me to keep my head up and that he knows this is going to be a tough game to get over. He told me that I played my heart out and gave it all I got. So many emotions went into the game, and we were deserving of winning. It's sad to see it all happen the way it did."

Basketball is both more popular and more naked than most other sports. Not only do players wear less clothing, but because of the ticking clock and scoring frequency, there is a greater chance of emotional moments where a season, or career, hinges on one play. College football has more fans, but players are hidden under helmets, there are few win-or-go-home games, and outcomes are rarely decided in the final seconds. Pro basketball players don't cry, except when they win awards or championships–those massive paychecks are a great security blanket.

Today, Black pop culture is dominated by rap's stone-faced ethos. Jay-Z rhymed about making the song cry rather than himself. Drake felt the need to have his mom dispel accusations about his leaky eyes. On the screen, Black male tears often come only when a man is stripped of everything. After his father abandoned him on *The Fresh Prince of Bel-Air*, Will Smith broke down only after trying to cope through jokes and defiance. Denzel Washington clinched his first Oscar playing a man with a soul so callused, he sheds only a single tear during a vicious slave whipping.

Barack Obama cried publicly several times during his presidency, and he was sometimes mocked for it or accused of faking. Michael Jordan let down his impenetrable guard for a moment while being inducted into basketball's Hall of Fame, and he was punished with the GOAT internet meme.

The concept of stoic masculinity is not limited to Black men, of course. Matt Damon finally allowing his character to cry in *Good Will Hunting* comes from the same kind of socialization as Derek Luke surrendering to his pain in *Antwone Fisher*. But this repressive construct can be exacerbated in Black men who experience a disproportionate amount of unique traumas while society gives them little, if any, sympathy. Hiding emotions is a survival tactic in a cruel world.

In *Native Son*, Richard Wright's masterpiece of Black anguish, fictional protagonist Bigger Thomas tells his lawyer as he faces execution: "I'm all right, Mr. Max. Just go and tell Ma I was all right and not to worry none, see? Tell her I was all right and wasn't crying none."

After being chosen to play in the 2016 NBA All-Star Game, Draymond Green said, "I almost started crying, but I knew I was on TV and I ain't want them to kill me on Instagram."

Green probably would have been forgiven for crying over his teams loss in Game 7 of that season's NBA finals. We understand that athletes pour everything they have into these games. We appreciate their skill, passion, and commitment, and when it's not rewarded, we extend our sympathy.

College basketball allows us to empathize with the same young Black men who get little love in the streets, the classroom, or the workplace. Basketball allows us to see that beneath all their hair and tattoos and bravado, these are teens and young adults who deserve the freedom to make mistakes.

This is the special sports sympathy that flooded over the UCF players who cried after leading top-seeded Duke by three points with eighteen seconds left but lost 77-76.

"We always said it's gonna end two ways when you invest like we invest. We gonna end celebrating or we gonna end crying, we gonna end in tears," Head Coach Johnny Dawkins told his sobbing players in the locker room.

"We end in tears."

Originally published March 28, 2019

AFTERWORD

Back in 2016, a website called *The Undefeated* launched with a majority Black newsroom focused on the intersections of sports, race, and culture. We planned from the beginning to be more and to have as expansive a view of the world as the Black folks who read us every day. Six years and a name change later–we're now called Andscape–we're committed to examining and celebrating Black life in all its infinite manifestations. As one of the early editors to join on, I'm more familiar than most with the talented people at *Andscape* and the ambition of their work. Still, rereading these essays after a year (or two or three) reminded me how smart and perceptive they are and how important it is to bring these voices out into the world.

This book represents only a taste of what we do, of course. If it seems like your thing–and if you're reading an afterword, it must be!–I invite you to check us out daily online at Andscape.com or on Instagram, Twitter, Facebook, TikTok, and YouTube.

Putting out a daily website and social media report is an unrelenting task that requires soul and muscle from many people who rarely see their names in print or pixels. Huge respect to these current and former Andscape editors who were among those who helped shepherd and hone the essays that originally appeared on Andscape.com: Karin D. Berry, Danielle Cadet, Aaron Dodson, Morgan Jerkins, Monique Jones, Kevin Merida, John X. Miller, Danyel Smith, Josiah S. Turner, Matt

Wong, Jenisha Watts, Khari Williams, and Lisa Wilson. And heartfelt thanks to these folks at Andscape and ESPN who do the work that makes us look so good: Anna Gramling, Sean Hintz, Kristine LaManna, Ashley Melfi, Rami Moghadam, Peter E. Scher, and Beth Stojkov.

—*Steve Reiss*
May 2022

CONTRIBUTORS TO BLACKTOLD

JERRY BEMBRY is a senior writer at Andscape. His bucket list items include being serenaded by Lizz Wright and watching the Knicks play a MEANINGFUL NBA game in June.

KARIN D. BERRY is copy chief for Andscape. She's way too short for the basketball court, but she's got mad editing skills and a mean red pen.

DWAYNE BRAY is a senior writer for Andscape. He writes about topics ranging from general sports to race relations to poverty. He previously ran ESPN television's award-winning investigative team and is a die-hard Cleveland sports fan.

DANIELLE CADET is a fan of good food, good novels, and good manners and has seen every episode of *Frasier* at least twelve times.

KELLEY L. CARTER is a senior entertainment reporter and the host of *Another Act* at Andscape. She can act out every episode of the U.S. version of *The Office*, she can and will sing the Michigan State University fight song on command, and she is very much immune to Hollywood hotness.

DAVID DENNIS JR. is a senior writer at Andscape and an American Mosaic Journalism Prize recipient. He is the author of *The Movement Made Us* and a graduate of Davidson College.

MICHAEL A. FLETCHER is a senior writer at ESPN. He is a native New Yorker and longtime Baltimorean who enjoys live music and theater.

DOMONIQUE FOXWORTH is a senior writer at Andscape. He is a recovering pro athlete and superficial intellectual.

ROBERTO JOSÉ ANDRADE FRANCO is a fronterizo from the El Paso/Juárez borderlands.

DOUG GLANVILLE was a first-round draft pick by the Chicago Cubs and an outfielder with the Cubs, Texas Rangers, and Philadelphia Phillies. He is the author of *The Game from Where I Stand*. Glanville is currently a baseball analyst for both ESPN and Marquee Sports Network and is an adjunct professor at the University of Connecticut.

MINDA HONEY is a Louisville, Kentucky–based writer and founder of the publication *TAUNT*. She spends her free time living beyond her emotional means and hyping up her friends on social media.

MARTENZIE JOHNSON is a senior writer for Andscape. His favorite cinematic moment is when Django said, "Y'all want to see somethin'?"

RAINA KELLEY is the editor-in-chief of Andscape and is obsessed with Whitney Houston, armchair mountaineering, and the MCU, among too many obsessions to count. She also would have made an excellent homicide detective.

SORAYA NADIA MCDONALD is the senior culture critic for Andscape. She writes about pop culture, fashion, the arts and literature. She is the 2020 winner of the George Jean Nathan prize for dramatic criticism, a 2020 finalist for the Pulitzer Prize in criticism, and the runner-up for the 2019 Vernon Jarrett Medal for outstanding reporting on Black life.

LONNAE O'NEAL is a senior writer at Andscape. She's an author, a former columnist, has a rack of kids, and she writes bird by bird.

ROGER REEVES is the author of *King Me* and *Best Barbarian*. He is the recipient of a Whiting Award and a Pushcart Prize, as well as fellowships from Cave Canem, the National Endowment for the Arts, the Poetry Foundation, and Princeton University.

WILLIAM C. RHODEN, the former award-winning sports columnist for the *New York Times* and author of *Forty Million Dollar Slaves*, is a writer-at-large for Andscape.

MARC J. SPEARS is the senior NBA writer for Andscape. He used to be able to dunk on you, but he hasn't been able to in years and his knees still hurt.

BRANDO SIMEO STARKEY is an associate editor at Andscape and the author of *In Defense of Uncle Tom: Why Blacks Must Police Racial Loyalty*. He crawled through a river of books and came out brilliant on the other side.

JUSTIN TINSLEY is a senior culture writer for Andscape. He firmly believes "Cash Money Records takin' ova for da '99 and da 2000" is the single most impactful statement of his generation.

JESSE WASHINGTON is a journalist and documentary filmmaker. He still gets buckets.

JENISHA WATTS'S Twitter bio quotes the late Toni Cade Bambara: "Don't leave the arena to the fools."

MICHAEL WILLIAMS is a writer, radio host, and television commentator based in Washington, D.C. He covers politics for Voice of America and is a member of the USGA Golf Journal editorial board. He met the Dalai Lama and Mike Tyson in the same year.

CLINTON YATES is a tastemaker at Andscape. He likes rap, rock, reggae, R&B, and remixes–in that order.